Baedeker

Italian Lakes
Lombardy · Milan

www.baedeker.com

Verlag Karl Baedeker

SIGHTSEEING HIGHLIGHTS ★ ★

Glorious seaside scenery that calls to mind the Mediterranean, magnificent villas, art-historical highlights, impressive mountain landscapes, picturesque towns. All this and the capital Milan, which is not just the economic centre of northern Italy but also the country's fashion capital and an important centre for art. Lombardy has plenty to offer, and we present here the top destinations that you should on no account miss.

Isole Borromeo
Wonderful parks on Isola Bella

SWITZERLAND

9 Parco Nazionale
dello Stelvio

3 Locarno
2 Ascona
1 Lago
aggiore   6 Lugano   7 Lago di Como

8 Bellagio   10 Parco Nazionale delle
Incisioni Rupestri

4 Isole
rromee   5 Lago
di Lugano

Lago d'Iseo   Lago d'Idro

16 Bergamo   11 Lago di Garda

17 Brescia

13 Milan   12 Sirmione

14 Certosa
di Pavia
15 Pavia   18 Cremona   19 Mantua

3 ✴✴ Lago di Garda
Goethe was one of those impressed by the lake's »delightful spectacle«.
► page 183

12 ✴✴ Sirmione
The main attraction of the much-visited holiday resort is the mighty Rocca Scaligera. ► page 193

13 ✴✴ Milan
The buzzing capital of Lombardy is a paradise for fans of culture and shopping. ► page 261

14 ✴✴ Certosa die Pavia
The former Carthusian monastery is among Lombardy's architectural and artistic highlights. ► page 145

15 ✴✴ Pavia
A historically important town with an attractive old quarter ► page 293

16 ✴✴ Bergamo
The old town is especially picturesque. ► page 122

17 ✴✴ Brescia
This important industrial city has preserved its historic centre. ► page 135

18 ✴✴ Cremona
Violin-making has made this town world famous. ► page 163

19 ✴✴ Mantua
The city is home to jewels of Renaissance architecture. ► page 246

BAEDEKER'S BEST TIPS

We have chosen the most interesting of Baedeker's tips in this book and listed them for you here. Experience and enjoy the best that Lombardy has to offer!

■ For lovers of piano music ...
... the Festival Pianistico Benedetti Michelangeli, which takes place in Bergamo in the spring, is recommended.
► **page 130**

■ Experience the caves
A characteristic feature of Chiavenna are the grotti, in which you can buy typical products of the region. Some have been fitted out as rustic bars.
► **page 152**

■ A stimulating break
Tasty espresso coffee is on sale in Caffè & Caffè in Como. ► **page 160**

■ On the trail of the betrothed
One tour in Lecco follows the events in Alessandro Manzoni's famous novel *The Betrothed*. ► **page 180**

■ Lakeside market
Those who enjoy looking around a market should head for Desenzano on Lago di Garda on Tuesdays. ► **page 198**

■ In Hermann Hesse's footsteps
Guided walks in Montagnola bring to life the world of the writer Hermann Hesse.
► **page 213**

Espresso
The perfect pick-me-up while seeing the sights

Lazise on Lago di Garda
A truly Mediterranean atmosphere

▉ Musical highlights
Fans of classical music should make space in their diary for a concert at the Settimane Musicali di Stresa on Lago Maggiore.
▶ page 227

▉ Film festival
The Locarno Film Festival enjoys international renown.   ▶ page 233

▉ For lovers of jazz
Lugano is a Mecca for fans of jazz.
▶ page 244

▉ Amaretto
Amaretto, a sweet liqueur that tastes of almonds, is made in Saronno.
▶ page 293

▉ Life in prehistoric times
The Archeodromo at Cemma in Valcamonica gives visitors an impression of life in the Stone Age.
▶ page 307

▉ Bresaola
This air-dried beef is a speciality of Valtellina.   ▶ page 314

Bresaola
Try this delicious air-dried beef

Al fresco dining is an essential part of an enjoyable holiday
► **page 77**

BACKGROUND

PRACTICALITIES

Price categories

► **Hotels**
Luxury over €250
Mid-range €100–250
Budget under €100
For a double room

► **Restaurants**
Expensive over €40
Moderate €20–40
Inexpensive under €20
For a meal

The elaborately decorated façade of Milan Cathedral ► page 271

TOURS

SIGHTS FROM A to Z

Background

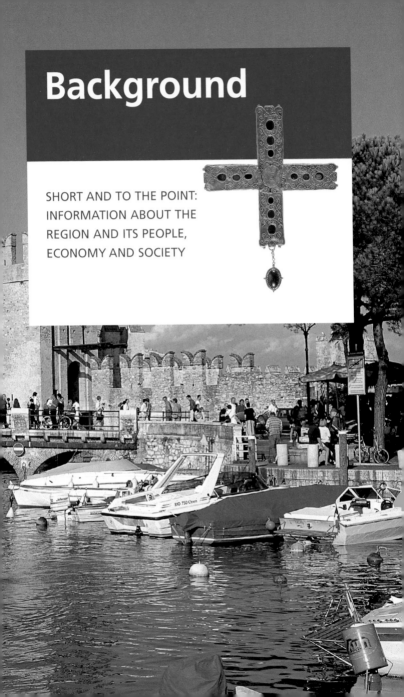

SHORT AND TO THE POINT:
INFORMATION ABOUT THE
REGION AND ITS PEOPLE,
ECONOMY AND SOCIETY

RICH AND BEAUTIFUL

Between the Alpine peaks and the plain of the river Po lies a delightful region where lemon trees blossom and at the same time more than one fifth of Italy's national income is earned. Here Mediterranean flora and fauna compete with industrial activity, and making money has priority over leisure.

But even the hardest-working inhabitants of the area, the Ambrosiani, as the people of Milan are respectfully called after their militant 4th-century bishop, have retained their love of the natural beauty and magnificent scenery of this region. The lakes, whether Lago Maggiore, Lago di Como, Lago d'Iseo or Lago di Lugano, are the loveliest part of Lombardy. As long ago as the 7th century, the Lombards were so enchanted by the scent of blossom here that they abandoned all plans for further conquest. In Pavia, once the place where the Lombard kings were crowned and now a buzzing university town, and in Monza, where the iron crown of the Lombards was kept, visitors can still feel the aura of early medieval history.

Caffè
There is always time for a quick espresso

Culture and Nature

In this area where trade always flourished, they were followed by Frankish rulers and Holy Roman emperors, Spanish viceroys and Austrian regents, whose intentions were not always peaceful as they fought for privileges with the local dynasties, the Visconti, Sforza, Gonzaga, Colleoni and Borromeo. At the same time, thanks to the cosmopolitan outlook of the merchant elite and princely patronage of art, Lombardy became one of Europe's outstanding cultural regions. A wealth of innovations, from Leonardo da Vinci's *Last Supper* to Alessandro Volta's battery, from Stradivari's violins to the creative fashions of Versace and brands such as San Pellegrino and Campari, has enriched European civilization. It was not until the 18th century that the landscape and culture of the north Italian lakes gained broad appeal as a place of leisure. Aristocrats in search of education, artists and nature lovers sang the praises of this Garden of Eden. For some, the attractions of Lombardy are the 4000m/13,000ft peaks of the Bernina range in Valtellina, a paradise for hikers and

←Castello Scaligero in Sirmione

Relaxation
Combine an active holiday with relaxation and enjoyment of nature

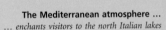

The Mediterranean atmosphere ...
... enchants visitors to the north Italian lakes

Beautiful parks
A lake and a park is an irresistible combination: here Villa Melzi on Lago di Como

Shopping
Milan is the top shopping destination in Lombardy

Milan Cathedral
It took centuries to complete Italy's second-largest church

Park of Villa d'Este
A fitting setting for the lakeside hotel in Cernobbio on Lago di Como

skiers; others come here for subtropical vegetation of blossoms and palm trees, white-painted villas behind laurel hedges, towered and fortified castelli in groves of cypress and pine, or high-class hotels and sailing trips on the lakes.

The Key to Italy

Lombardy has always been regarded as the key to Italy – from Roman times to the age of the Holy Roman Empire and the era of the competing great powers of early modern Europe, from the Risorgimento movement to Mussolini's puppet state in Salò. Even the recent political campaign against corruption began in Milan. This city of luxury and fashion, perhaps the unofficial capital of Italy, calls the tune. Here the forces that shape society – labour and capital, media and commerce, creativity and consumption – are engaged in a perpetual process of change and shifting equilibrium. In terms of cultural heritage Lombardy is a veritable treasure chest, filled with gems from all eras. The sights range widely from 6000-year-old rock carvings in Valcamonica, imposing Roman ruins and crenellated castles to picturesque medieval town centres with impressive palazzi, where frescoes adorn brick-built churches, and from romantic little squares to the very latest architecture. Many cities possess rich artistic treasures but hide their charms behind faceless suburbs and grey industrial zones. However, advanced industrial activities, crafts and art all have essential parts to play in Lombardy. Do not let the

Windsurfing
Lago di Garda is ideal for this sport

industry spoil cultural treats such as the Brera Gallery in Milan, the trompe l'oeil paintings of the ducal palace in Mantua, the bustling lanes of the old quarter of Bergamo and, last but not least, a cup of good cappuccino on the magnificent Piazza Ducale in Vigevano. To enjoy music and theatre go to the Piccolo Teatro and the world-famous La Scala. For culinary delights try the tasty cuisine of Milan and other areas, the relatively unknown wines of Lombardy and, as a pick-me-up, caffè with a shot of amaretto.

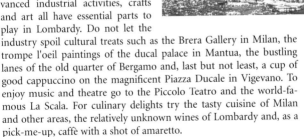

Facts

The landscapes of Lombardy are varied. They range from high Alpine mountains to the pretty north Italian lakes with their Mediterranean flora. Lombardy is also one of the most densely populated and economically prosperous regions of Italy.

Natural Environment

Lombardy is divided into two distinct areas of landscape, with the **north Italian lakes** as a transitional zone between. The north takes its character from mountains that rise to over 4000m/13,000ft and their foothills, while the broad Po valley extends across the southern half. The uplands to the far south-west beyond the Po are part of the Apennines.

Contrasting scenery

The Alps were formed during the Cretaceous and Tertiary periods by folding of the earth's crust. In the course of several phases layers of rock were detached from their original location, lifted and thrust over other rock deposits, in some cases moving more than 100km/ 60mi. The later **ice ages**, when the whole region was reshaped, had an important influence on the appearance of the landscape today. The **Alpine valleys** were filled with layers of ice between 500m and 1200m (1500–4000ft) thick. The ice cut mountain ridges, making them sharp-edged and narrow, and scoured out narrow depressions into wide valleys. Glaciers deepened tectonic trenches. The largest depressions have now been filled by the **north Italian lakes**. The southern boundaries of these lakes, i.e. the lower slopes of the Alpine foothills with many small lakes, were formed by moraine deposits. The plain of the Po was once the furthest north-west extent of the Adriatic Sea, which separated the Alps from the Apennines. Elevation of the earth's crust and alluvial deposit of coarse material carried by the rivers gradually created an expanse of land. In the Middle Ages there were still areas of wetland here.

Geology

> **?** **DID YOU KNOW …?**
>
> ■ The name Lombardy derives from a Germanic tribe known as the Lombards (»long beards«), who reached the Alpine valleys and Po plain in AD 569 and established an important kingdom there. »Lombard« was the name used for an Italian merchant or moneylender in the Middle Ages. Lombard Street in the City of London is a reminder of this old usage.

The highest summits of the Lombard Alps are in the far north of the Bernina range. They are the border to the neighbouring cantons of Switzerland and also form the watershed dividing areas that drain north into the Rhine and the Inn from those draining to the Adda in the south. The **Bergamasche Alps**, with their highest elevation at Pizzo di Coca (3052m/10,014ft), extend south of the Adda from Lago di Como in the west to Valcamonica, a valley to the east. To the east and north-east of Valcamonica rise the summits of **Adamello** (3554m/11,661ft) and the **Ortles range** – the highest peak of the Or-

Mountains

← *A superb variety of plants in the botanical garden on the Brissago Islands in Lago Maggiore*

Facts and Figures Lombardy

Lombardy

©Baedeker

► mountains 40.6%, hills 12.5%, plains 46.9%
highest point: Punta Perrucchetti (4021m/13,193ft) in the Bernina massif
lowest point: near Quatrelle (11m/36ft)

Government
► 12 provinces: Bergamo (2771 sq km/ 1069 sq mi), Brescia (4784 sq km/1846 sq mi), Como (1251 sq km/483 sq mi), Cremona (1770 sq km/683 sq mi), Lecco (816 sq km/315 sq mi), Lodi (782 sq km/302 sq mi), Mantova (2339 sq km/902 sq mi), Milano (1983 sq km/ 765 sq mi), Monza and Brianza (363 sq km/140 sq mi), Pavia (2965 sq km/1144 sq mi), Sondrio (3212 sq km/1239 sq mi) and Varese (1199 sq km/463 sq mi)
► 1546 communes

Population
► 9.4 million
(394 per sq km/1021 per sq mi)

Economy
► 20% of GDP of Italy
► 30% of exports and 37% of imports of Italy

Capital city
► Milano · Milan

Area
► 23,872 sq km/9210 sq mi

tles (3905m/12,810ft) is actually in South Tyrol (Alto Adige). West of Lago di Como lies the eastern part of the **Ticino Alps**, reaching altitudes of 2245m/7366ft (Pizzo di Gino).

The **Lombard foreland**, which in contrast to the higher Alpine regions consists not of crystalline but of sedimentary rock (mainly limestone), extends from Varese to Lago di Garda via Como, Bergamo and Brescia.

Passes   Since time immemorial the Alpine passes, once a laborious and dangerous route for the passage of humans and goods, have connected north and south through a realm of inaccessible mountains. The main passes in Lombardy are **Passo dello Stelvio** (2757m/9046ft), **Passo dello Spluga** (2113m/6932ft), **Passo di San Marco** (1985m/ 6513ft), **Passo del Tonale** (1884m/6181ft) and **Passo dell'Aprica** (1176m/3858ft).

The **north Italian lakes**, which owe their strangely elongated shape to the glaciers of the ice age, are lined up like a chain from west to east: **Lago di Orta** (18 sq km/7 sq mi; depth 143m/469ft), **Lago Maggiore** (212 sq km/82 sq mi; depth 372m/1221ft), **Lago di Lugano**, (51 sq km/20 sq mi; depth 288m/945ft), **Lago di Como** (146 sq km/56 sq mi; depth 410m/1345ft), **Lago d'Iseo** (65 sq km/25 sq mi; depth 251m/824ft), **Lago d'Idro** (11 sq km/4 sq mi; depth 122m/400ft), and the longest and largest lake, **Lago di Garda** (370 sq km/143 sq mi; depth 346m/1135ft). The smaller, round lakes are **Lago di Varese** (15 sq km/6 sq mi; depth 26m/85ft), **Lago di Comabbio** and **Lago di Monate** to the west near Varese, **Lago di Annone** (6 sq km/2.3 sq mi; depth 11m/36ft), **Lago di Pusiano** (5 sq km/1.9 sq mi; depth 24m/79ft) and **Lago di Alserio** south-west of Lecco, as well as the lakes south of Lecco which are fed by the Adda: **Lago di Garlate** and **Lago di Olginate**. To the west of Lago d'Iseo lies **Lago di Endine**.

Lakes

With a total length of 652km/405mi, the Po is the longest river in Italy. Its source is in Piedmont, south-west of Turin in the Cottian

Po

For centuries the lovely lakes to the south of the Alps have attracted famous visitors to »the land where the lemon trees flower«

Alps, and it flows into the Adriatic Sea south of Venice in a wide delta. The Po is navigable from its confluence with the Ticino near Pavia. The name of the river today derives from the Latin »Padus«, as it was called in Roman times. The Greeks called it »Eridanos« (bringer of gifts).

Many rivers flow through Lombardy, all of them direct or indirect **tributaries** of the Po. The largest of them flow into and out of the north Italian lakes: the Adda, the fourth-longest river in Italy with a length of 313km/194mi, flows through Lago di Como, the Ticino (248km/154mi) through Lago Maggiore, the Oglio (280km/174mi) through Lago d' Iseo, and the Chiese through Lago d' Idro. Other rivers of Lombardy include the Olona, the Lambro and the Mella, a tributary of the Oglio, as well as the Brembo and the Serio, both tributaries of the Adda. In addition to the longest river in Italy, Lombardy also has the shortest: near Varenna the **Fiumelatte**, which is only 250m/800ft long, enters Lago di Como. It roars down a 36% gradient, which gives it a milky colour and its name, »milk river«. It disappears each year in October and starts to flow again in the second half of March. There is thought to be a large reservoir inside the mountain which overflows into the river when the snow melts.

Plain of the Po The plain of the Po (pianura padana or Padania) south of the Alps is more than 400km/250mi long and up to 150km/100mi wide. It collects the waters of all the rivers that flow out of the Alps, and many large channels of water cross the plain. It is noticeable that there are no sizeable towns on the banks of the Po. The river has an existence of its own away from the cities, as time and again it has had to find a new course through the sand and clay soils of low-lying bassa pianura.

While settlements elsewhere were founded on rivers and in river valleys, life on the Po was always too dangerous. The river is therefore not directly integrated into the life of the cities and the transport network, even though it is the vital artery of the region. As it continually carries suspended materials and sand, which are deposited due to its low gradient, the river bed is rising all the time. This means that the average water level is several metres above the surrounding land in places. **Devastating floods** with burst dykes and large areas under water used to be a common occurrence after heavy rainfall and when the snows melted. During the flood disaster of 1951, further east in the Po delta, 50,000 people were made homeless. It is now thought that the construction of dykes has brought the flooding under control.

Apennines South of the Po, in Oltrepò Pavese, the plain gives way to the south to a region that is initially hilly, then mountainous. Here Lombardy stretches to the northern foothills of the Apennines, which then run all the way down the »boot« of Italy. The highest point of the Lombard part of the Apennines is Monte Lesima (1724m/5656ft).

Many hot mineral springs, most of which were already used in Roman times, rise in the mountains of Lombardy. The springs of **S. Pellegrino Terme**, which contain sodium bicarbonate and sulphur, are the best known in the region. The sulphur and salt springs at **Bormio** (1225m/4020ft) have the highest elevation, and further south in Valcamonica there are sulphur and lime springs at **Boario Terme** and the neighbouring **Angolo Terme**. The radioactive sulphurous springs in **Sirmione** on Lago di Garda, which have a temperature of 69°C/156°F, have attracted visitors since antiquity. **Salice Terme**, with hot springs on the northern edge of the Apennines, is also a popular spa.

Hot springs

Flora and Fauna

Plants

Nature is still largely unspoilt in a few less accessible areas of the Alps. **Valtellina** in particular has an extremely varied flora. Below the barren zone of rocks and low vegetation grow forests of larch and fir, with bearberry and juniper at their margins. The deciduous zone below this is colonized by woods of beech and oak, with ash, lime, chestnut and sycamore in between. The Alpine flowers that grow here include ten species of gentian, members of the buttercup family (Ranunculus), various kinds of violet such as the marsh violet (Viola palustris), twin-flowered violet (Viola biflora) and pansy (Viola tricolor), the alpenrose, pasque flower, aquilegia and primulas such as the fragrant primrose.

Alpine vegetation

The **north Italian lakes** have their own special flora. Here – sometimes only on particular stretches of the lake shore – the mild climate permits luxuriant Mediterranean vegetation to grow. There are orange and lemon trees, cypresses, olive groves, orchards with apple, cherry and peach trees, almond trees, and even cork oak and carob trees, agaves and palms, mimosas, azaleas, camellias and agapanthus – i.e. a **typical Mediterranean flora**.

Subtropical vegetation

The plain of the Po is almost entirely cultivated, as the soil is suitable for growing rice, maize, cereals, soya and sunflowers. Poplars in groves and endless rows mark this country where habitats for wild animals and plants hardly exist.

Po plain

In the foothills of the Apennines the vegetation is Mediterranean, but differs from that around the lakes in that it grows wild. Boxwood, the Judas tree, pines and a macchia of bushes such as rock rose, arbutus, laurel and myrtle are the typical plants. Vines and fruit trees are cultivated.

Apennine foothills

Poplars are the characteristic trees on the plain of the river Po

Animals

High Alps Where its natural habitat has not been destroyed by deforestation or other human intervention, a **typical Alpine fauna** still lives in the higher mountain regions. The larger mammals are chamois, which live in groups and are known for their ability to climb; ibex, which spend the summer above the tree line and the winter at lower altitudes; and red deer. Marmots like the sunny Alpine slopes. Golden eagles, ravens and Alpine choughs – members of the raven family which often appear in large numbers around mountain huts – can be spotted. Valtellina is home to almost 240 bird species. The Alpine salamander and Alpine newt are also characteristic animals of the region, the protected black Alpine salamander being the only species of amphibian that reproduces out of water. There are also some conspicuous butterflies. The most commonly seen are two types of Apollo butterfly: the Apollo with a wingspan of 7–8cm (approx. 3in) and the somewhat smaller, red-black Alpine Apollo butterfly.

Fish In the many lakes and rivers of Lombardy there are not only large numbers of fish but also, on closer inspection, a great variety of different piscine species. Lago di Como, for example, harbours carp, tench, pike and eels. In Lago di Garda, by contrast, the conditions are hardly suitable for fish. Trout are plentiful in the upper Adda and its tributaries.

The **plain of the Po** is heavily urbanized and therefore covered by a network of roads. The large cities suffer from industrial and traffic exhaust gases, which create a layer of smog above the plain. The creation of car-free city centres represents a first step towards improving the air quality. The Po is one of Europe's dirtiest rivers. Pollution of its water and banks by untreated or inadequately treated sewage and by agricultural pesticides, the drying and concreting of old channels, and the planting of poplars for industrial use instead of the natural trees of the water meadows, have caused huge damage and are a threat to the ecology of the whole region. In the **Alps** large-scale deforestation, the straightening of the courses of streams and the bulldozing of slopes for skiing have had a severe effect. The consequences are erosion, landslides and of course, in the mountains and the valleys, elimination of the habitat of plants and animals. In order to at least begin to halt the destruction of the natural environment, 23 areas of Lombardy have been declared protected zones, and a further 60 nature reserves have been established.

Protection of nature

Population · Politics · Economy

Lombardy has 9.4 million inhabitants and an average population density of 394 persons per sq km/1021 per sq mi. By way of comparison: Tuscany, which is about the same size, has a population density of just 157 per sq km/407 per sq mi, and the national average is 189 per sq km/489 per sq mi. Between 1951 and 1971 there was marked immigration into Lombardy, and the population rose from 6.5 to 8.5 million. This increase was the prerequisite for and also the result of the economic growth of this period. In the 1970s growth was lower, and in the 1980s even negative at times. The most densely populated part of Lombardy is the province of Milan, with 1954 persons per sq km/5060 per sq mi; only the province of Naples, with 2637 per sq km/6829 per sq mi, surpasses this. Although there is a shortage of housing, strong pressure from immigration remains. At the other extreme, the province of Sondrio in the north-east has just 55 inhabitants per sq km/143 per sq mi, almost as low as anywhere in Italy.

Population, population density

The official language is Italian, but the people of Lombardy and the neighbouring regions speak **Gallo-Italian dialects** that are significantly different from those spoken further south. A small minority in the remote mountain region of Livigno in the north-east speaks a completely different language, **Ladin or Rhaeto-Romance**.

Language

Almost the entire population is Roman Catholic, but in 1984 Catholicism ceased to be the state religion. However, in Milan, as in other leading European cities, there is a great variety of smaller religious communities, from Anglicans to Buddhists.

Religion

Some places are still male-dominated – this caffè, for example

For most Italians their **family and place of birth** are extremely important. Those who do not move away for studies or training usually live with their parents until they get married. This is partly a matter of tradition, but also a result of the scarcity of housing. Strong family relationships have survived almost everywhere, especially in rural areas. However, in the cities it has become acceptable for couples to live together without marrying. Since the early 1970s divorce has been possible in Italy, and since 1977 there has been legislation on equality of the sexes at work.

The marked **difference in living standards between the north and the south** is a severe problem for Italy. Many north Italians feel they have little in common with the people of central and southern Italy. There are great disparities, which are partly connected to the industrialization of the north, in political, economic and social terms. Women, for example, are much more involved in working life in the north than in the south. This fact and the greater influence of the church are the reasons why family ties are stronger in southern Italy.

Political system Rome is the seat of the Italian parliament, which consists of the 315 members of the senate and the 630 members of the chamber of deputies. Members of parliament represent the 20 regions of Italy and are elected every five years. Both chambers take part in legislation and monitoring the government. Since the franchise reform of 1993 three quarters of the senators have been elected on a simple majority and one quarter by proportional representation. The government consists of the prime minister and his ministers. The Italian president, who is elected for a period of seven years, has wider powers than his purely representational functions. He can influence legislation by means of a delaying veto and dissolve parliament. Draft legislation can only be introduced to parliament with his consent, and he nominates the prime minister.

Economy and Transport

Lombardy Provinces

Today Lombardy is economically the strongest region of Italy. In the early 20th century the **Lombard economy** was still dominated by agriculture and trade. From the 1950s rapid, broadly based industrial development took place. The boom years were mainly between 1950 and 1970, and by the late 1980s about one fifth of all Italian goods and services were produced in the Milan region. In the 1990s Veneto, Emilia-Romagna, Trentino-Alto Adige and Marche experienced higher levels of growth, but Lombardy is still regarded as the **powerhouse of the Italian economy**.

The general economic expansion was essentially dependent on the development of industry. Engineering, textile production, chemicals, wood processing and the production of food are the strongest sectors. Industry in Lombardy is characterized by the presence of a wide range of different activities. **Engineering** is concentrated in the provinces of Milan, Varese and Brescia, the **textile industry** in the provinces of Como and Varese, wood processing and furniture manufacture around Como and north of Milan in Brianza. **Chemical and petrochemical companies** are based in the provinces of Milan, Pavia, Cremona and Mantua. Some sectors developed in a small geographical area and are still concentrated there: Valtrompia north of Brescia is traditionally known for making **weapons**, Como for **silk production** and Vigevano for **shoes**. Following a number of factory closures in the 1990s, for example by the tyre manufacturer Pirelli on the northern edge of Milan and the computer company Olivetti in the small town of Crema, an initiative to promote investment was launched. New agreements to establish joint ventures and attract foreign firms are intended to strengthen the regional economy. **Industry**

A large number of small and medium-sized craft companies operate in Lombardy. The most important group of these are engaged in **woodworking**. Cremona is world-famous for the production of **violins**. **Crafts**

Since the 1950s agriculture has expanded, although not as strongly as industry. Lombardy is now **one of the most important agricultural areas** in Italy. In the mid-1990s the region's agricultural output for the first time exceeded that of its neighbouring region Emilia- **Agriculture**

Elegant shoes of the finest quality are manufactured in Pavia

Romagna, which previously held first place. Most agricultural production is based in the well-watered plain of the river Po, where rice, maize, soya, cereals and sunflowers are the most important crops. A good deal of Parma ham, a product of Emilia-Romagna, is actually made in the Lombard province of Mantua.

DOC quality **wines** (denominazione d'origine controllata) are made in 13 wine-growing areas of Lombardy, which produce 1.5 million hectolitres (40 million US gallons) annually of the 51 million hectolitres (1.35 billion US gallons) produced in the whole of Italy. Lombardy is thus not one of the major Italian wine regions. The main **areas of grape cultivation** are in Valtellina (Sondrio province) in the north, in Franciacorta (Brescia province) south of Lago d'Iseo, at the southern end of Lago di Garda and in Oltrepò Pavese (Pavia province) in the southwest.

Tourism   Tourism in Lombardy is not particularly significant in national terms: 15 million visitors come to the region each year. The **main tourist areas** are Lago di Garda and the skiing resorts in Bormio, Livigno and Valtellina. In rural areas many small farmers try to supplement their earnings by offering »agriturismo«.

Transport   Thanks to its location between the Alps and the Mediterranean, Lombardy has always been an important area of transit where there have been routes for commerce, but also for the many peoples who have passed through or invaded the region, since time immemorial. The first roads to be built were those of the Romans. The opening and improvement of the **Alpine passes**, which could only be used by mules, horses and – right up to the First World War – by coaches was a significant boost to trade between the countries north of the Alps and those of the Mediterranean. In 1237 the St Gotthard Pass was opened, in 1881 the Gotthard Rail Tunnel. The famous road over the Stilfser Joch was built between 1820 and 1825. The **waterways** were also important trade routes. In some places around the north Italian lakes there were no asphalted roads until the 1930s, and much transport, including traffic to the passes, went by water. The canals that cross the plain of the river Po were also an extremely important transport system, which originated in Roman times. In the Renaissance the network of canals and rivers was extended to the point that Milan was connected to Venice by water – an age-old dream of the rulers of Milan, who possessed no major river and therefore no direct link to the sea. The Naviglio Grande, which connects Milan to Ticino and Lago Maggiore, was built around 1200. **Leonardo da Vinci** is said to have worked on canal engineering, and parts of the irrigation system of Lomellina are attributed to him. Today only a small part of this canal system still exists, as in the 1930s most man-made waterways were filled in. Today Milan is connected by canals and rivers to Lago Maggiore, Lago di Como and the Po, and thus with the Adriatic Sea.

Wine growing is important to the economy of Lombardy

History

In the course of its history, northern Italy has been a gateway for incursions by many different peoples and a pawn of great powers. The period of migration after the collapse of Rome brought the Lombards to this region. Later Lombardy had a variety of rulers, ranging from the Franks to the Austrians.

Early History and Antiquity

4000 BC	First evidence of settlers
6th–5th century BC	Etruscans and Celts move into the region.
c200 BC	The Romans conquer northern Italy.

The first traces of humans from this region, dating from about 4000 BC, were found in the Alps. They probably relate to the prehistoric tribe known as the **Camunni**. The first known inhabitants of northern Italy were the **Ligurians**, who settled around 1600 BC in the region between the coast that is named after them and the north-west plain of the Po. In the 6th century BC the **Etruscans** came from the south and occupied the area near Mantua. They were founders of cities, talented craftsmen and successful traders. From the 5th century BC northern Italy was inundated by the great **Celtic invasion** from the north. The armies of **Rome** opposed their advance and brought northern Italy under their control piece by piece, making it into the province of Gallia Cisalpina. To reinforce their rule the Romans built a network of roads, including the Via Aemilia from Rimini to Piacenza. Originally these roads were military routes with army bases spaced at a distance of one day's march. The bases quickly became prosperous settlements such as Pavia (Ticinum), Como (Novum Comum), Lodi Vecchio (Laus Pompeia) and Brescia (Brixia). Milan's status rose and rose: in 15 BC under **Augustus** the city became the main urban centre of the region, which was to be one of the most highly developed of the Roman Empire thanks to its agricultural wealth and strategic position for communications. In AD 286 Milan even gained the status of a capital city. The Edict of Milan in 313 introduced toleration of Christianity. Gratian, Valentinian and Theodosius I made Milan their imperial residence.

First humans

Age of Migrations

From 3rd century	Start of the age of migrations
568	The Lombards enter northern Italy.
774	Charlemagne conquers the Lombard kingdom.

In the course of the migrations that began in the 3rd century, and especially between the 5th and 9th centuries AD, invaders came across

Invaders in northern Italy

← *Castello Sforzesco in Milan: renowned artists and architects worked on the construction of this mighty castle*

the Alps into northern Italy. Rome, so insecure that the emperor moved to Ravenna in 404, was looted by the **Visigoths** in 410. In 452 Milan suffered the same fate at the hands of the **Huns**. Finally in 476 the Germanic chieftain **Odoacer** deposed the last West Roman emperor and declared himself king of Italy but was defeated in 493 by the Ostrogoth king **Theoderic**, who was acting on behalf of the East Roman emperor. Until 526 Theoderic ruled an Ostrogoth kingdom in Italy from his residence in Pavia.

Lombards

In 568 new invaders appeared in northern Italy: the Lombards, who derived from Pannonia (now Hungary). These »longbeards« quickly conquered all of northern and central Italy and made Pavia the capital of their kingdom in 572. They gave their name to Lombardy, defended it against attacks by other peoples, rebuilt the cities that had been destroyed in the wars of the Goths, and adopted both the old administrative structure and the religion of the native population. By the late 7th century the Lombard aristocracy had become fully Romanic in terms of language and culture.

Bent on expansion, they came into conflict with the **popes**, who feared losing their influence and made their intentions clear through one of the most famous forgeries in European history: between 750 and 760 papal scholars produced documents relating to a donation by Emperor Constantine to Pope Sylvester that had never taken place. The forgery was intended to prove that the city of Rome and the western half of the Roman Empire had been granted to the papacy by Constantine. Citing these documents, in 754 the pope called on the help of **Pepin, king of the Franks**. In the course of several campaigns Pepin, who had in fact been an ally of the Lombards, forced them to cede territory to the pope. This went down in history as the so-called **Donation of Pepin** and led to the establishment of a papal state. Pepin's son **Charlemagne** finally destroyed the Lombard kingdom and placed the Iron Crown of the Lombards on his own head in Pavia in 774. In 800 Pope Leo III crowned him as Roman Emperor.

Medieval City Republics

951	Otto I defeats the last Italian king.
11th century	Social tensions between aristocracy and middle class
12–13th centuries	The cities of northern Italy defend their privileges against Holy Roman Emperors Frederick I and Frederick II.
13th century	Conflicts between Ghibellines and Guelphs

Political conflicts

For the 70 years after the coronation of Charlemagne, northern Italy was part of the Frankish kingdom, which was partitioned in 843. Northern Italy then fell under the influence of the east Frankish kingdom, from which the Holy Roman Empire emerged. As a result of the lack of a central power, various rival dynasties succeeded each other between 888 and 962 as **rex Italiae**, so-called kings of Italy. As the situation became ever more confused, elements of the aristocracy and the pope called for the help of the German king. In 951 **Otto I** defeated the last rex Italiae and in 962 was crowned Holy Roman Emperor in his role as protector of the church and guarantor of order in Italy. Over the next 100 years an open conflict for primacy in Italy broke out between the emperor and the pope. Its dramatic climax was the **Investiture Controversy** (1075–1122). When Pope Gregory VII denied to Emperor Henry IV any influence in the appointment of bishops, the emperor was forced to give way. In winter 1077 he walked barefoot to **Canossa** wearing a hair shirt, and submitted to the pope. During the Investiture Controversy the urban communities (comuni) succeeded in gaining their freedom from feudal rule and creating their own organs of administration.

Social conflict

It is clear that in 11th-century northern Italy this could not take place without social conflict. Trade and industry, and the profitable crusades, had made the cities prosperous. A new social class had taken its place alongside the nobility: the **middle class**, which included merchants and craftsmen as well as lawyers, the so-called judices and notarii. As time passed their status and their interest in greater independence grew. They formed an alliance with the lesser nobility (valvassores), who wanted to make their fiefs hereditary against the express wishes of church prelates and the high aristocracy, most of whom were Franks. Emperor Conrad II, who was called on to mediate, took the side of the valvassores and declared the fiefs of the lesser nobility to be hereditary in 1037.

◀ Pataria

The Pataria, a **popular movement** that began in Milan and extended to the rest of Lombardy, also fomented unrest. Originally religious, later revolutionary in political terms, it attacked the rule of the prelates and aristocrats, who had been appointed by the emperor, and denounced abuses in the church such as the marriage of priests and the sale of ecclesiastical offices (simony). At times the papacy used the Pataria for its own ends, but later distanced itself when the movement began to turn against the Church of Rome. The beneficiaries of all these quarrels were the cities. As one party or another attempted to win them over, they were granted more and more concessions and gained secular rights such as the rights to levy customs, mint coins, operate harbours and hold courts and markets.

◀ Comune

The culmination of these developments was that Milan became an autonomous city republic, a comune, with its own organs of government. Harking back to the ancient Roman tradition, many cities elected consuls, who were the true political heads of the comune.

City councils with 500 to 1000 members were formed. An elected podestà, who had to come from another city in order to guarantee his independence, had the power to enforce law and order for a period of six to twelve months. There was also a publicly monitored financial officer. As wider circles of the population acquired influence, they were given their own representative, the capitano del popolo. The first consuls were chosen in Cremona as early as 1031, in Pavia in 1084, in Milan in 1097 and in Como in 1109.

Emperors and city republics

For almost 20 years no German ruler had made an appearance in Italy. The city republics grew strong. They no longer restricted their claims to government of the territory of the city, but extended them to the surrounding country, which led to violent conflicts with neighbouring comuni. This coincided with the accession in Germany of an emperor from the Hohenstaufen family, **Frederick I** (Frederick Barbarossa, ruled 1151–90), a man who aimed to restore imperial authority towards the pope as well as the city republics. Under the pretence of maintaining order, Barbarossa arrived in northern Italy in 1154. His intention was to demand from the cities the cession of all rights for which they possessed no documentary evidence. The comuni were divided: powerful cities such as Milan pursued a radical anti-imperial policy, while other, smaller cities such as Como, Pavia and Cremona hoped that by showing support for the emperor they

Over 200 family towers looked down on medieval Pavia

would get assistance in their struggle against expansionist neighbouring communities. The battle was initially fought in court. This changed in 1162: Frederick besieged Milan. The city was eventually forced to surrender and razed to the ground. Resistance now formed, supported by the pope. In 1167 the papal legates succeeded in bringing together the previously divided cities to found the **Lombard League** against the emperor at the monastery of Pontida near Bergamo. The united forces of the league inflicted a devastating defeat on the imperial army at the Battle of Legnano in 1176. In later campaigns Frederick also failed to defeat the comuni, which had formed alliances. At the Peace of Constance in 1183 he was obliged to acknowledge the cities' freedom to elect consuls and to guarantee their other rights within the city walls. 60 years later the Hohenstaufen dynasty was again defeated when the north Italian cities formed a second league against **Frederick II** (ruled 1212–50) and cut off his line of withdrawal. When Frederick died in southern Italy in 1250, the ambition of the Hohenstaufen emperors to establish an empire encompassing Italy and Germany expired with him.

During this period of political uncertainty the economy of Lombardy grew. In the 12th and 13th centuries the construction of the Naviglio Grande, the first large canal, contributed to the drainage and irrigation of the land; the opening of the St Gotthard Pass in 1237 was a further boost to trade. Within the cities, however, conflicts between rival dynasties raged. These families were divided into the **Ghibelline** (imperial) and **Guelph** (papal) parties, their allegiance dependent on the question of which side gave them their privileges. Testimony to these turbulent times survives in the form of family towers, tall structures standing close together in which families could take refuge during their feuds. These clan wars destroyed the foundations of the city republics, and the comuni were succeeded by **signorias**. A signoria was at first no more than government for a fixed period by a man experienced in war, who was given office in order to keep the conflicting parties from each other's throats. However, those who exercised this rule by force for a limited time then used their office to seize power themselves. By the end of the 13th century families had taken control of several comuni and established themselves as ruling dynasties. In order to reinforce their position, the signori had recourse to any means, from terror, violence, murder and war to diplomacy and displays of magnificence.

Fall of the city republics

The most successful of them were the much-feared Visconti of Milan, who from 1311 conquered an enormous north Italian territory, including Como, Bergamo, Piacenza, Pavia, Cremona, Vercelli, Tortona and Alessandria. They employed architects, sculptors, painters and poets to celebrate their triumphs in stone, on canvas and in verse. In 1395 **Gian Galeazzo Visconti** even purchased the title of duke. This was the age of the condottiere, the mercenary generals,

Visconti in Milan

whose assistance princes used to maintain their power. The Visconti seemed to have an insatiable appetite for hegemony until the second leading power in northern Italy, Venice, entered the contest and triggered the great north Italian war between the two cities. It was not until the **Peace of Lodi in 1454** that equilibrium was established for the next 40 years between the leading powers in Italy: Milan (the Sforza), Venice (a city republic), Florence (the Medici), Genoa (a city republic), the Papal States and the Kingdom of Naples and Sicily.

From the 15th Century to the Present

1525	The conflict between France and the Habsburgs is decided in favour of Emperor Charles V at the Battle of Pavia.
1714	Spanish territories in Italy are awarded to Austria.
1805	After Napoleon's conquests northern Italy becomes part of the Kingdom of Italy.
1815	The Congress of Vienna restores Austrian power in the shape of the Kingdom of Lombardy-Venetia.
1859–61	After the Battle of Solferino Austria is forced to cede Lombardy to Sardinia-Piedmont.
1870	Following the final expulsion of the Austrians from Lombardy in 1861, Italy is united.
1914–18	First World War
1922–45	Fascism and the Second World War

Il Moro Sforza of Milan

While Venice and the cities of Bergamo, Brescia and Verona, which were subject to its rule, enjoyed peace until the late 18th century, the Duchy of Milan experienced catastrophe, becoming a pawn in the struggle between France and the Habsburgs for mastery in Europe. Initially, however, the city had a period of peace under the condottiere **Francesco Sforza** (ruled c1450–66), the son-in-law of the last Visconti ruler, and his successor **Ludovico Sforza, known as il Moro** (ruled 1494–1500). Milan was the most populous city in Europe. Ludovico Sforza brought the architect Bramante and Leonardo da Vinci to his court. He was also successful economically, for example initiating the cultivation of rice and the planting of mulberry trees. The breeding of silkworms opened new markets, and silk from Milan acquired a worldwide reputation. However, the claims of the house of Orléans to rule Milan led King Charles VIII of France to invade Italy in 1491. He was repulsed, but just a few years later the army of **Louis XII** marched to the gates of Milan. Louis took Ludovico Sforza back to France, where he died in prison in 1508, and seized the duchy for the French crown. The threat of a foreign power ruling Italy caused the pope to ask the principal opponent of France at that time, the Habsburg emperor **Charles V**, for assistance. He also gained assurances of military aid from the Swiss Confederation. In a war against François I that devastated half of Lombardy and was decided at the Battle of Pavia in 1525, the Habsburg armies were victorious. The French were driven from Italy and **Francesco Sforza** was installed as Duke of Milan in 1529. When he died without an heir, the emperor declared Milan to be an imperial fief that had reverted to his dominion. The duchy fell into the hands of the Spanish Habsburgs. The support of the Swiss Confederation also had its price: Bellinzona, Locarno and Lugano, which now belong to Ticino, became part of Switzerland. In 1559 the continued division of Italy into a number of states was sealed in an agreement between Philip II of Spain and Henri II of France. From that time on, northern Italy no longer played any important role in European politics.

Austrian rule in northern Italy

The War of the Spanish Succession (1701–14) brought the dominance of Spain in northern Italy to an end. Lombardy passed to the Austrian Habsburgs. In 1735 the territories south of the Po (Oltrepò Pavese, Lomellina and Novara) fell to the ruler of Savoy, **Carlo Emanuele III**, King of Sardinia-Piedmont. During the reigns of **Maria Theresia** (ruled 1745–90) and her son **Joseph II** the privileges of the nobles in the Duchy of Milan were restricted. New roads, canals and irrigation systems were built, and schooling was made available to all. In 1760 the number of students in Pavia was a mere 150, but the introduction of the school reform increased this to 1000.

Napoleon

Despite these reforms the ideas and demands of the French Revolution were welcomed by most of the people of Lombardy, and when Napoleon marched his army into Italy and entered Milan in 1796, many gave him an enthusiastic reception. Lombardy, Valtellina and the territories of Bologna, Ferrara, Modena and Reggio were combined to form the **Cisalpine Republic** with Milan as its capital. In 1801–02 the Cisalpine Republic was converted into an Italian Republic and, after Bonaparte crowned himself emperor in 1804, became the **Kingdom of Italy** in 1805. The country was given its own constitution based on that of the French Republic of 1795, including a guarantee of freedom of the press. The constitution separated legislative and executive powers, and enshrined the sovereignty of the people and citizens' equality. Napoleon also introduced prefectures, thus creating the administrative districts which exist to the present day.

Restoration and Risorgimento

After the fall of Napoleon, the Congress of Vienna in 1814–15 decided to hand Lombardy back to Austria. The restoration of the ancien régime in the new Kingdom of Lombardy-Venetia was wind in the sails of the Risorgimento, the movement for national unification. Milan was the intellectual centre of the Risorgimento, which took its name from a magazine founded in 1847 and was led by **Count Camillo Cavour** and **Giuseppe Garibaldi**. In a number of campaigns supported by France and Sardinia-Piedmont – including the Battle of Solferino – between 1859 and 1861 the Austrians were driven from northern Italy, and Lombardy became part of the Kingdom of Sardinia-Piedmont. In 1861 Vittorio Emanuele II of Sardinia-Piedmont took the title »King of Italy« in accordance with a vote of the first, newly elected Italian parliament.

First World War In 1882 Italy was reconciled with Austria and, together with Germany, formed the Triple Alliance. When the First World War broke out, Italy initially proclaimed its neutrality, but entered the war on the side of the entente after gaining assurances of support for its territorial claims from England and France in a secret agreement. In May 1915 it declared war on Austria-Hungary, in August 1916 on Germany. In fighting on the Isonzo which caused great loss of life, the Italians attempted to storm the Austrian Alpine front. In 1919 Italy was awarded the South Tirol (Alto Adige), Trentino, Venezia-Giulia, Trieste and Istria (except for Fiume), as well as several Dalmatian islands.

Fascism Enormous economic and social problems after the First World War
Second created the conditions for the rise of Fascism. With **Benito Mussoli-**
World War **ni's »March on Rome«** in 1922 and his subsequent appointment to the office of prime minister, the Fascists took power. In 1940 Italy entered the Second World War on the German side. After Mussolini was toppled in July 1943, Italy signed an armistice with the Allies. Mussolini retreated to German-occupied northern Italy and founded the Repubblica Sociale Italiana in September in Salò on Lago di Garda; in April 1945 he was killed by partisans while fleeing near Tremezzo on Lago di Como.

Republic of Italy ▶ Following a referendum in June 1946, in which 64.1% of the voters in Lombardy voted for a republic, King Vittorio Emanuele III abdicated.

Today Since the unification of Italy, the north of the country has risen rapidly to become one of Europe's economic powerhouses. Milan's status as the business and cultural centre of Italy is undisputed. The collapse of communist eastern Europe up to 1990 and large-scale investigations into corruption in Milan in 1992, a campaign by Milanese judges to clean up politics, opened the floodgates and swept away a sclerotic party system that had existed for almost 50 years. Since then political battles have been fought out not between the parties but between centre-left and conservative groupings. In the parliamentary elections of 2001 a centre-right alliance led by the media mogul **Silvio Berlusconi**, the richest man in Italy, was victorious. In 2006 a centre-left coalition under **Romano Prodi** was elected, but in 2008

Berlusconi returned to power. His attacks on the freedom of the press and the judicial system have been met by frequent protests.

In 1996 Umberto Bossi's separatist Lega Nord caused a stir when Bossi called for the independence of Padania, the northern part of Italy through which the river Po (»Padus« in Latin) flows. In the parliamentary elections of 1996, 3.77 million north Italians cast their vote for the Lega. The danger of the north seceding from Italy is, however, not great, as few support Bossi's aims of creating an independent republic, ending the status of Italian as the official language of state and introducing English for external communications and local dialects for internal matters. Nevertheless, the Lega has forced the country to face up to some urgent problems: the glaring contrasts between north and south Italy and the inefficiency of the central government. Three rich regions in the north, Lombardy, Piedmont and Venetia, bear the main burden of taxation which helps to pay for the expensive but ineffective **Mezzogiorno policy**.

Padania libera

Art and Culture

Where did the basilica, which influenced Christian architecture for centuries, originate? Which peoples helped shape the history of art in Lombardy? Where did the universal genius Leonardo da Vinci work? What is the region's design capital?

History of Art

Lombardy's earliest cultural traces are to be found in the Alpine region. **Valcamonica**, a valley north of Lago d'Iseo, was home to members of a probably half-nomadic tribe generally referred to as the **Camunni** or ancient Camunians. Whether they were of Celtic or Ligurian origin is not really clear. It is certain, however, that they left to posterity a rich heritage of cultural   treasures. From the Neolithic Age onwards, rock carvings were made here that not only give evidence of settlement from about the 4th millennium BC but also provide an idea of life at the time. On the basis of the depictions, the carvings can be dated quite precisely: Stone Age, Bronze Age and Iron Age culture find expression on the rocks.

Prehistoric traces

The whole valley is full of rock carvings, and new sites are being discovered all the time. The best known are the carvings in the national park near **Capo di Ponte** (► Baedeker Special p.308). The Massi di Cemmo on the edge of Capo di Ponte, on which an artful and systematically arranged composition of deer can be seen, may be considered the most beautiful of the sites. Further traces of the Neolithic Age in **Valtellina** are freely accessible in the Parco delle Incisioni Rupestri near Grosio, in which the Rupe Magna rock bears figures that can be identified relatively easily. In the Palazzo Besta in Teglio there are very well-preserved Neolithic stelae on which game animals, sun symbols and spiral characters are depicted. Roman characters below the rock carvings in **Valcamonica** make it clear that these cult sites were still used in Roman times. In addition Christian cross symbols have been discovered.

◄ Sites of finds

Cultural traces of other peoples who moved into Lombardy in the pre-Roman period are scant in comparison. Between 800 and 200 BC northern Italy was shaped by the **Golasecca culture**, named after the site of a burial ground found near Somma Lombardo south of Lago Maggiore. The Golasecca culture was influenced from the 6th century BC by the Etruscans, who advanced from the south into southern Lombardy. The **Celtic Cenomanes**, who came from the north over the Alps into areas of northern Italy after the 5th century BC, brought the La Tène culture into the southern Alpine region.

In the 3rd century BC the Romans asserted claims to northern Italy, and until around AD 400 they shaped the cultural scene of the region. During their rule an excellent road system was created across the whole Roman Empire. In northern Italy the important Via Aemilia was built somewhat south of Lombardy between Rimini and Piacenza in 187 BC. Smaller roads connected Roman cities in Lombardy such as **Brixia (Brescia)**, **Novum Comum (Como)**, **Laus Pompeia (Lodi Vecchio)**, **Mediolanum (Milan)** and **Ticinum (Pavia)**. The system of

Romans

← *Galleria Vittorio Emanuele in Milan and its impressive glass dome*

canals, too, which would be extended impressively in later centuries, was initiated at this time. Imposing temples, amphitheatres, spas and city gates were built. Roman noble families built villas in the most beautiful areas, such as the Alpine foothills near Varese and, of course, on the lakes of northern Italy. The famous Pliny family had several country seats at Lago di Como. Evidence of this rich culture is comparatively rare in Lombardy today, but a good impression of the building style and way of living of the time can be acquired in Brescia and at Lago di Garda in Sirmione, as well as in Desenzano. In Sirmione the villa known as the **Grotte di Catullo** was built around AD 1, and the villa in Desenzano dates from AD 4. In Brescia parts of the Roman forum and the Capitoline Temple have been preserved.

Early Christian period
When the construction of churches began some time after the toleration of Christianity in AD 313, elements of Roman architecture were adopted.

There are no longer any complete churches in Lombardy from the early Christian period, i.e. from the 4th century AD: as a rule they were replaced by later buildings in subsequent centuries. However several important churches go back to places of worship founded during this time, including the **Milanese churches of S. Ambrogio and S. Lorenzo Maggiore**, which were constructed under Archbishop Ambrose (▶ Famous People). Pre-Romanesque parts of the church of S. Ambrogio are still preserved in the form of a campanile and the vestibule. In the interior there is a depiction of St Ambrose on the ceiling of the funerary chapel of S. Vittore in Ciel d' Oro from 470, an impressive example of an early Christian mosaic. The sarcophagus of Stilicho, made for Flavius Stilicho, the Roman regent in the West, dates from the early 5th century.

? **DID YOU KNOW …?**

■ In the search for a suitable space in which Christian congregations could assemble, the Roman market hall or hall for court hearings, known as a basilica, was adopted. It is from this building form that the early Christian **basilica** derives, with the apse, which served as a podium for the market overseer or judge, normally on the east side of the choir. The basic plan of the basilica, with variations, was retained for centuries, with the transept, vestibule and belfry being added in the course of time. Columns and round arches were taken from the Roman repertoire of architectural forms.

Lombardy boasts a very interesting work in the history of Western church architecture with Milan's church of S. Lorenzo Maggiore, which also derives from an original 4th-century church and is one of the earliest Christian buildings with a central ground plan.

Lombards
After the turmoil of the invasions of the Roman Empire and the destruction of cities through military conflict, the Lombards were the first people to take over government for an extended period, and as such from 568 they shaped the culture of northern Italy. With them

they brought their own funerary art and gold jewellery, characterized by a strong tendency toward abstract ornamentation. Braided motifs and stylized plants of all kinds are the main elements. The notable preference for rich decoration at this time continued to have an effect in Lombardy in almost all style epochs. Because of this tradition the Gothic style, for example, with its pronounced ornamentation, lasted significantly longer in Lombardy than any other region of Italy.

In keeping with the Lombard love of ornament, important architecture of the Lombard Renaissance, such as the façade of the **Certosa di Pavia** and the crossing tower of S. Maria delle Grazie in **Milan**, exhibits markedly filigree decoration in comparison to the austerity of Renaissance work in other parts of the country. Fine examples of the Lombard art of gold jewellery are to be seen in **Monza**. The »Iron Crown« of Lombardy, with which a great variety of rulers, including eventually Napoleon, had themselves crowned king of Italy, is kept in the cathedral there. The town of **Castelseprio**, whose remains were excavated after the Second World War, was very important in Lombard times. A quite spectacular 7th-century cycle of frescoes has survived the passing of time here, and the fact that it exhibits a Byzantine style presents several riddles. Today it is assumed that in Lombard times itinerant artists from Byzantium were active in Lombardy.

Some testimony to the ensuing Carolingian epoch in the 8th and 9th centuries also remains. Two major 9th-century works can be seen in S. Ambrogio in Milan: the Altare d'Oro with relief work of gilded sheet silver and the altar baldachin with rich decoration of painted stucco. The Croce di Desiderio, a cross in **Brescia**, is probably the most impressive piece from this period.

Carolingians

Through revived agriculture and thriving trade the towns grew in size between the 11th and 13th centuries. Their cathedrals, with market places in front of them, became the focal points of religious and societal life. The first small town halls were built. In the Lombardy of the 7th to the 12th centuries architecture and stonemasonry are primarily linked with the Maestri Comacini and Maestri Intelvesi, stonemasons who were named after their places of origin (► Baedeker Special p.158). **S. Michele in Pavia** is one of the oldest Romanesque basilicas. Built in the 12th century, this place of worship served as the coronation church of the Lombards. What marked out S. Michele was its outstanding Romanesque architectural sculpture, today all but destroyed by air pollution. Comparable features are also to be found elsewhere in Lombardy. Capitals and especially doorways, with their floral and figurative decorations shaped from stone, represent a world of their own. The doorway in particular was the preferred place for figurative representation in Romanesque architecture. A nice example can be seen above the entrance to S. Michele, where

Romanesque
◄ Architecture

Lavish Romanesque sculpture on the church of S. Michele in Pavia

the archangel Gabriel holds down the malevolent lindworm with his foot. Through depictions, it was thought, the demons could be brought closer to reason and the divine. A further important feature of Lombard Romanesque is the dwarf gallery, which stretches along the line of the gable and can be found in numerous Lombard churches. It was developed in Lombardy in the 12th century and found its way to the whole of Europe.

S. Ambrogio in Milan, too, is an important example of Lombard Romanesque. Here, for the first time in Italy, a ribbed vault was used for the construction of the ceiling instead of the barrel vaulting common up until that point, and S. Ambrogio consequently became a model for many other churches. Characteristically for Romanesque buildings in Lombardy, it has no transept. A completely different construction was chosen for two 11th-century churches in **Mantua** and **Brescia**, which were erected as rotundas; the small **round church of S. Bartolomeo in Almenno** near Bergamo was built in the 12th century. Such churches with a central ground plan were generally modelled on the Church of the Holy Sepulchre in Jerusalem and on the ancient tradition of burying rulers in rotundas – a custom that had entered into Christian culture. In the Alpine valleys there are numerous small Romanesque churches, usually with a very archaic appearance which stems from the building material – rough stone blocks – and a lack of decoration. Two fine examples are the churches of S. Siro and S. Salvatore in **Capo di Ponte** in the Valcamonica valley.

Painting ▶ The double-sided icon-like Tavola di S. Agata (13th century) in **Cremona** is considered to be a high point of Romanesque painting.

Gothic
Architecture ▶ While many Romanesque buildings continued to sprout in the first half of the 12th century, the Gothic style came to Lombardy with the Cistercians in 1135. In that year **Chiaravalle Milanese** abbey was founded and built according to French models in plain Cistercian

Gothic style. The decision to construct new Gothic cathedrals was made only in towns that at this time were experiencing a marked economic upswing; in most other centres there was already a Romanesque cathedral, which was extended or remodelled at most. The remarkable Gothic love of detail evident on the great French cathedrals functioned as a model. In Lombardy, where the art of ornament was ever present, decoration and embellishment could now used to full effect. Finally **Milan Cathedral**, too, testifies to typical Lombard tendencies, its construction meticulously concluded with over 3000 figures on the outer walls. **Monza Cathedral**, whose façade unites elements of Lombard and Tuscan style, is a pièce de resistance of Gothic church architecture.

In the transitional period from late Gothic to the Renaissance two important Lombard architects of the 15th century were working in Milan and the surrounding areas. **Guiniforte Solari** (1429–81) and **Giovanni Solari** (c1440–1484) were substantially involved in this phase of the building of Milan Cathedral. Guiniforte Solari designed the balanced late Gothic western part of S. Maria delle Grazie church in Milan. At the end of the 14th century the Certosa di Pavia, one of the most impressive churches in Lombardy, was begun; Guiniforte und Giovanni Solari were employed as master builders here, too.

From the 13th century secular buildings were also increasingly being built in the town centres, giving clear evidence of the growing political and economic might of the comuni. Among the most impressive are the prestigious palaces in the centre of **Mantua**. The Loggia dei Militi in **Cremona**, with its open hall on the lower floor, is a beautiful 13th-century building. The old town halls, mostly named Palazzo Broletto, that stand on the central squares in almost all Lombard towns were built in part during this time – perhaps the most beautiful example is the old town hall of **Mantua**; the **Broletto of Pavia**, begun as early as the 11th century, is the oldest town hall in Lombardy. Gothic fortress architecture from the 13th and 14th centuries can be seen in Milan (Castello Sforzesco), Mantua (Castello S. Giorgio), Pavia (Castello Visconteo) and Vigevano (Castello Sforzesco). The last surviving family towers, which served a defensive purpose and as places of refuge in the clashes between Guelphs and Ghibellines, also date from the Middle Ages.

◄ Painting

Gothic wall paintings have been preserved in various churches. The most impressive example is without doubt the fresco cycle by Masolino in the baptistery in **Castiglione Olona**. It was created in the transitional period: though it is clearly in the spirit of late Gothic art, the beginnings of the Renaissance are evident in the depiction of human figures.

Renaissance

◄ Architecture

The theories of the Renaissance architects from Florence and Rome – recourse to the ideas of antiquity – were taken up in Lombardy only slowly. The first Renaissance building in Lombardy is considered to be the church of S. Andrea in **Mantua**. S. Andrea was built from

A Sisyphean task lasting 21 years: the restoration of Leonardo da Vinci's famous »Last Supper«

WITH PATIENCE AND SOLVENT

One of the most famous paintings in the world gleams with unusual radiance. The restoration work on Leonardo da Vinci's *Last Supper* took more than twenty years and cost about 7 million euros.

The work carried out by Giuseppina Brambilla, Italy's most renowned restoration expert, and her employees involved removing the traces left behind by their predecessors, who used other methods of restoration or simply painted over the original. Having recognized that for centuries a falsified work had been on display, the restorer now attempted to expose and fix the original that lay under dirt, dust and several layers of paint and varnish: a job that requires hours of painstaking labour with tweezers and scalpel. Later, on the places where nothing at all had been preserved, a neutral colour – which merged in with the others in that part of the picture – was applied with the finest paintbrush. How exhausting this work was – both physically and mentally – the layman can only guess. An international committee followed and monitored the process. Even after the restoration had been under way for only a short period of time, people were already speaking of »the wonder of Milan«. When part of the right half was restored, a completely new painting suddenly emerged in this area.

The **colours of the original** were considerably brighter and flatter – as if thinned out – and for some art lovers, who missed the mysterious depth and dignified aura of the former centuries-old patina, it took some getting used to at first. All of a sudden the faces were clear, there was embroidery in the table cloth, a sliced orange, reflections of the garments in pewter plates, tapestries in the background. Above all, the expressions on the faces became much finer and full of feeling.

Seventh restoration

The long history of the attempts to save the masterpiece began in the 18th century. For a long time it was considered appropriate to paint over areas that had peeled off. The beard of Simon on the far right must have been created in this way – it can still be seen on old illustrations. The first attempt at cleaning took place in 1908. In 1943 a bomb hit the monastery complex, but the carefully protected painting survived unscathed. After the restoration work of the 1950s it was thought that Leonardo's painting had been saved for ever –

until, a good ten years later, a fine micro-flora was again discovered on the surface. The most recent project to preserve the *Last Supper*, sponsored by Olivetti, began after an alarm bell rang: at the end of the 1970s a 2m/6ft-long crack was discovered in the wall bearing the world-famous painting. It was caused by the traffic on Corso Magenta, especially the trams, which shook all the buildings – a situation that continues today. Now the attempts to save the painting are aimed at stabilizing the structure of the 70cm/28in-thick wall. Still more dangerous for the painting is the concentration of dust and smog in the air of Milan, which for a long time entered the refectory unhindered. A two-door lock system, which allows only a handful of visitors to slowly pass through it, should now confine exhaust and dust to the exterior. However, some dust and damp will still enter and threaten to destroy Brambilla's efforts. Along with all the external trials and tribulations, a further problem emerged after the restoration work had been running for some years: it was feared that further cleaning would remove the last of the paint from some areas. After ten years of work Brambilla

reported that under some over-painted areas she had found **no original** at all, especially on the left half of the picture. Only the composition was by Leonardo da Vinci. Judas's head, for example, was actually no longer there. In this case the restorers had to make do with the false version.

Artistic experiment

Ludovico il Moro, who commissioned the work, is said to have been angry at the slowness with which **Leonardo** worked – he needed about three years to complete the *Last Supper*. Again and again he interrupted the work for long periods, and he would sometimes stand on the scaffolding for hours and consider the painting without even taking out a paintbrush. The reason for this slow progress was that Leonardo did not use the common fresco paints, which are applied to plaster when it is still wet and then bind inseparably to the wall, thereby enabling work to proceed rapidly. In order to be able to paint more slowly, he used tempera paints, then untested, which react strongly to damp conditions – and exhibited the first signs of peeling after just ten years. The painting was thus an artistic experiment that went decidedly wrong.

1472 to plans by **Leon Battista Alberti** (c1404–72), who was known both as an architect and an innovative art theorist. In Milan/**Leonardo da Vinci** (1452–1519) and **Donato Bramante** (1444–1514) worked at the court of Ludovico il Moro.

The crossing of S. Maria delle Grazie, designed by Bramante, is one of the most beautiful examples of Renaissance sacred architecture. This harmoniously composed and richly decorated crossing tower with a surrounding gallery served several architects as a blueprint for churches in Lombardy – this function as a role model is especially clear in Crema. In general the church of S. Maria delle Grazie is the best example of the juxtaposition of late Gothic and early Renaissance. The eastern part was created as of 1490 in the style of the early Renaissance only about 20 years after the completion of the late Gothic western part (1463–69), but it is clear that they belong to different style epochs. One very versatile artist of the 16th century was the painter, architect and sculptor **Pellegrino Tibaldi** (around 1527–96), who was employed as the favoured master builder of Archbishop Carlo Borromeo in Milan, working on the cathedral among other buildings. In Como and the surrounding areas, too, as well as in Monza and Lodi, works of his have been preserved.

Numerous **city palaces** were built in the Renaissance. The Gonzaga family in Mantua had the final extension and decoration work on their Palazzo Ducale carried out in Renaissance style. In Cremona there are several palaces of the late 15th and early 16th centuries, some by **Bernardino de Lera** (died 1518), a highly regarded architect in the city at the time. In **Sabbioneta** near Mantua in the 16th century an »ideal city« was created, a blueprint for urban development founded on the architectural doctrines of Vitruvius (1st century AD).

Worthy of mention, too, are the public squares of the Renaissance, such as the Piazza Ducale in **Vigevano**, built at the end of the 15th century, probably to plans by Bramante, and considered the most beautiful early Renaissance square in Italy. The Piazza della Loggia in **Brescia** was laid out between the late 15th and the 16th century under Venetian influence.

Painting ► One of the most famous paintings of the Renaissance – *The Last Supper* by **Leonardo da Vinci** – can be seen in Milan in the refectory of the church of S. Maria delle Grazie (► Baedeker Special p.42–43). The frescoes of **Andrea Mantegna** (1431–1506), which have gone down in art history as epoch-making works, are preserved in the Palazzo Ducale in Mantua; in the Camera degli Sposi, Mantegna executed an illusionist oculus in the ceiling, completely new at the time and thereupon imitated by other artists. A considerable number of Lombard artists made a name within the region at this time. In the 15th and 16th centuries many painter families were at work, passing their knowledge on to the next generation – a typical example is the **Campi family** of Cremona: Antonio Campi (1522/23–87), Bernardino Campi (1522–91) and Giulio Campi (c1502–72). Visitors to Lombardy will often come across the works of **Vincenzo Foppa** (1430–*c*1515), **Gerolamo Savoldo** (1480–*c*1548), Alessandro Bonvicino, known as **Moretto** (1498–1554), and **Gerolamo Romanino** (1484–*c*1559) from Brescia, in whose works Lombard and Venetian stylistic elements were mixed. There are also paintings by **Gian Francesco Bembo** (1460–1526), **Bonifacio Bembo** (1447–78), Bernardino Gatti (1495–1575), **Boccaccio Boccaccino** (*c*1466–1525), **Camillo Boccaccino** (1501–46) and lastly by painters who worked mostly in Milan such as **Bernardino Luini** (1480/85–1532), **Andrea Solario** (*c*1460–1524), **Ambrogio Bergognone** (*c*1453–*c*1523) and **Gaudenzio Ferrari** (1480–1546).

As a style form of the late Renaissance, Mannerism found special expression in 16th-century Lombardy. At that time the best-known palace of the epoch was erected before the gates of **Mantua**: the **Palazzo del Tè**, built on the orders of Federico II Gonzaga by Giulio Romano (1499–1546), a pupil of Raphael and the most famous Lombard architect of his time, between 1525 and 1535. His design, in which the playful treatment of the forms of antiquity is fascinating,

Mannerism

The gods knew how to party – Renaissance fresco from Mantua's Palazzo del Tè, designed by Guilio Romana and his pupils

made architectural history as one of the most important north Italian Mannerist edifices. The frescoes, too, which Romano designed for the Palazzo del Tè, in particular those in the Sala di Psiche and the Sala dei Giganti with a depiction of the battle of the Titans against the gods on Olympus, have become famous well beyond the borders of Mantua.

17th and 18th centuries

The Baroque and Neoclassical periods left fewer important architectural traces in Lombardy. In the case of Milan one of the reasons may be the outbreak of the plague in 1630, which killed almost half the population of the city. In the Baroque period, nevertheless, many interiors of old churches were decorated, though some decoration, considered unsuitably ornate, was removed later. Still preserved is the rich decoration in the pilgrimage church in **Tirano** in the Valtellina region. The cathedrals in Mantua and Vigevano received Baroque façades. Finally, in the 17th century, came the chapel complex of the **Sacro Monte** near Varese, with its 15 small buildings on a central ground plan. **Pietro Ligari** (1686–1752) from Sondrio, who worked in Valtellina and Milan, made a name for himself as an architect and painter.

Probably the most important 18th-century building is **La Scala in Milan**, designed by **Giuseppe Piermarini** (1734–1808), a very well-known Milan architect of the time. The **Palazzo Reale** near Monza is also his work.

Especially worthy of mention among the palazzi of the 18th century are the magnificent and opulently designed villas on Lake Como, for instance the classical **Villa Carlotta** with a terraced garden in Italian style, **Villa d'Olmo** and the remodelled parts of **Villa Serbelloni** in Bellagio.

19th and 20th centuries

Perhaps the best known Lombard building from the second half of the 19th century is the **Galleria Vittorio Emanuele II in Milan**, a famous arcade constructed from glass, as was common in Europe at that time, and exhibiting Neoclassical elements in its decoration. In the same period the **Cimitero Monumentale in Milan** was laid out, where Historicism par excellence is to be seen; in a way that today appears odd, every conceivable manner of imitation was explored here. The less well-known **bridges** over the river Po must also be mentioned – some, such as the Ponte della Becca (1912) south of Pavia, were modelled on large French iron constructions of the second half of the 19th century. Milan's railway station, the **Stazione Centrale**, was built between 1912 and 1931 and exhibits exaggerated Neoclassical and Art Nouveau elements.

Art Nouveau ▶

The greatest architect of Art Nouveau (Stile Liberty in Italian) was **Giuseppe Sommaruga** (1867–1917). Among his works were several residential buildings in Milan. In S. Pellegrino Terme a well-known Art Nouveau ensemble consisting of the Grand Hotel, spa buildings and a casino was built by **Romolo Squadrelli** and **Luigi Mazzocchi**.

In 1910 a meeting of Italian painters took place in Milan: Carlo Carrà, Umberto Boccioni, Luigi Russolo and Tommaso Marinetti were among those present. A **Futurist manifesto** was adopted, which was also signed by the Rome-based Giacomo Balla. Futurism opposed all kinds of tradition and declared a universal dynamism in architecture, painting and music. Many works of these artists can be seen in Milan's art collections of the 20th century.

◄ Futurism

During the period of fascism many commissions were awarded to architects working in the Neoclassical style. There are notable urban sites of the 1930s in **Brescia** (Piazza della Vittoria) and **Varese** (Piazza Monte Grappa). Mussolini's favoured architect was **Marcello Piacentini**.

◄ Fascist architecture

Among the architects of recent decades **Marco Zanuso** (1916–2001; new building for the Nuovo Piccolo Teatro in Milan) and **Vittorio Gregotti** (b. 1927; headquarters of the Feltrinelli Foundation in Milan) have made a name for themselves in Lombardy. **Aldo Rossi**, born in 1931 in Milan and killed in an accident in 1997, was Italy's best-known contemporary architect. However he did very little work in Lombardy. At the beginning of the 1970s he designed the Gallaratese block of flats in **Milan**, conceived less as a functional building, more as a kind of large-scale sculpture. Many contemporary architects work as designers at the same time, there being a lot of crossover between the two fields. In the past decades, **Mario Botta** (b. 1943) from Switzerland has designed both in his home country and in Lombardy buildings that have caused a stir, most recently the new casino in Campione d'Italia on Lago di Lugano and the new La Scala building in Milan.

◄ Recent architecture

Design

Italian design is identified primarily with Milan, where the leading designers have or had their offices. The origins of Italian design in the 20th century, too, lie in the Lombard metropolis. Various social, economic and cultural factors played a role: the relatively cool and industrial design ethic of Milan signified a turn towards the post-war dominance of rational and liberal tendencies in Europe, and expressed a critical distance to the country's own rather tradition-bound, academic and provincial culture. Secondly, Milanese design mirrored the convergence of the industrial world and that of the creative designer. The first to see a need for designers were the industrialist Adriano Olivetti and leaders of the burgeoning craft industry in Brianza, who paid close attention to design in the 1960s in order to distinguish their products from others. **Ettore Sottsass** (1917–2007), who came to Milan after the Second World War, worked at Olivetti for years and led a new form of collaboration between designer and

Industrial design

industrialist – in such a way that the designer is directly involved with production instead of being temporarily called in as an outside expert to address creative issues.

One of his best-known items – one of the most popular Italian designs of its time – is the »Valentine« typewriter, designed in 1969 for Olivetti. Sottsass also designed, for example, business premises for the clothing firm Esprit and various articles for Alessi. **Aldo Rossi** and **Achille Castiglioni** (1918–2002) are among those who worked

Shop in Milan, Italy's design capital

for Alessi. Castiglioni's concept of the late 1950s and the 1960s aimed to present everyday and familiar objects in a new way – accordingly, a bicycle seat was altered to make a stylish stool. An important event in the world of Milan design was the founding of the **Memphis Group** of architects and designers by Sottsass in the 1970s. He himself belonged to the group for four years. Memphis's concept opposed common practice up to that point, namely that form follows function. Sottsass was therefore attacking the very procedure he had himself followed for many years. Now, reason alone was not to be taken into consideration; instead the group wanted at last to work to please the senses. It was in this connection that Sottsass's well-known »Carlton« room dividers were created. **Matteo Thun** (b. 1952) from Alto Adige, also a member of the group, achieved his breakthrough with the »Chicago Tribune« floor lamp – its appearance paid homage to Adolf Loos, resembling that architect's design for the newspaper giant's new highrise, which remained unbuilt. Like many of his design colleagues, Thun is also an architect.

For years, **Marco Zanuso** (1916–2001) and the German **Richard Sapper** (b. 1932) were a successful duo: their first great success was the »TS 502« portable radio. **Alessandro Mendini** (b. 1931) developed the »Proust armchair«, covered in Pointillist dots – it became Mendini's trademark. The design of Italian cars was undertaken by **Rodolfo Bonetto** (Ferrari, Lancia, Fiat) and **Giorgetto Giugiario** (Alfa Romeo, Fiat). The Milanese architect and designer **Gae Aulenti** (b. 1927) is also internationally known.

Fashion

Lombardy lay on trade routes on which materials from the Orient were transported for centuries. Como was a major trading centre and later an important place for textile production. In the 18th century mulberry trees were planted in Lombardy for silkworm breeding, and the first silk mills were established. Today silk is primarily processed in the large factories in Como. The raw material is imported, while designs are supplied by Milan couturiers.

Silk

Milan fashion has enjoyed an outstanding reputation worldwide since the 1970s: when fashion designers from Milan present their newest creations, celebrities swarm in from every direction. The »Milano Collezioni« fashion trade show is also world famous. The »king of Milan fashion« is **Giorgio Armani**, a »world champion in leaving things out, simplifying, reducing to the essentials«. His classical style stands in contrast to the designs of **Gianni Versace**: wild, colourful and patterned, sometimes unrestrained and excessive. The significance the fashion designers have in their home town was made

Fashion designers

Versace: one of the great Italian fashion designers

clear after the deadly attack on Gianni Versace in 1997 – the news left no-one cold. Alongside his work in fashion, Gianni Versace also designed theatre costumes for La Scala. **Rosita und Tai Missoni** have risen to prominence as a husband-and-wife fashion designer team. They began their life's work together in Varese, where they produced uncomplicated striped patterns on simple looms. Stripes and zigzag patterns are their trade marks. **Krizia** (b. 1933)started her career in Milan, and is known for her animal motifs. A brilliant fashion rebel, a punk among the designers, the Milanese **Franco Moschino** (1950–1994) works with provocative slogans and copies the designs of other couturiers. A younger generation of fashion designers is represented by **Domenico Dolce** (b. 1959) and **Stefano Gabbana** (b. 1963), who first showed their models in 1985 at a »Milano Collezione« talent show. Dolce & Gabbana shops are these days to be found throughout the world.

Arts and Crafts

Musical instruments

Stringed instruments are built in Cremona, following in the great tradition of the famous Amati, Guarneri and Stradivari families (► Baedeker Special p.169). Since 1937 there has been a **violin-making school** here, and at the present time there are more than 30 workshops. Those interested in the intricate manufacture of stringed instruments have the opportunity in Cremona to watch an instrument being made. Organs are made in Crema, north-west of Cremona.

Shoes

Italian shoemaking has its centre in **Vigevano** near Pavia. With a little luck, here and in Milan it is still possible to find workshops in which shoes are not produced by machine but made to measure by hand.

Soapstone products

The north of Lombardy is known for its products of soapstone (pietra ollare), which are primarily made in the **Valtellina** region and in neighbouring **Valmalenco**. The greenish soapstone was already

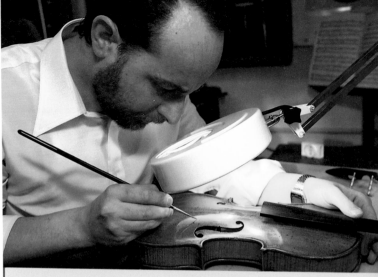

In Cremona, violins are still hand-made piece by piece in the tradition of Stradivari and Guarneri

known in Roman times. Today in Valtellina casseroles and other crockery are made from it on a lathe.

The »pezzotto« rag rug is also a well known product of the Valtellina **Rag rugs** region. Pieces of fabric made of wool, silk, cotton and linen serve as material for the rugs. In former times items of clothing were cut into strips and made into rugs on looms. By weaving the pezzotti rugs, the mountain people were able to earn their money at home during the long winter months. Today, pezzotti rugs with modern designs are manufactured in small workshops.

Music

As a consequence of the Edict of Milan of 313, which legalized Chris- **Church music** tianity, early Christian church music developed very quickly in this region. At this time **St Ambrose** (▶Famous People) wrote his hymns in support of the orthodox Christians in their battle with the Arians. The »Milanese« or »Ambrosian chants« of the liturgy have persisted to this day. Gregorian chants, introduced in the 6th century by Pope Gregory the Great, are derived from the Ambrosian liturgy. **Boethius** drew up a work of music theory, *De Institutione Musicae*, around the year 500. Singing in harmony began around the year 1000. The Milan Treatise of about 1100 heralded a new emphasis in the history of polyphony: for the first time, a crossing-over of parts was introduced so that the voices no longer followed a parallel course as had previously been the case.

Secular songs At the courts of the northern Italian cities, above all in Milan at the residences of the Visconti and Sforza and in Mantua with the Gonzaga family, the art of the secular song blossomed from the 14th century on. The decisive factor was the evolution of Italian to a language of literature; priority was accorded to setting to music texts by Petrarch and Boccaccio. Ballads and madrigals were sung about shepherd idylls and love, as well as caccia songs about hunting or other events. Two composers at the court of the Gonzaga family around 1600 were **Claudio Monteverdi** (► Famous People) from Cremona and Mantua-born **Salomone Rossi** (c1570–1630), who wrote sonatas and polyphonic madrigals.

Still up-to-date today: Monteverdi's opera »L'Orfeo« – this is a performance by the Staatsoper Berlin from 2004

The emancipation of purely instrumental music took place on Italian soil in the 16th century. It was now an independent genre alongside singing. Sonatas, concerti grossi, overtures, suites and solo pieces were composed. The importance of instrumental music led to phenomena such as the blossoming of **violin-making in Cremona** and the virtuosity of Italian violinists.

Instrumental music

It was also on Italian soil – in Florence – that opera emerged around 1600. It developed from court functions and the pastoral dramas of the 16th century. **Monteverdi's *L'Orfeo***, performed for the first time in Mantua in 1607, is considered the first work of Baroque opera. In the 18th century, the main type of opera was opera seria, featuring an alternation between the recitative, in which the plot was described, and da capo arias to portray emotions. At the beginning of the 18th century – emerging from Naples and Rome – opera buffa developed from amusing intermezzi in the meanwhile moribund opera seria. The texts of opera buffa were linked to some extent with the commedia dell'arte. Although a strong operatic culture developed in other European countries, the international significance of Italian opera persisted – in the 19th century with works by **Gioachino Rossini** (1792–1868) and **Gaetano Donizetti** (► Famous People), and eventually with operas by **Giuseppe Verdi** (► Famous People) and **Giacomo Puccini** (1858–1924).

Opera

Luigi Nono (1924–90) from Venice was among the most important composers of the 20th century. Between 1955 and 1962 he wrote numerous choral pieces with anti-fascist texts. From the 1970s he began his experiments with space dynamics und microtonal intervals.

20th century

Famous People

With whom was the gifted actress Eleonora Duse romantically linked? Who made Mantua a centre for art? Why was Claudio Monteverdi one of the most brilliant composers in music history? Short written memorials for those whose life's work has enriched Lombardy.

St Ambrose (c339–397)

Ambrose was born the son of a Roman official in Trier around 339. He embarked upon a career as a civil servant, firstly as governor in Liguria and Aemilia. In 374 he was elected to the office of bishop of Milan. Under his leadership the Milanese church was held in high esteem and achieved a certain independence from Rome. Emperor Constantine had proclaimed the teachings of the Christian Arians to be the generally valid doctrine. As Bishop of Milan, Ambrose began a merciless struggle against the followers of the Arian teachings. By introducing hymnal choral singing – which probably came from Syria – to the church, he contributed considerably to the development of early Christian music. **St Augustine** was converted to Christianity by Ambrose and baptized by him in 387. On the insistence of Ambrose, in 391 Emperor Theodosius elevated Christianity to be the sole state religion. On 4 April 397 Ambrose died in Milan. The city chose the bishop as its patron saint and celebrates his feast day on 7 December.

Bishop of Milan

Gaetano Donizetti (1797–1848)

Jokingly called »Dozzinetti« (»dozzina« means »dozen«) because of his workaholic productivity, Gaetano Donizetti was born in a poor part of Bergamo in 1797. He died in Palazzo Scotti 51 years later, a highly regarded and wealthy man. Along with his contemporary Vincenzo Bellini, Donizetti is among the most important composers of Italian melodrama. However his restless and inwardly torn life had its consequences: his mania for work – he composed 611 works, including masses, marches, songs and quartets, piano pieces, madrigals, concertos and 71 operas – his immense appetite for life and his at times fantastic egotism all took their toll. When he was taken to Bergamo almost by force from a sanatorium near Paris, where dubious friends were keeping him locked up, it was already too late. He died only two years later in a state of mental derangement. Among his undisputed principal works are *The Elixir of Love* (1832), *Lucia di Lammermoor* (1835) and *Don Pasquale* (1842).

Composer

Eleonora Duse (1858–1924)

Eleonora Duse, born in Vigevano in 1858, came from an acting family and was performing in her father's company of actors by the age of twelve. At 15 she took on the role of Juliet in Shakespeare's *Romeo und Juliet*, performed in the Verona Arena. As a character actress she embodied the female characters in dramas by Dumas, Ibsen, Maeterlinck and **Gabriele d'Annunzio**. Her love affair with d'Annunzio (▶ Baedeker Special p.202), with whom she hoped to reform Italian the-

Actress

← *Dario Fo proudly shows off his Nobel Prize for Literature in 1997*

atre, began in 1894 and lasted for years. George Bernard Shaw, who saw Duse in Paris, was highly impressed by her and said: »Duse has confirmed my frequently faltering belief that a theatre critic really is a servant … of a high art.« From 1906 to 1921 Duse took a break from stage work. In 1924 she travelled for a guest performance to Pittsburgh in the USA, where she died in the same year and was buried according to her wishes in a small cemetery in Asolo. While the actress was celebrated by many, her life was at times overshadowed by anxiety and depression.

Isabella d' Este (1474–1539)

Marchioness of Mantua

Isabella d' Este is considered one of the foremost female figures of the Renaissance. Born in Ferrara in 1474 the daughter of Eleonora of Aragon and Ercole I, at the age of 16 she married the Marquis of Mantua, Francesco Gonzaga. Just like her sister **Beatrice d' Este**, who married Ludovico il Moro in Milan and died very young, Isabella d' Este is described as intellectual and highly educated. Under the leadership of this self-assured woman the court of Mantua developed into one of the most glittering of the period, with an atmosphere marked by humanist ideals.

Leonardo da Vinci and Titian painted portraits of her, and Andrea Mantegna worked for her. Her living quarters in the Palazzo Ducale, with the study that she furnished according to her own very specific ideas, are well known. Preserved in these rooms are her numerous epigrams and symbols, some of them difficult to decipher – she devoted much time to their invention. She corresponded with countless people, and approximately 2000 letters still exist today. Isabella d' Este had three daughters and three sons. She died in 1539 – 20 years after her husband.

? DID YOU KNOW …?

■ Isabella d' Este summoned the leading artists and musicians of the time to Mantua and thus made the city into a cultural centre of the Italian Renaissance. She was the **first art collector of the Renaissance** and commanded outstanding knowledge of the subject; she acquired the most valuable paintings for her court.

Dario Fo (born 1926)

Actor, set designer, dramatist

»I didn't want to play Hamlet, I wanted to be a clown« – this comment says a lot about the great man of 20th-century Italian literature. Dario Fo was born in 1926 in S. Giano/Leggiuno on Lago Maggiore, his father a railway worker, his mother a peasant farmer. From the early 1950s the trained architect wrote plays that mirror the history of Italy. At first he devised satirical political revues for radio and television; from 1958, working together with his wife **Franca Rame**, he developed folksy farces in the tradition of the commedia dell' arte. From 1970 he performed political theatre with his own acting company La Comune.

Until now he has written about 70 plays, which have been translated into 30 languages and performed countless times. Stinging criticism of the ruling classes and the clergy, and satire based on the double standards of the bourgeoisie, are common to all of them, but so is the ironic portrayal of a credulous people who are taken for a ride so easily. Again and again his performances are marked by direct contact with the public and a provocative approach. As a consequence he has faced court proceedings over 40 times, been arrested on stage and been banned from television appearances. In 1997 Dario Fo was awarded the **Nobel Prize for Literature**. Among his best-known plays are *Mistero Buffo* (1969), *Can't Pay? Won't Pay!* (1974), *The Accidental Death of an Anarchist* (1978), *The Open Couple* (1983), *Heroine* and lastly *The Devil with Boobs* (1997).

Claudio Monteverdi (1567–1643)

Claudio Monteverdi was born on 15 May 1567 in Cremona. He is considered the most innovative composer of his time and **one of the most brilliant figures in music history**. From 1590 to 1612 he worked as court musician to the Gonzaga family in Mantua, at first as a singer and viola player, then from 1601 as musical director. Afterwards he spent 30 years in Venice, where he was maestro di cappella at St Mark's Basilica until his death on 29 November 1643. Difficult times cast a shadow over is life. His wife died when he was 40 years old, his youngest son was arrested by the Inquisition, and he lived through a major plague epidemic in Venice.

Court musician, composer

Monteverdi's importance lies above all in the development of a new style. Having mastered the polyphony of the late Middle Ages and the Renaissance completely, as his early pieces show, he was quick to shift the emphasis onto a single main voice accompanied by chords. The words and their meaning now had decisive significance; the music took on a subordinate role and not the other way round. He understood language as being the entire range of human and passionate expression. This he attempted to transpose into musical motifs, an unheard-of novelty at the end of the 16th century. The fact that he also worked with daring harmony and produced dissonance for the ears of the time provoked the critics: he contravenes the laws of music, they complained. Monteverdi's new style found a home in opera, a field in which he could realize his **»stile espressivo«**. The pioneering opera **Orfeo**, which introduced the Baroque era, was first performed in Mantua in 1607.

Pliny the Elder (23/24–79)

Historian, writer

One of the best known figures of antiquity, the historian and writer Pliny the Elder was born in AD 23 or 24 in Como. Gaius Plinius Secundus came from a prosperous dynasty of knights. He held positions as an imperial official and officer, and finally as fleet commander. The 37 books of the *Naturalis Historia*, one of his two great scientific works, have survived the ravages of time and served as an important source of knowledge into the 18th century. Today they convey an outstanding impression of the state of knowledge and conception of the world during that period. Pliny the Elder died in Stabiae on 24 August 79 during the eruption of Vesuvius. **Pliny the Younger** (61/62–113) was his nephew and adopted son. He worked as a jurist, statesman and writer.

Giuseppe Verdi (1813–1901)

Opera composer

Giuseppe Verdi was born on 10 October 1813 in Le Roncole near Busseto (Parma), the son of an innkeeper. At the age of seven a patron noticed his talent and arranged for him to have music lessons. Later, Verdi was to marry his benefactor's daughter. Verdi's musical career took its course. He became the conductor of the local orchestra early on. At the age of 26 he attracted attention as a guest conductor in La Scala. The staging of ***Rigoletto*** (1851) – an opera set in Mantua – in Venice heralded a series of ever-increasing stage successes. He gained international fame with *Il Trovatore* (1853), *La Traviata* (1853) and finally ***Aida*** (1871). Verdi was a sympathizer with the Risorgimento, the national unification movement; his early works such as ***Nabucco*** are connected with this. Described as somewhat reserved and withdrawn, Verdi spent most of his private time on his estate near Busseto, where he often dedicated himself to farming and gardening. The composer involved himself in social issues early on. His first wife and his two children died, and his second marriage remained childless. At the end of his life Verdi lived in Milan in a suite of the Grand Hotel de Milan, where he died on 27 January 1901. In line with the composer's wishes, part of his fortune today still funds an old people's home for impoverished musicians in Milan.

Virgil (70–19 BC)

Poet

On 15 October 70 BC Publius Vergilius Maro was born in Andes, today's Pietole, near Mantua and grew up there on the estate of his parents in the belt of land named after him: Virgilio. The estate was lost when the land was taken for the veterans of Octavian's army, and Virgil moved to Rome, where he found a patron in Maecenas, a wealthy art-loving friend of Emperor Augustus.

From this time on Virgil, who moved to Naples, devoted his life to his poetic works. In his pastorals, in which he expresses the longing for a natural life on the land, he reveals himself as an empathetic observer of nature. With these works he touched a nerve of the overstimulated society of the capital. He dedicated the **Georgics**, a didactic poem about farming, to his patron. The *Georgics*, which explain to the population of the city the interrelations and order of the world of the countryside and inform them about weather, cultivating trees, bee-keeping and arable farming, is considered one of the most beautiful works of Roman literature. The best known, however, is his **Aeneid**, a heroic epic, on which he worked for eleven years. Shortly before completing it Virgil died in Brundisium (today's Brindisi) after returning from a trip to Greece; he was buried in Naples.

? DID YOU KNOW ...?

■ ... that the name of Virgil's wealthy patron, Maecenas, has become a word used to denote a cultural benefactor? It appears in a number of languages: *mecenaat* in Dutch, *mesenaatti* in Finnish, *mécénat* in French, *Mäzen* in German, *mecenate* in Italian, *mecenat* in Romanian, *mecen* in Slovenian, *mecenas* in Spanish, and *меценат* in Russian.

Alessandro Volta (1745–1827)

The physicist Count Alessandro Volta came from Como, where he was born in 1745. Volta worked as a professor in Como and at the renowned university in Pavia. He made pioneering discoveries in the field of electricity: the anatomist Luigi Galvani from Bologna may have discovered electric current, but it was Alessandro Volta who first succeeded in explaining the phenomenon. He developed the **voltaic pile** – named after him – a series connection of elements producing electrical potential, considered to be the first truly functioning source of electricity. The physicist's name is immortalized in the unit for electrical potential, the volt. The Tempio Voltiano in Como, in which several of his inventions can be seen, is dedicated to him. Alessandro Volta died in Como on 5 March 1827.

Physicist

Practicalities

WHAT SHOULD YOU ON NO ACCOUNT LEAVE BEHIND? HOW DO YOU SAY »I AM LOOKING FOR A ROOM« IN ITALIAN? WHAT IS THE SPEED LIMIT ON ITALY'S ROADS? LOOK IT UP HERE!

Accommodation

Hotels

In addition to hotels, guest houses and holiday homes, accommodation in the country is available (agriturismo, see below). Lists of hotels are available from the ENIT offices and from regional and local tourist offices (►Information).

Reservations When trade fairs are held, hotel beds are scarce in Milan, and on the north Italian lakes in summer it is advisable to book rooms well in advance. Reservations can be made by phone or fax, via a travel agent, hotel reservation service or directly, and online.

> ### *i* Hotel price categories
>
> - Luxury: from €250
> - Mid-range: €100–250
> - Budget: up to €100
>
> for a double room

Italian hotels are graded according to **five official categories**, from a five-star luxury hotel to simple accommodation with one star. There are also some smaller, unclassified guesthouses with a perfectly acceptable standard.

Bed & Breakfast Bed & Breakfast Italia is worth considering as an alternative to hotels. They range from rooms with shared bathrooms (2 corone) to en-suite rooms in important historic buildings (4 corone).

Price categories Hotel prices vary according to the season and are generally higher in larger cities. A double room of a reasonable standard seldom costs less than €60; the widest range is available in the category between €120 and €160. A single room costs 20 to 25% less than a double.

Agriturismo · Country Holidays

»Agriturismo« is rural accommodation that ranges from camping and rooms on a farm to well-equipped apartments in villas or on wine farms in rural surroundings. For information contact tourist offices (►Information) and the agriturismo headquarters in Rome.

Camping and Caravanning

Camp sites In Lombardy there are almost 200 camp sites, most of them around the north Italian lakes. Plots for a mobile home or caravan are often let for a year here, which restricts the spaces available for short-term guests. It is advisable to book in advance if travelling in the high sea-

For residing in true lordly style, few places are better than →
Hotel Villa Serbelloni in Bellagio on Lago di Como

son from mid-July to mid-September. Many camp sites are open only during the summer months. There is a general ban on wild camping. Visitors travelling in a **mobile home or caravan** can stay for one night at a car park, roadside services or by the roadside if this is not explicitly prohibited.

Youth Hostels

Italian youth hostels (alberghi per la gioventù) are part of the international youth hostel federation. They are open to everyone who possesses an international youth hostel card. Prices vary from one place to another, usually between €8 and €15 per person per day. In the high season early booking is recommended.

For information about mountain huts in the north of Lombardy contact the APT in Sondrio, Como or Lecco (▶Information).

 ACCOMMODATION

AGRITURISMO

▶ **Agriturist**
Corso Vittorio Emanuele 101
I-00186 Roma
Tel. 0 66 85 23 42, fax 0 66 85 24 24
www.agriturist.it

BED & BREAKFAST

▶ **Bed & Breakfast**
Association of Rome
Via A. Picinotti, I-00146 Rom
Tel. 06 55 30 22 48
Fax 06 55 30 22 59
www.b-b.rm.it

CAMPING

▶ **Federazione Italiana del Campeggio e del Caravaning**
Via Vittorio Emanuele 11
I-50041 Calenzano
Tel. 0 55 88 23 91
Fax 05 58 82 59 18
www.federcampeggio.it
www.camping.it

HOTELS

▶ **Central reservations**
Tel. 06 42 03 15 55

Numero verde (toll free)
Tel. 01 80 5 47 70 00
www.hotelme.it

▶ **Other addresses:**
www.initalia.it
www.italypass.com
www.familyhotels.com

YOUTH HOSTELS

▶ **Information worldwide**
www.hihostels.com

▶ **Information in Italy**
Associazione Italiana Alberghi per la Gioventù
Via Cavour 44
I-00184 Roma
Tel. 0 64 87 11 52, fax 0 64 88 04 92
www.ostellionline.org

▶ **Information in UK**
Youth Hostels Association
Trevelyan House, Matlock
Derbyshire, DE4 3YH
Tel. (0 16 29) 59 27 00
Fax (0 16 29) 59 27 01
www.yha.org.uk

Arrival · Planning the Trip

The quickest way across the English Channel to France is via the Eurotunnel. Passengers drive their cars onto the train, *Le Shuttle*, which covers the distance from Folkestone to Coquelles near Calais in 35 minutes. At peak times there are four trains every hour (tel. 0870 535 3535; www.eurotunnel.com). Drivers can also take their cars across the Channel by ferry.

There are no car-carrying »motorail« trains from Calais or Paris to Italy, so motorists will normally need to make the long journey on European highways. In summer, in particular at the beginning of August, the start of the holidays in France and Italy, there is likely to be heavy traffic on motorways heading south. Those driving south-east through France can go south to Lyon, then cross the Alps on the E70 to Turin; alternatively take a route further north past Geneva and through the Mont Blanc tunnel to Turin (E25). The coastal road is the E80 from the south of France parallel to the shore of the Mediterranean to Genoa, La Spezia and Livorno.

Drivers who have been in the Swiss or Austrian Alps or are coming from Germany or other points further north have a number of options. One is to take the St Bernard Pass, entering Italy at Chiasso and continuing to Milan. Alternatives from Switzerland are the Simplon Pass and St Gotthard Pass. Further east the E45 runs from Munich to Innsbruck and over the Brenner Pass. A toll is payable on this stretch of motorway.

A toll is normally charged for the use of motorways in France, Austria, Switzerland and Italy. In France it can be paid either in cash or by credit card (but not with a Maestro card) at the »CB« counter. The so-called **»vignettes«** for Austrian and Swiss motorways are available from tobacconists, post offices and local automobile clubs, and automobile clubs can supply them in other countries. They are also sold at petrol stations near the border crossings. In Italy, motorway (autostrada) tolls (pedaggio) can be paid in cash, by credit card or with a Viacard. The Viacard is obtained from automobile clubs, ACI offices at the border crossings, at motorway toll stations (»Punto Blu«), in tabacchi, and at motorway services and petrol stations.

Those travelling by train are best advised to take a Eurostar from London to Paris and then a TGV on to Milan, either via south-eastern France or via Switzerland (booking online: www.raileurope.co.uk), a journey that takes about 12 hours. TGVs arrive at **Milan Central Station** (Stazione Centrale di Milano). From Milan, trains and buses head out to all cities in Lombardy and to the north Italian lakes.

There are also rail connections to Trento and Verona, from where buses leave for Lago di Garda. For further connections within Lombardy, which are not always direct, enquire at the departure station in question.

By car
◀ From the west

◀ From the north

◀ Motorway tolls

By rail

Stazione Centrale in Milan: a hub for train travellers in Lombardy

By bus or coach   Eurolines run several coaches daily from London Victoria to Paris. Further Eurolines services continue to Milan. The total journey time is about 26 hours.

By air   There are **direct flights** to Milan from all major international European airports as well as from airports in North America and elsewhere in the world. British Airways flies direct from London Heathrow to Milan Malpensa, as do bmi British Midland and others. A number of low-cost airlines fly direct from UK and Irish airports to the Milan region. At the time of writing these routes include Easyjet from London and Edinburgh, Flybe from Manchester and Birmingham, Jet2.com from Leeds-Bradford, and Ryanair from Dublin, Glasgow, Liverpool and Luton to Bergamo. Bear in mind that this is a rapidly changing market in which services open and close frequently.

Malpensa ▶   Most air traffic lands at Milan Malpensa, located approximately 50km/30mi north-west of the city centre. Two alternating bus services run every 10 minutes to the air terminal at the main station. Travel time is about 50 minutes.

Linate ▶   Milan Linate (10km/6mi east of the city centre) primarily serves flights to and from Rome, but the now merged Alitalia and Air One also offer direct flights here from London Heathrow. STAM buses leave Linate for the main station every 20 minutes, with a journey time of about 30 minutes. The number 73 city bus service goes to the centrally located Piazza S. Babila.

► **USEFUL INFORMATION**

AIRLINES

► **Alitalia**
Tel. 0870 225 5000
www.alitalia.com

► **Air One**
Tel. 020 8939 2434
www.flyairone.it

► **bmi**
Tel. 0870 6070 555,
www.flybmi.com

► **British Airways**
Tel. 0844 493 0787
www.britishairways.com

► **Easyjet**
Tel. 0871 244 2366
www.easyjet.com

► **Flybe**
Tel. 0871 700 2000
www.flybe.co.uk

► **Jet2.com**
Tel. 0871 226 1737
www.jet2.com

► **Ryanair**
Tel. 0871 246 0000
www.ryanair.com

AIRPORTS

► **Milan Malpensa**
50km/30mi north-west of Milan
Tel. 0 23 66 43 01 28
www.malpensa.it

Express trains into the city centre:
www.malpensaexpress.it
Express buses into the city centre:
www.malpensashuttle.it

BY BUS

► **Eurolines**
Bookings online and in UK
through National Express
Tel. 087 05 80 80 80;
www.eurolines.com and
www.nationalexpress.com

BY RAIL

► **In London**
Rail Europe Travel Centre
178 Piccadilly, London W1V 0BA
Tel. 0870 8 37 13 71
www.raileurope.co.uk

► **In Italy**
Trenitalia
Tel. 89 20 21
http://www.ferroviedellostato.it/
homepage_en.html

Travel Documents

The identity cards and passports of EU citizens are often no longer checked. However, since random inspections are carried out at the border and identification is required at airports, all visitors should be able to show their **passports** when they enter the country. Children under 16 years of age must carry a children's passport or be entered in the parent's passport.

Personal documents

Always carry your driving licence, the motor vehicle registration and the international green insurance card when driving in Italy. Motor

Car documents

vehicles must have the oval sticker showing nationality unless they have a Euro licence plate.

Pets and travel

Those who wish to bring pets (dogs, cats) to Italy require a **pet pass**. Among other things, it contains an official veterinary statement of health (no more than 30 days old), a rabies vaccination certificate that is at least 20 days and no more than eleven months old, and a passport photo. In addition, the animal must have a microchip or tattoo. A muzzle and leash are required at all times for dogs.

Customs Regulations

Duty-free zone

In Livigno in northwest Lombardy there is a duty-free shopping zone with about 200 duty-free shops.

Regulations for EU citizens

The European Union member states (including Italy) form a common economic area within which the movement of goods for private purposes is largely duty-free. There are merely certain maximum quantities which apply: 800 cigarettes, 400 cigarillos, 200 cigars, 1 kilogramme of tobacco, 10 litres of spirits, 20 litres of other alcoholic beverages with up to 22% alcohol; 90 litres of wine (of which a maximum of 60 litres can be sparkling), and 110 litres of beer. Should a customs inspection occur, a plausible explanation for the intended private use of the goods is required.

Regulations for non-EU citizens

For travellers from outside the EU, the following duty-free quantities apply: 200 cigarettes or 100 cigarillos or 50 cigars or 250g of tobacco; also 2 litres of wine and 2 litres of sparkling wine or 1 litre of spirits with an alcohol content of more than 22% vol.; 500g of coffee or 200g of coffee extracts, 100g of tea or 40g of tea extract, 50ml of perfume or 0.25 litres of eau de toilette. Gifts up to a value of €175 are also duty-free.

Travel Insurance

Health insurance

Citizens of EU countries are entitled to treatment in Italy in case of illness on production of their **European health insurance card**. Even with this card, some of the medical care costs and prescribed medication must be paid by the patient.

Upon presentation of receipts the health insurance at home covers the costs – but not for all treatments. Citizens of non-EU countries must pay for medical treatment and medicine themselves and should take out private health insurance.

Private travel insurance

Since some of the costs for medical treatment and medication typically have to be covered by the patient, and the costs for return transportation may not be covered by the normal health insurance, additional travel insurance is recommended.

Children in Italy

The Italians are particularly fond of children. Because the noise level in public places in Italy tends to be higher anyway, children are permitted to be both seen and heard. At the top of the list of recommendations for families with children is of course a **holiday by the lakes** of northern Italy, where children are welcome and good preparations have been made for families with younger holidaymakers. There is a wide choice of holiday flats, apartments, guest houses and hotels with rooms with enough beds for a whole family. Day trips by boat or on horseback make a nice change, and bicycles can be rented in various places. **Leisure and amusement parks** provide entertainment for young and old alike.

▶ ACTIVITIES FOR CHILDREN

LEISURE PARKS

▶ **Fantasyworld**
►Tip p.134

▶ **Gardaland**
p.192

▶ **Parco della Preistoria Rivolta d' Adda**
►Cremona, surroundings

▶ **Swissminiatur**
►Tip p.214

The secret ingredient for a successful holiday with children

MUSEUMS

▶ **Museo della Bambola**
   ▶ p.228

▶ **Museo Europeo dei Transporti**
   Via Alberto 99, Ranco (bei Angera)
   Open: Tue–Sun 10am–noon,
   3pm–5pm.
   The range of »mobile« exhibits in this transport museum extends from the horse-drawn carriage to the spaceship; the huge model railway, which is in operation on Sunday afternoons, is a big attraction for both young and old.

WATER PARKS

▶ **Canevaworld**
   ▶Tip p.192

▶ **Aquapark California**
   Balerna (near Chiasso)
   Via San Gottardo 4
   Tel. 9 16 95 70 00
   www.california-aquapark.ch
   Open: Mon–Fri 8.30am–10pm,
   Sat, Sun 9am–8pm
   While the children have fun on the water slide, their parents can relax in the jacuzzi.

ANIMAL PARK

▶ **Parco Natura Viva**
   ▶p.192

Electricity

The Italian grid generally supplies 220-volt electricity. Due to the variety of sockets all visitors, especially who are not from mainland Europe, are advised to take an **adapter** (reduzione).

Emergency

The first pages of local telephone directories (elenco telefonico) list local emergency numbers under the heading »Avantielenco«.

▶ USEFUL PHONE NUMBERS

▶ **General emergency number**
   Tel. 1 13 (national number)

▶ **Police**
   (carabinieri, soccorso pubblico)
   Tel. 1 12 (national)

▶ **Fire**
   (vigili fuoco)
   Tel. 1 15 (national)

▶ **Medical emergency number**
   Tel. 38 83

▶ **Ambulance**
   Tel. 1 18 (national)

▶ **ACI breakdown service**
   (soccorso stradale)
   Tel. 80 31 16
   (toll-free)

Etiquette and Customs

In restaurants and cafes it is usual to tip 5–10% of the amount on the bill. If you pay by cheque or credit card, leave the tip in cash on the table or on the plate provided. Taxi drivers (€0.50–1.00), city guides (€1–2), toilet attendants and room service personnel are also pleased to receive a tip.

Tipping

Since January 2005 a smoking ban has been in force in all public buildings, which includes restaurants and cafes. Smoking is permitted only if there is an enclosed, well-ventilated smoking zone with automatic doors. Smoking is also prohibited outdoors.

No smoking

Even if you speak only a little Italian, it is worth learning two phrases which can often be used: »permesso« and »scusi«. These are the equivalent of saying »excuse me«, for example when you want to pass or get around somebody.

Permesso, scusi

»Bella figura«, a beautiful appearance, is a deep-seated need for most Italians. Everyone who goes out in public likes to dress up, even for a trip to the post office or market, following Coco Chanel's motto: always be dressed to meet the love of your life. When there is a choice, money is always spent on fashion (and good food) rather than furniture or a coat of paint for the house. Tourists who stroll into cathedrals with flip-flops on their feet, wear shorts to visit the art gallery, sit in a restaurant in sandals or even dare to stroll through the old town with a naked chest are looked down upon, either with amusement or a complete lack of comprehension.

Bella figura

This is not always the way to create a »bella figura«

Festivals, Holidays and Events

▶ DATES

▶ **1 January**
New Year (Capodanno)

▶ **6 January**
Epiphany (Epifania)

▶ **25 April**
Liberation Day 1945
(Festa della Liberazione)

▶ **March/April**
Easter

▶ **1 May**
Labour Day
(Festa del Primo Maggio)

▶ **15 August**
Assumption of the Virgin
(Assunzione/Ferragosto)

▶ **1 November**
All Saints Day
(Ognissanti)

▶ **8 December**
Immaculate Conception
(Immacolata Concezione)

▶ **25–26 December**
Christmas (Natale)

EVENTS IN JANUARY

▶ **Albaville**
On the last Thursday in January
the Gubiana festival is celebrated;
a puppet symbolizing winter is
carried through the village and
then burnt; music, dancing, food
and drink.

▶ **Lodi**
19 January: festival of the city's
patron S. Bassiano with processions and markets

IN FEBRUARY/MARCH

▶ **Bagolino**
Carnival with historical dancing
and costumes

▶ **Milan**
Carnevale Ambrosiana: city car-
neval (late Feb. until early March,
1st Sat. in Lent

IN MARCH

▶ **Limone**
Festa di Mezzaquaresima: age-old
festival halfway through Lent with
wine, polenta and fish from Lago
di Garda

▶ **Pescarolo**
During the last weekend in
March in celebration of the
Senigola festival flowers are sold
in the streets across the whole
region and typical food is
served.

AT EASTER

▶ **In many places**
Good Friday procession

▶ **Bormio**
I Pasquali: every quarter of the city
brings a lamb to the Easter Mass,
and afterwards there is roast lamb
to eat.

IN MAY

▶ Rogarò
3rd Sunday in May: asparagus festival with a harvest service in the church consecrated to the Black Madonna; asparagus is eaten in the restaurants in the evening.

▶ Legnano
Last Sunday in May: Sagra del Caroccio. Historical costumes are worn at a procession with an ox-drawn cart. The event is in celebration of the victory of the Lombard League in 1176.

IN JUNE

▶ Milan
1st Sunday in June: Festivale dei Navigli in the Navigli quarter with swimming competitions and games in the water

▶ Abbiategrasso
Fish festival: with fish and wine – along the bank of the Ticino

▶ Limone
Last Sunday in June: folk festival in honour of St Peter with plenty of fish and local wine, and music and dancing in the open air

▶ Lago di Como/Isola Comacina
Sagra di San Giovanni: Midsummer's Eve is celebrated with an illuminated boat procession and fireworks.

▶ Lago di Orta
Festival of ancient music on Isola San Giulio or in Orta; Italian and international orchestras play on original instruments and in historical costumes.

▶ Ascona
End of June/beginning of July: New Orleans festival with various styles of jazz held in the old town of Ascona

IN JULY – AUGUST

▶ Milan
Milano d'Estate: cultural events in Sempione Park

IN JULY

▶ Lugano
Jazz festival ▶Tip p.244

▶ Casalmaggiore
First ten days in July: festival with concerts, fireworks and rowing regattas on the Po

▶ Locarno
End of July/beginning of August: international film festival, partly in the open air

▶ Lago di Lugano
End of July: a night-time lake festival with illuminations and fireworks in many places

▶ Gardone Riviera
Concerts and open-air performances in the Vittoriale degli Italiani

▶ Salò
Classical concerts on the cathedral square

▶ Iseo
End of July/beginning of August: jazz festival

▶ Casteldidone
Last Saturday: Festa di Melone, a folk festival in the Castello Mina

▶ Salò
Last Saturday: Carnevale del Sole, a summer carnival

A procession during the Palio delle Contrade in Garda

IN AUGUST

► **Introbio**
5 August: festival of the Madonna of Biadino with a procession to the Madonna della Neve pilgrimage church

► **In many places**
Processions on 15 August (ferragosto, Assumption of the Virgin)

► **Locarno**
Film festvial ►Tip p.233

► **Lumezzane**
16 August: Molete festival (festival of knife grinders); visitors come from the whole area come to celebrate this region's oldest trade.

► **Curtatone**
13–17 August: Fiera di Grazie, competition for pavement artists with a big festival

► **Garda**
15 August: Palio delle Contrade, a parade in historical costumes and boat races

► **Ascona**
End of August to mid-October: classical concerts in various locations

IN SEPTEMBER

► **Lugano**
Blues to Bop & world music festival on the open-air stage on Piazza Riforma

► **Ascona**
Marionette festival with puppeteers from all over the world

► **Desenzano**
1 Sunday: duck festival with music, food and drink

► **Mezzegra**
Mid-September: at the Missoltino festival on the church square

agricultural products of the region are put up for auction; afterwards visitors eat »missoltino«, the salted, dried fish from Lago di Como.

► **Chiavenna**
3 Sunday: at this festival in the grottoes there is local wine and regional specialities.

► **Gerola Alta**
Bitto festival at which the tasty bitto cheese is accompanied by plenty of music

► **Lago Maggiore**
Settimane Musicali: festival for classical music in Stresa and on Isola Bella

► **Bardolino**
Last weekend: Festa dell' uva, wine and grape festival

IN OCTOBER/NOVEMBER

► **Milan**
Popular concert cycle for ancient music in S. Maurizio on Corso Magenta

IN DECEMBER

► **Milan**
7 December: St Ambrose's Day; the patron saint of the city is celebrated with a procession and markets; the season also begins at La Scala on this date; around Sant' Ambrogio the »O bej, o bej« festival takes place, named after the jubilant cry of the children meaning »Oh, how lovely«.

Food and Drink

The local cuisine is as diverse as the landscape of the Lombard provinces. It is based primarily on **pasta** and the **rice** grown around Pavia and Milan. In addition polenta, the golden-yellow cornmeal (ground maize) porridge from the rural cuisine of the Valtellina region, has a large role to play. In the Alpine valleys, good substantial fare is served: butter, for example, is used instead of olive oil for frying. Milan offers typical dishes not only from all the provinces of Lombardy but also from the whole range of Italian cuisine – it doesn't enjoy a reputation as a Mecca for gourmets for nothing. On the plain of the Po there are a large number of pig, rabbit and poultry breeders; the geese from Mortara are well known throughout Europe. Lombard farmers produce excellent olive oil; moreover, almost one in two Italian cheeses comes from this region.

Pasta, rice and polenta

The Italian **breakfast** (prima colazione) often amounts to no more than a cappuccino (espresso with foamed milk), espresso or caffè

---

i   **Historical fare**

■ Products of certain rural regions and their outstanding quality have historical roots. Ruling families such as the Gonzaga in Mantua or the Sforza in Milan insisted upon the best ingredients for their foods; foie gras, for example, was known in Lombardy well before it found its way onto French menus.

(strong espresso) with pastries, for instance a small croissant (cornetto). However, hotels are usually geared to the habits of their guests and provide a more or less extensive breakfast buffet. Breakfast in a normal bar is still recommended: taken at the counter, it consists of a tramezzino, focaccia or similar served with ham, salami, cheese, tuna with egg or even an insalata russa. Those who still fancy something sweet can choose from the delicious dolci. **Lunch** (pranzo) normally consists of an antipasto (starter), primo (pasta, rice or soup), secondo (meat or fish) with vegetables (contorno) or salad (insalata). After that there is a choice between cheese (formaggio), a sweet dessert (dolce), ice cream (gelato) and fruit (frutta). An espresso rounds off the meal, sometimes in the form of a »corretto« (»corrected« with grappa, cognac amaro or sambuco).

The **evening meal** (cena), with the same succession of courses as at midday, is seldom served before 7.30pm.

Restaurants   Along with **restaurants** (ristorante) there are the establishments known as **trattoria**, **osteria** and **»tavola calda«** (warm food). Pizzerias and self-service restaurants are found in the towns and cities. Go to a cafe or stand at the counter in a bar for a snack or a cup of coffee between meals. One Italian peculiarity is the **enoteca**, a wine tavern in which typical local food is served and wines of the region can be sampled.

It is not customary to choose a table for yourself in Italian restaurants; diners wait instead for the waiter to show them to their place. A service (servizio) and/or a cover charge (coperto) will sometimes be added to the normal price of the food. Lay the tip on the plate for change separately from the amount on the bill. An important point: except in holiday resorts, many eateries are closed in August.

Lombard Cuisine

Antipasti   **Olives**, **artichokes** (carciofi), **sausage** (salame) and **ham** (prosciutto) are often served as antipasti. In Mantua another antipasto on offer is a kind of ravioli in bouillon (**agnolini in brodo**). In Valtellina starters include **sciatt**, dumplings with a cheese filling, and at Lago di Como air-dried fish, **missoltitt** (missoltini), is a speciality. **Bresaola**, an air-dried salted beef served in thin slices and sometimes marinated, is a speciality from the north of Lombardy.

Pasta   For the primo piatto diners almost always have the choice of spaghetti, macaroni, lasagne, ravioli or tagliatelle. Special ways of preparing pasta include **tortelli di zucca**, pasta shells with a pumpkin

An important part of any holiday in the south: eating al fresco in the evening

filling, and **gnocchi di zucca**, pumpkin dumplings, which are served in Mantua. **Pizzoccheri**, ribbon noodles made of buckwheat flour, are eaten in the north of Lombardy, especially in Valtellina. They are prepared with potatoes, cabbage and melted cheese. In Brescia there is **casonsei**, pasta cases with sausage and cheese. **Marubini**, also a type of ravioli, is served up in Cremona.

Soups

As an alternative to pasta the first course can also consist of a tasty soup, to which pasta is often added. Soups are usually served with various types of vegetable (**minestroni**); **bean soup** (zuppa di fagioli) and now and then also **chickpea soup** (zuppa di ceci) are also on the menu. Those who have a taste for offal can order a **trippa** soup. The Milanese version is called **busecca** and is particularly strongly seasoned. A **stracciatella** is a beef tea with custard royale.

Risotto

The rice grown on the plain of the Po forms the basis of a variety of risotto dishes. A good risotto requires special rice: cooking should make the outside of the grain soft, but the inside should remain solid. The arborio, carnaroli and baldo varieties enjoy the best reputations in the Lomellina region. The best-known dishes are **risotto alla milanese** with saffron and **risotto alla mantovana**, which is served with pieces of salami. Those who order **risotto con le rane** in the province of Pavia should be aware that it comes with frogs' legs. **Risotto alla certosina** is also enriched with frog meat, along with bass, freshwater shrimps and vegetables.

Risotto: an essential part of Lombard cuisine

Polenta dishes Meat dishes are often served with polenta, as is the case for ossobuco, a typical Lombard dish with knuckle of veal steamed in vegetables, which comes from Valtellina. **Polenta e osei alla bergamasca**, a polenta dish prepared with wildfowl, butter and sage, is a speciality in Bergamo. Cassoeula, a stew with pork, cabbage, celeriac and carrots, is also eaten with polenta. **Polenta rustica fried with butter and onions** is served as a main course, while a strong cheese is added to **polenta taragna**.

Meat and fish Various types of grilled meat can be ordered as »grigliata mista«. **Lombata** is a piece of loin, while **stracotto**, a pot roast, is prepared differently from region to region. **Bollito misto**, a traditional stew made of veal, chicken and beef, often along with tongue and sausage, is served according to region with either with salsa or with mustard fruits such as mostarda di Cremona or mostarda mantovana: these are cherries, apricots, pineapple and so on cured and cooked in spices and mustard. Typical of Mantuan cuisine are dishes with donkey and horse meat, which are generally served as a pot roast. **Carpaccio** is very thinly sliced raw meat or raw fish and is served with olive oil and basil or another marinade.

Around the north Italian lakes, fish dishes predominate. **Sturgeon** (storione), **carp** (carpa), **tench** (tinca), **eel** (anguilla), **salmon** (salmone) and **trout** (trota) are all on the menu. At Lago di Como,

BLESSED BY THE SUN

»God may have created the lemon, but it was Conte Carlo Bettoni-Cazzago who gave it juice and strength.« The count made the lemon indigenous on Lago di Garda, which thanks to him became famous as the »garden of Italy«. Even today, especially on the lake's western bank, the remains of limonaie, the former lemon houses, are still to be seen.

Citrus fruits had already been brought to Lago di Garda by the Romans. In the Renaissance the little trees that bore yellow fruit four times a year were popular as ornamental plants in geometrically arranged gardens. Commercial cultivation however did not take place because of frequent night frosts, until in the 18th century Conte Carlo Bettoni-Cazzago, a resident of Bogliaco, invented the lemon house, allegedly inspired by French orangeries. Before this, in 1768, he had founded an agrarian academy in Salò. Here he dedicated himself to the investigation of lemon cultivation, and with some success: on the western slopes, above Bogliaco, he had the land terraced and soil transported from the eastern shore of the lake. On a area of 20 sq m/215 sq ft, the campi, three trees were planted one behind the other. In order to create a favourable climate for them all year round, the side and rear walls of the lemon houses were closed off with wooden beams, with only the front remaining open. In winter they also received roofs. By the end of the 18th century thousands of such limonaie had been built. The Garda lemon distinguished itself from its Sicilian sister by the fact that it kept longer, had more juice and higher amount of vitamin C. However it was to be the Sicilian lemon that put an end to the Garda fruit. After 1866, when Lombardy became part of the united Italy, protective duty was done away with when the borders fell, and Sicily was able to supply the market with cheaper products.

Today

The final blow came shortly before the end of the First World War. The Italian government occupied the campi in order to build barracks for the army. During the especially hard winter of 1928–29 almost all the lemon trees on Lago di Garda froze. Today there are only a few limonaie: in Gargnano the remains of them are under a preservation order, while in Tignale and Limone they have been re-cultivated.

marinated and baked **shad** (agone alla comasca) is a speciality. As curadura, the same fish has been promoted from being a food for the poor to a delicacy for gourmets: it is preserved in bay leaves and compressed in a wooden cask.

Dolce   The most delicious dessert is without doubt **zabaione**, a simple, fluffy custard dish made with egg yolk. **Cotizze** are deep-fried pieces of apple; **cassata** is a layered dessert with ricotta cheese and sponge cake, and **gelato** is ice cream. The thin, crumbly cake that often accompanies coffee in Mantua is known as **sbrisolona**.

Formaggio   A number of cheeses come from Lombardy. In addition to **taleggio**, **gorgonzola** and **mascarpone**, try **grana padano**, a fine hard cheese ideal for grating, or the soft **bel casale**. **Bitto**, produced in a side valley of Valtellina, is very mild as a young hard cheese, but later becomes solid and strong and can eventually be grated. **Casera** and **scimud**, produced from skimmed cow's milk, are slightly sharp-tasting and piquant. **Bagoss**, a tasty hard cheese, comes from Bagolino near Lago d'Idro. The goat's cheese **cingherlin**, which is produced in the strip of land between Varese and Como, is also to be recommended.

Drinks   Italy is the land of the aperitif. **Campari**, from Milan, can be drunk with soda or orange juice. Standard drinks with meals are **wine** (vino) and **mineral water** (acqua minerale), either carbonated or non-carbonated (con or senza gas). The water from the San Pellegrino spring is the best-known regional mineral water. In addition lemonades (limonata) or **fruit juices** (succo di ...) and diverse **beers** (birra) are available. Along with the light Italian beer, there is a variety of brews from abroad.

Wines   Table wines are served by the carafe – 1 litre (un litro), 0.5 litres (mezzo litro) or 0.25 litres (quarto litro) – or by the glass (un bicchiere). More expensive wines are brought to the table in corked bottles bearing a label. Among Lombard wines, the **red wines** from the Oltrepò Pavese region (Barbera, Bonarda, Buttafuoco, Sangue di Giuda) are very popular, but also the **white Riesling, Pinot and Moscato wines.** In Oltrepò Pavese and Franciacorta outstanding **sparkling wines** (spumante) are produced. In Valtellina, robust fruity wines are made from the Nebbiolo grape. The best-known are Sassella, Grumello and Inferno. Lugana is a pleasant and refreshing white wine from the regions to the south of Lago di Garda. The Lambrusco from the province of Mantua in no way takes second place to the famous wines of the same type from Emilia-Romagna. Several Lombard wines are **DOC wines** (Denominazione di Origine Controllata). In contrast to table wines (vino da tavola) they come from a precisely defined growing area, are subject to production regulations and must be submitted for analysis and tasting before being put on the market.

Classification ▸

Health

In many places there is a Guardia Medica for medical help. The medical emergency service at night (8pm–8am) and on holidays is provided by the Guardia Medica notturna e festiva. Medical emergency help or first aid (pronto soccorso) outside hospitals (ospedali) comes from the White Cross (Croce Bianca), Green Cross (Croce Verde) and Red Cross (Croce Rossa Italiana), whose addresses can be found on the first pages of the telephone book (Avantielenco). Dentists can be found in the telephone book under "medici dentisti".

Medical help

Pharmacies (farmacie) are generally open Mon–Fri 8.30am–12.30pm and 3pm–7.30pm. They are closed either on Wednesdays or Saturdays. Every pharmacy displays in the window or door a list of pharmacies (farmacie di turno) which are open at night and on holidays.

Pharmacies

Information

IN ITALY

▶ **ENIT**
(Ente Nazionale Italiano per il Turismo)
Via Marghera 2
I-00185 Roma
Tel. 06 44 49 91
www.enit.it

IN AUSTRALIA

▶ **ENIT**
Level 4, 46 Market Street
Sydney NSW 2000
Tel. 02 92621666, fax 02 92621677
Email: italia@italiantourism.com.au

IN CANADA

▶ **ENIT**
175 Bloor Street E. – Suite 907
South Tower
Toronto M4W 3R8
Tel. 1 416 9254882
Fax 1 416 9254799
Email: enitto@italiantourism.com

IN THE UK

▶ **ENIT**
(Italian state tourist board)
1, Princes Street
London W1B 2AY
Tel. 020 7408 1254
Fax 020 7399 3567
Email: italy@italiantouristboard.co.uk

IN THE USA

▶ **ENIT**
630, Fifth Avenue – Suite 1565
New York NY 10111
Tel. 1 212 2455618
Fax 1 212 5869249
Email: enitny@italiantourism.com

12400, Wilshire Blvd. – Suite 550
Los Angeles CA 90025
Tel. 1 310 8201898
Fax 1 310 8206357
Email: enitla@italiantourism.com

▶ **Assessorato Regionale al
Turismo Lombardia**

Via Sassetti 32
I-20124 Milano
Tel. 0 26 75 61
Fax 02 67 66 62 92
www.regione.lombardia.it

▶ **Province of Bergamo**
APT
Viale Vittorio Emanuele 20
I-24121 Bergamo
Tel. 0 35 21 31 85
Fax 0 35 21 31 84
www.apt.bergamo.it

▶ **Province of Brescia**
Ufficio Informazioni e Accoglienza
Turistica
Via Musei 32
I-25121 Brescia
Tel. 03 03 74 98 38
Fax 03 03 74 99 82
www.provincia.brescia.it

▶ **Province of Como**
APT
Piazza Cavour 17
I-22100 Como
Tel. 0 31 3 30.01 11
www.lakecomo.com

▶ **Province of Cremona**
APT
Piazza del Comune 5
I-26100 Cremona
Tel. 0 37 22 32 33
Fax 03 72 53 40 80
www.aptcremona.it

▶ **Province of Lecco**
APT
Via N. Sauro 6
I-22053 Lecco
Tel. 03 41 36 23 60

Fax 03 41 28 62 31
www.aptlecco.com

▶ **Province of Lodi**
APT
Piazza Broletto 4
I-26900 Lodi
Tel. 03 71 42 13 91
Fax 03 71 42 13 13
www.apt.lodi.it

▶ **Province of Mantova**
APT
Piazza A. Mantegna 6
I-46100 Mantova
Tel. 03 76 43 24 32
Fax 03 76 43 24 33
www.turismo.mantova.it

▶ **Province of Milano**
APT
Via Marconi 1
I-20123 Milano
Tel. 02 72 52 41
Fax 02 72 52 42 50
www.milanoinfotourist.it

▶ **Province of Pavia**
APT
Via Fabio Filzi 2
I-27100 Pavia
Tel. 0 38 22 21 56
Fax 0 38 23 22 21
www.apt.pv.it

▶ **Province of Sondrio**
Via C. Barttisti 12
I-23100 Sondrio
Tel. 03 42 51 25 00
Fax 03 42 21 25 90
www.valtellina.com

▶ **Province of Varese**
APT
Via Carrobio 2
I-21100 Varese
Tel. 03 32 28 36 04
www.varesottoturismo.com

TOURIST OFFICES
IN SWITZERLAND

▶ **Switzerland Tourism**
Tel. 00 800 100 200 30
Fax 00 800 100 200 31
www.myswitzerland.com

▶ **Ticino Turismo**
Via Lugano 12
CH-6500 Bellinzona
Tel. 091 8 25 70 56
Fax 091 8 25 36 14
www.ticino-tourism.ch

INTERNET

▶ **www.regione.lombardia.it**
Background, political and administrative information on the region

▶ **www.italiantouristboard.co.uk**
www.italiantourism.com
The official ENIT websites provide a wealth of information on accommodation, museums, and travel within Italy, as well as a calendar of events and the latest news.

▶ **www.welcometoitaly.com**
Descriptions in English of museums and accommodation

▶ **www.beniculturali.it**
www.museionline.it
Plenty of information in Italian on museums, cultural events and exhibitions

▶ **www.italiamia.com**
A good source of links and background information

▶ **www.deliciousitaly.com**
Recipes, restaurants, cooking holidays

▶ **www.parks.it**
Information on Italy's nature parks

EMBASSIES IN ITALY

▶ **Australian embassy in Rome**
Via Antonio Bosio 5
Tel. 06 85 27 21
www.italy.embassy.gov.au

▶ **British embassy in Rome**
Via XX Settembre 80A
Tel. 06 422 00 001
www.britishembassy.gov.uk

▶ **Canadian embassy in Rome**
Via Zara 30
Tel. 06 44 59 81
www.canada.it

▶ **Embassy of the Republic of Ireland in Rome**
Piazza Campitelli 3
Tel. 069 697 91 21

Language

Italian evolved from Latin and is closer to it than any other of the Romance languages. A large number of dialects developed, including in the course of the 13th and 14th centuries Tuscan, which is now the standard form of written Italian.

c, cc before »e, i« like an English »ch«, e.g. dieci; otherwise like »k«   Pronunciation
ch, cch »k«, e.g. pacchi, che

ci, ce like English »ch«, e.g. ciao, cioccolata
g, gg before »e, i« like the English »j« in jungle, e.g. gente
gl like lli in »million«, e.g. figlio
gn as in »cognac«, e.g. bagno
sc before »e, i« like the English »sh«, e.g. uscita
sch wie »sk«in »skip«, e.g. Ischia
sci before »a, o, u« like the English »sh«, e.g. lasciare
z as »ds«

Stress   In words of several syllables the second-last syllable is usually stressed; in cases where the last syllable is stressed, it is normally marked with an accent (e.g. città). When the stress falls on the third-last syllable, this can also be shown by means of an accent, a practice followed in this guide at the first mention of a place name.

Italian Phrase Book

At a glance

Sì / No	Yes / No
Per favore / Grazie	Please / Thank you
Non c'è di che	You're welcome
Scusi! / Scusa!	Excuse me!
Come dice?	Pardon?
Non La / ti capisco	I don't understand you
Parlo solo un po' di ...	I only speak a little
Mi può aiutare, per favore?	Could you help me?
Vorrei ...	I would like ...
(Non) mi piace	I (don't) like that
Ha ...?	Do you have ...?
Quanto costa?	How much does it cost?
Che ore sono? / Che ora è?	What time is it?
Come sta? / Come stai?	How are you?
Bene, grazie. E Lei / tu?	Fine, thanks. And you?

Travelling

a sinistra	left
a destra	right
diritto	straight ahead
vicino / lontano	close / far
Quanti chilometri sono?	How far is it (in kilometres)?
Vorrei noleggiare ...	I would like to rent ...
... una macchina	... a car
... una bicicletta	... a bicycle
... una barca	... a boat

Scusi, dov'è ...?	Excuse me, where is ...?
la stazione centrale	the main railway station
la metro(politana)	the underground
l'aeroporto	the airport
all'albergo	to the hotel
Ho un guasto.	I had a breakdown.
Mi potrebbe mandare ...	Could you send me ...
... un carro-attrezzi?	... a tow truck?
Scusi, c'è un'officina qui?	Is there a garage here?
Dov'è la prossima stazione di servizio?	Where is the next petrol station?
benzina normale	Normal petrol
super / gasolio	Super / diesel
deviazione	detour
senso unico	one-way street
sbarrato	closed
rallentare	drive slowly
tutti direzioni	all directions
tenere la destra	drive right
zona di silenzio	honking not allowed
zona tutelata inizio	no parking zone
aiuto!	help!
attenzione!	careful!
Chiami subito ...	Please call ... quickly
... un'autoambulanza	... an ambulance
... la polizia	... the police

Going Out

Scusi, mi potrebbe indicare ...?	Where is there ...?
... un buon ristorante?	... a good restaurant?
... un locale tipico?	... a typical restaurant?
C'è una gelateria qui vicino?	Is there an ice-cream shop here?
Può riservarci per stasera	Could I reserve a table for to-night
... un tavolo per quattro persone?	... for four people?
Alla Sua salute!	Cheers!
Il conto, per favore.	The bill, please.
Andava bene?	Did it taste good?
Il mangiare era eccellente.	The food was excellent.
Ha un programma delle manifestazioni?	Do you have a calendar of events?

Shopping

Dov'è si può trovare ...?	Where can I find ...?
... una farmacia	... a pharmacy
... un panificio	... a bakery

... un negozio di articoli fotografici	... a photography shop
... un grande magazzino	... a department store?
... un negozio di generi alimentari	... a grocery shop
... il mercato	... the market
... il supermercato	... the supermarket
... il tabaccaio	... the tobacconist
... il giornalaio	... the newspaper stand

Accommodation

Scusi, potrebbe consigliarmi ...?	Could you please ... recommend?
... un albergo	... a hotel
... una pensione	... a guesthouse
Ho prenotato una camera.	I have reserved a room.
È libera ...?	Do you still have ...?
... una singola	... a single room
... una doppia	... a double room
... con doccia / bagno	... with shower / bath
... per una notte	... for one night
... per una settimana	... for one week
... con vista sul mare	... with a sea view
Quanto costa la camera ...?	How much does the room cost ...?
... con la prima colazione?	... with breakfast?
... a mezza pensione?	... with half board?

Doctor and Pharmacy

Mi può consigliare un buon medico?	Could you recommend a good doctor?
Mi può dare una medicina per ...	Please give me medicine for ...
Soffro di diarrea.	I have diarrhoea.
Ho mal di pancia.	I have a stomach ache.
... mal di testa	... head ache
... mal di gola	... sore throat
... mal di denti	... tooth ache
... influenza	... the flu
... tosse	... a cough
... la febbre	... a fever
... scottatura solare	... sunburn
... costipazione	... constipation

Numbers

zero	0

uno	1
due	2
tre	3
quattro	4
cinque	5
sei	6
sette	7
otto	8
nove	9
dieci	10
undici	11
dodici	12
tredici	13
quattordici	14
quindici	15
sedici	16
diciassette	17
diciotto	18
diciannove	19
venti	20
ventuno	21
trenta	30
quaranta	40
cinquanta	50
sessanta	60
settanta	70
ottanta	80
novanta	90
cento	100
centouno	101
mille	1000
duemille	2000
diecimila	10 000
un quarto	1/4
un mezzo	1/2

Menu

Prima colazione	*breakfast*
caffè, espresso	small coffee, no milk
caffè macchiato	small coffee, a little milk
caffe latte	coffee with milk
cappuccino	coffee with foamy milk
tè al latte / al limone	tea with milk / lemon
cioccolata	hot chocolate
frittata	omelette/pancake
pane / panino / pane tostato	bread / roll / toast

burro	butter
salame	sausage
prosciutto	ham
miele	honey
marmellata	jam
iogurt	yoghurt

antipasti	*starters*
affettato misto	mixed cold meats
anguilla affumicata	smoked eel
melone e prosciutto	melon with ham
vitello tonnato	cold roast veal with tuna sauce

primi piatti	*pasta and rice dishes, soups*
pasta	noodles
fettuccine / tagliatelle	ribbon noodles
gnocchi	small potato dumplings
polenta (alla valdostana)	maize porridge (with cheese)
vermicelli	thin spaghetti
minestrone	thick vegetable soup
pastina in brodo	meat broth with thin noodles
zuppa di pesce	fish soup

carni e pesce	*meat and fish*
agnello	lamb
ai ferri / alla griglia	from the grill
aragosta	lobster
brasato	roast
coniglio	rabbit
cozze / vongole	mussels / clams
fegato	liver
fritto di pesce	fried fish
gambero, granchio	shrimp
maiale	pork
manzo / bue	beef / ox
pesce spada	swordfish
platessa	plaice
pollo	chicken
rognoni	kidneys
salmone	salmon
scampi fritti	fried langoustines
sogliola	sole

tonno	tuna
trota	trout
vitello	veal

verdura	*vegetables*
asparagi	asparagus
carciofi	artichoke
carote	carrot
cavolfiore	cauliflower
cavolo	cabbage
cicoria belga	chicory
cipolle	onions
fagioli	white beans
fagiolini	green beans
finocchi	fennel
funghi	mushrooms
insalata mista / verde	mixed / green salad
lenticchie	lentils
melanzane	aubergine
patate	potatoes
patatine fritte	French fries
peperoni	paprika
pomodori	tomatoes
spinaci	spinach
zucca	pumpkin

formaggi	*cheese*
parmigiano	Parmesan
pecorino	sheep's cheese
ricotta	cottage cheese
dolci e frutta	sweets and fruit
cassata	ice cream with candied fruit
coppa assortita	mixed ice cream cup
coppa con panna	ice cream cup with whipped cream
tirami su	sponge with mascarpone cream
zabaione	egg cream
zuppa inglese	trifle

bevande	*beverages*
acqua minerale	mineral water
aranciata	orangeade
bibita	refreshment
bicchiere	glass

birra scura / chiara	dark / light beer
birra alla spina	draught beer
birra senza alcool	non-alcoholic beer
bottiglia	bottle
con ghiaccio	with ice
digestivo	after-dinner liqueur
gassata/con gas	carbonated
liscia/senza gas	not carbonated
secco	dry
spumante	sparkling wine
succo	fruit juice
vino bianco / rosato / rosso	white / rosé- / red wine
vino della casa	house wine

Literature

Non-fiction

Anderson, Burton: *Wines of Italy* (Mitchell Beazley Pocket Guides). Almost 3000 wines and producers described by an international authority on Italian wine.

Brown, David Alan: *The Legacy of Leonardo: Painters in Lombardy 1490–1530*. A scholarly work for those with a serious interest in the art of this region.

Burke, Peter: *The Italian Renaissance: Culture and Society in Italy*. A standard work on a great period in the history of Italy.

Parks, Tim: *A Season with Verona*. The author looks at modern Italy from the perspective of a football fan.

Procacci, Giuliano: *History of the Italian People*. A good general history of the peninsula from the Middle Ages to the post-war period.

Fiction and literature

Boccaccio, Giovanni: *The Decameron*. A collection of 100 stories which were written after the great plague in Florence in 1348 and are considered to be the genesis of Italian prose.

Colvin, Clare: *The Masque of the Gonzagas*.
A historical novel about a love affair of Vincenzo, Duke of Mantua, set at the magnificent court of the Gonzaga dynasty. The author's detailed knowledge of the place and period bring the story to life.

Manzoni, Alessandro:: *The Betrothed*. One of the great works of Italian literature, a love story with a political message set in Lombardy in the period of Spanish occupation in the early 17th century.

Umberto Eco: *Baudolino*. Novel about the fictional son of a peasant from Piedmont, who in 1155 was taken to be a child of Emperor Frederick Barbarossa and witnessed all the great historical events of the following 50 years.

Media

The main national newspapers are *Corriere della Sera*, which is published in Milan, *La Repubblica* (on Thursdays with the weekly section *Tutto Milano* with events and cinema programs) and *La Stampa*.

Italian newspapers

English-language newspapers and magazines are readily available in Milan, and can usually also be found in other places that attract international visitors.

Media in English

The state broadcaster RAI (Radio Televisione Italiana) has no great reputation for political independence or quality of programming. English-language channels are widely available via cable or satellite.
For those who understand Italian, the RAI radio channels broadcast pop, light and classical music, and have regular traffic reports (RAI-1 89.7 FM, RAI-2 91.7 FM, RAI-3 93.7 FM).

Radio and TV

Money

Since 2002 the euro has been the official currency of Italy.

Euro

Citizens of EU members countries may import to and export from Italy unlimited amounts in euros.

Currency regulations

As a rule banks are open Mon–Fri 8.30am–1pm; afternoon opening times vary (about 2.30pm–3.30pm). On days before holidays (prefestivi) the banks close at 11.20am.

Banks

Cash is available at **ATM machines** round the clock by using **credit and debit cards** with a PIN. Credit cards have limits.
Loss of a card must be reported immediately.

i Exchange rates

- 1 € = 1.33 US$
  1 US$ = 0.75 €
  1 £ = 1.17 €
  1 € = 0.84 £

Most international credit cards are accepted by banks, hotels, restaurants, car rentals and many shops. While Visa and Eurocard are common, American Express and Diners Club are not accepted everywhere.

Credit cards

In Italy customers are required to request and keep a receipt (ricevuta fiscale or scontrino). It can happen that a customer is asked to show a receipt after leaving a shop– this is intended to make tax evasion more difficult.

Receipts

▶ CONTACT DETAILS FOR CREDIT CARDS

In the event of lost bank or credit cards you can contact the following numbers in UK and USA (phone numbers when dialling from Italy):

▶ **Eurocard/MasterCard**
Tel. 001 / 636 7227 111

▶ **Visa**
Tel. 001 / 410 581 336

▶ **American Express UK**
Tel. 0044 / 1273 696 933

▶ **American Express USA**
Tel. 001 / 800 528 4800

▶ **Diners Club UK**
Tel. 0044 / 1252 513 500

▶ **Diners Club USA**
Tel. 001 / 303 799 9000
Have the bank sort code, account number and card number as well as the expiry date ready.

The following numbers of UK banks (dialling from Italy) can be used to report and stop lost or stolen bank and credit cards issued by those banks:

▶ **HSBC**
Tel. 0044 / 1442 422 929

▶ **Barclaycard**
Tel. 0044 / 1604 230 230

▶ **NatWest**
Tel. 0044 / 142 370 0545

▶ **Lloyds TSB**
Tel. 0044 / 1702 278 270

Personal Safety

Beware of pickpockets! Petty crime is widespread in Lombardy, especially in Milan and the centres of tourism. Keep an eye on bags, suitcases, cameras and other valuable items. Cars – even hire cars with Italian registration plates – and especially caravans, camping vans and luxury cars, are often broken into or stolen. Never leave valuables, papers, money, bank cards or keys in a parked car – it is better to keep them with you. Empty the glove compartment and boot rather than locking them, and make efforts to park in a locked garage overnight.

... and if the worst happens The Italian police are helpful but more or less powerless in the face of organized crime. After a robbery the police produce a document which is important for making an insurance claim.

Post · Communications

Italian post offices offer regular mail and package delivery services as well as postal banking services. They are open Mon–Fri 8.30am–1.30pm and Sat 8.30am–noon. Post offices close at noon on the last day of the month. The following post offices in Milan have longer opening hours: Via Cordusio 4, Mon–Fri 8am–7.30pm and Sat 8am–5pm; in main railway station, Mon–Fri 8.15am–7.30pm and Sat 8.15am–3.30pm.

Post offices

Postage stamps (francobolli) can be bought in post offices or – quicker – in tobacco shops, which have the T sign (tabacchi). Letters up to 20g/0.7oz and postcards within Italy and to EU countries cost 0.65 euros.

Postage stamps

Phone calls to other countries can be made from public telephone booths with an orange telephone receiver symbol. Few work with coins; most accept only telephone cards (carta telefonica), which can be bought in bars, newspapers stands or tobacco shops.

Telephoning

Important: area codes are part of the Italian telephone numbers. This means that the area code including the initial 0 must always be dialled when calling from another country as well as locally (the exceptions to this are mobile phone numbers, which do not begin with a zero, emergency numbers, and toll-free service numbers beginning with 800).

Important

COUNTRY CODES

▶ **From Italy**
to other countries: 00 followed by the country code, e.g.
to Australia: tel. 0061
to the Republic of Ireland:
tel. 00353
to UK: 0044
to USA: 001

▶ **From other countries to Italy:**
+39

CITY AREA CODES

The local area codes are part of the Italian telephone numbers. Both for local calls and when calling from foreign countries, the area code including the 0 must also be dialled. The exceptions to this are emergency, service and mobile phone numbers, which do not begin with 9. Service numbers with the code 800 are free of charge.

TELEPHONE DIRECTORY INQUIRIES

In Italy tel. 12
Abroad tel. 176

FEES

Cheaper rates apply daily from 10pm to 8am and at weekends.

Mobile phones
mobile phones
The use of mobile telephones from other countries is generally problem-free in Italy. The two most frequented telephone networks are Telecom Italia Mobile (number 2 22 01) and Omnitel Pronto Italia (number 2 22 10). If you spend much time in Italy, it may be worth buying a prepaid chip of Telecom Italia Mobile (TIM).

Prices and Discounts

Admission
Visitors from EU countries who are under 18 or retired have free admission to many sights. For 18 to 25-year-olds it is worth asking about reduced admission prices. Most larger cities offer savings in the form of tickets for admission to a number of sights.

► WHAT DOES IT COST?

Double room
from €60

Three-course meal
from €25

Simple meal
from €8

Coffee
€2

Petrol
approx. €1,30 per litre

Shopping

Shopping heaven
For shoes, clothes, household goods, designer items and food, bought either at markets or in boutiques, Lombardy is one big shopping heaven. The city of choice for quality-conscious shoppers is **Milan**, where many famous national and international fashion designers are represented. A good way of picking up bargains is to **buy directly from the factory outlets** (punto vendita diretto), for example Alessi (Crusinallo near Omegna on Lago di Orta) for household goods, Lanificio (Romagnano Sesia, near Varallo) for cashmere pullovers and Ratti (Guanzate, near Como) for ties, blouses and silk scarves. Guides to the factory outlets are available from all good bookshops. When shopping keep the receipt (scontrino), which has to be produced in case of checks by the tax authorities.

? DID YOU KNOW …?

■ Trading in pirated brand goods is illegal in Italy, and tourists who buy forged handbags or luxury watches bearing exclusive brand names are subject to heavy fines if caught!

Milan is shopping heaven for high-quality fashion →

Food   The local culinary specialities are excellent souvenirs: a sweet and sticky portion of **torrone** from Cremona, for example, **lime liqueur** from Brescia, a bottle of **Campari** from Milan or **Amaretto liqueur** from Saronno. Many agriturismo houses sell their home-made specialities: olive oil, jam, ravioli, sausage, cheese, wine and grappa. In Franciacorta in the Oltrepò Pavese area, south of Lago di Garda and in Valtellina many wine farmers and cellars sell their **regional wines**.

Crafts   The products made from **pietra ollare** (a type of steatite or **soapstone**) sold in Valtellina are excellent for preparing and storing food. The patchwork carpets made of pieces of coarse fabric known here as **pezzotti** are a characteristic product of the region.

Souvenirs   The copies of capitals and other architectural fragments sold in some places are heavy but durable souvenirs. A shop on Piazza Ducale in Sabbioneta has what is probably the largest range of them.

Furniture   Hand-made furniture is also sold in Lombardy. The cabinet makers from Cantù, where intarsia work is also on offer, have a particularly good reputation.

Music   Opera fans can buy CDs with historic recordings made at **La Scala** in Milan from the theatre museum. Books about opera are also on sale here. Lovers of stringed instruments can buy or place an order for a violin in a workshop in **Cremona**.

Spas

No other region of Italy has as many spas as Lombardy, where there are many thermal springs set in lovely scenery. The Regione Lombardia publishes a guide to all of these spas (►Information). More details are available from the APT offices of the province (►Information). A few of the leading spas are described below.

Bergamo province   S. Pellegrino Terme (400m/1300ft altitude)
Alkaline sodium bicarbonate and sulphur spring (26°C/79°F)
Recommended for: women's complaints, rheumatism and skin disease. Treatments: massage, water massage, mud baths, water for drinking and bathing, inhalation, heat treatment.

Brescia province   Boario Terme (221m/725ft altitude, www.termedipoario.it)
Alkaline salt, calcium and sulphate springs, colloidal waters with a catalytic and hypotonic effect.
Recommended for: digestive complaints, metabolic disease, gall bladder complaints. Treatments: drinking the waters, thermal baths, mud baths, inhalation.

Sirmione (68m/223ft altitude, www.termedisirmione.com)
Radioactive, sulphurous, hyperthermal spring with iodine, bromine and chlorine content (69°C/156°F).
Recommended for: diseases of the respiratory system, rheumatic complaints. Treatments: massage, water massage, mud baths and mud packs, bathing cures, heat treatment, inhalation.

Salice Terme (173m/568ft altitude, www.termedisalice.it)   Pavia province
Iodine salt spring and sulphurous waters.
Recommended for: rheumatic complaints, diseases of the respiratory system. Treatments: massage and water massage, mud baths and mud packs, baths, heat treatment, inhalation, mineral water for drinking.

Bagni di Bormio (1318m/4324ft altitude, www.bagnedibormio.it)   Sondrio province
Thermal springs with a temperature of 38–40°C/100–104°F
Recommended for: diseases of the respiratory system, digestive problems, rheumatic complaints. Treatments: beauty treatments, massage, water massage, mud baths and mud packs, inhalation, water for drinking and bathing.

Sport and Outdoors

Cyclists in Lombardy can choose from a broad range of options,   Cycling
from gentle rides on the plain and lakeshore circuits to mountain tours. The wonderful scenery of the nature parks Ticino, Mincio, Groane and Adda can be discovered by bike, and there are plenty of cycle hire points in the nature reserves of the Po plain. The APT offices a in Pavia, Mantua and Lodi provide more detailed information and, for some areas, maps on which the side roads are marked.
The **Touring Club Italiano** sells the English-language guidebook *Italy by Bike* via its website: www.touringclub.com.

There are some fine areas for hiking in Lombardy, such as the Chia-   Hiking
venna valley in the far north, Valtellina, the Malenco valley north of Sondrio, the Stelvio National Park, Valcamonica, Adamello, the west bank of Lago di Como, the Alpi Orobie north of Bergamo, Grigne and Resegone (Valsassina, eastern shore of Lago di Como), the foothills of the Alps near Varese and the northern Apennine regions of Oltrepò Pavese.
Huts for shelter can be found everywhere. ENIT and the local APT offices are useful sources for descriptions of hikes, information about huts, important telephone numbers, and maps with marked routes. For more detailed information contact the Club Alpino Italiano (CAI).

USEFUL ADDRESSES

CYCLING

► **Internet**
www.cycling.it

► **Touring Club Italiano**
Corso Italia 10
I-20122 Milano
Tel. 0 28 52 61
www.touringclub.it

HIKING

► **Club Alpino Italiano
(CAI)**
Via Petrella 19
I-20124 Milano
Tel. 02 2 05 72 31
Fax 02 2 05 72 32 01
www.cai.it

GOLF

► **Federazione Italiana Golf**
Viale Tiziano 74
I-00196 Roma (Lazio)
Tel. 0 63 23 18 25
www.federgolf.it

WATER SPORTS

► **WWWind Square Malcesine**
Loc. Sottodossi
Tel./Fax 0 45 7 40 04 13
www.wwwind.com

► **Windsurfcenter Domaso**
Domaso
Camping Paradiso
www.windsurfcenter-domaso.com

ANGLING

► **Federazione Italiana
Pesca Sportiva e
attivita subaque**
Viale Tiziano 70
I-00196 Roma
Tel. 0 63 20 17 11
www.portale.fipsas.it

WINTER SPORTS

► **Federazione Italiana
Sport Invernali**
Via Piranesi 44
I-20137 Milano
Tel. 02 75 731
Fax 02 7 57 33 68
www.fisi.org

Climbing   Lombardy has excellent places for climbing, including Valtellina, Valchiavenna, Val Brandet, Val di Campovecchio and the Stelvio National-al Park. Climbers from Milan favour the area around Lecco, where there is a well-known climbing school. The **limestone pinnacles in Grigna and the granite rocks of the Mello valley** are a climbers' paradise. The **world climbing championships** are held each year in September in Arco at the northern end of Lago di Garda.

Horse riding   Riding is often offered as part of an agriturismo holiday. Many participants in the agriturismo scheme offer horseback tours. There are some wonderful riding paths in the nature reserves of the lowland such as the Ticino Park. Since parts of the park are closed to motorized vehicles, a horseback ride will be all the more pleasant and offer opportunities to see the local flora and fauna. In the ENIT (►Information) brochures about agriturismo in Lombardy, all accommodation with riding holidays is listed.

There are 35 golf courses in Lombardy, most of them around Milan and the lakes. They are listed under www.1golf.eu.

Golf

Lombardy has good conditions and infrastructure for winter sports, especially in the high Alpine regions of Sondrio. In other areas, too, there are many smaller skiing resorts with slopes and tracks for downhill and cross-country skiing.

Winter sports

Water Sports

All the north Italian lakes are ideal for sailing and windsurfing. **Lago di Garda** in particular is known for its reliable and usually strong winds. There are countless schools of sailing and windsurfing on the lakes, and those who possess a licence can hire boats.

Windsurfing and sailing

Canoeing and kayaking are becoming increasingly popular. It is possible to take a long tour from Milan via the Naviglio Pavese, the Ticino and the Po to the Adriatic. The upper reaches of the Adda in Valtellina, the Brembo north of Bergamo and the Oglio north of Brescia are also excellent for canoeing and kayaking. For more detailed information refer to the Lombardy office of the Italian canoeing and kayak club in Milan.

Canoeing and kayaking

Anglers need a permit, which should be ordered in good time from the Federazione Italiana Pesca Sportiva e attivita subaque in Rome.

Angling

Windsurfers find conditions to suit them on Lago di Garda

Time

Italy is in the central European time zone (CET), one hour ahead of Greenwich Mean Time. For the summer months from the end of March to the end of October European Summer Time is used (CEST = CET+1 hour).

Transport

Road Traffic

Autostrada

Almost every motorway (autostrada) in Italy is a toll road (pedaggio); expect to pay about €5 per 100km/60mi. The **autostrada toll** can be paid in cash, by credit card or with a Viacard, which can be obtained in Italy from the automobile clubs, from ACI offices at the borders, at autostrada approach roads, at autostrada services (»punto blu«), and from tobacconists and petrol stations. Further information at www.autostrade.it.

Petrol stations

The import and transport of petrol in canisters is prohibited. Super (95 octane), superplus (98 octane) and diesel (gasolio) fuel is available. The usual opening times for petrol stations are 7am–noon and 2pm–8pm. 24-hour service is usual on motorways. At weekends and when petrol stations are closed, it is often possible to pay at a machine.

Traffic regulations

The **blood-alcohol limit** is 0.5mg/ml. On motorways and country roads dipped headlights must be used during daytime. In rain the speed limit on motorways is 110kmh/68mph rather than the usual 130kmh/80mph. Otherwise the **speed limits** are: cars, motorbikes and motor caravans of up to 3.5 tons 50kmh/30mph in built-up areas, 90kmh/56mph outside built-up areas, 110kmh/68mph on dual carriageways, 130kmh/80mph on a motorway (autostrada); vehicles over 3.5 tons 80kmh/50mph, on motorways 100kmh/62mph. Heavy fines are imposed for speeding. Private **towing** is not allowed on motorways. In case of **breakdown** the Italian automobile club ACI tows foreign drivers and motorbikes to the next garage free of charge. Riders of motorbikes over 50cc must wear a helmet. In case of an accident where the car is a complete write-off, the customs authorities must be informed.

Parking

It is not easy to find a parking space in any city in Lombardy, let alone one that is legal and safe. The centres of almost all towns are either completely traffic-free or subject to traffic-calming measures, but access to hotels is permitted. Close to the traffic-free zones of inner cities there are hardly any free parking spaces. Parking is permitted on the spaces marked in blue if a ticket has been purchased from a machine. Spaces marked in white are usually free for one hour.

To hire a car in Italy you have to be at least 21 years old, possess a credit card, and have had a national driving licence for at least one year. When hiring from the major international car hire firms, it is usually cheaper to book in advance from your home country. Local car-hire firms are listed in telephone directories under »Noleggio«.

Car hire

Boat Traffic

Boat trips operate on the north Italian lakes and the river Po, sometimes as packages including admission to sights. In the high season the boats usually run daily, in spring and autumn less often. Local tourist offices have details of prices and timetables. For information see also www.navigazionelaghi.it.

Trips

The best way to explore the lakes is to take a boat trip

Travellers with Disabilities

See www.accessible-italy.com for details of tours to some of the most popular destinations. www.everybody.co.uk has information about airlines. The Italian railways have a brochure on *Services for Disabled People*.

▶ TOURS FOR THE DISABLED

UNITED KINGDOM

▶ **Holidaycare**
Tourism for All
The Hawkins Suite
Enham Place, Enham Alamein
Andover SP11 6JS
Tel. 08 45 124 99 71
www.holidaycare.org.uk

USA

▶ **SATH**
(Society for the Advancement of Travel for the Handicapped)
347 5th Ave., no. 610
New York, NY 10016:
Tel. (21) 4 47 72 84
www.sath.org

When to Go

Climate

Mountains ▶ The mountain regions of the north have long winters with heavy snowfall. The snow cover in the winter sports areas is reliable, and snow falls here until March. April is generally a rainy month, but the average amount of rainfall varies greatly from one valley to another. The **most pleasant climate in Lombardy** is without a doubt that of the north Italian **lakes**. In the shadow of the Alps, they are screened from weather coming from the north. The summers are enjoyably warm without being too hot, and with average temperatures of 4°C/39°F or more the winters are not cold. The hours of sunshine in summer are twice as high around the north Italian lakes as on the **plain of the Po**, where the predominantly warm and moist climate of the summer months can become oppressively hot and humid. The winters are relatively cold: **Milan** has the lowest average annual temperature of any large Italian city (10.5°C/51°F), with a January average of 3.1°C/37.5°F and 21.8°C/71°F in July. The hours of sunshine here are 543 in spring, 757 in summer, 365 in autumn and 170 in

Apennines ▶ winter. The climate of the northern Apennine region is more temperate, with mild weather in both summer and winter, as this climatic zone is influenced by the Adriatic Sea and the Tyrrhenian Sea.

When to travel The ideal time season for travelling to the north Italian lakes is between May and the end of September, but the winter months too can be mild and beautiful. The highest temperatures are in July and ◀ North Italian lakes August, with an average of 21°C/70°F, but this is also the season when the most visitors come, so May and September are an advantageous time to see the lakes. Periods of sustained bad weather are unusual, but short heavy showers of rain can be expected at any time.

For a tour of the **Po plain** and the smaller cities of Lombardy, the months from April to October are suitable in principle, but as this area can be **very hot and humid**, and July and August are the main tourist season, it is better to come in the spring and autumn months. During Ferragosto (mid-August) many museums and other institutions in the cities close. In late autumn the first fogs appear. The plain of the Po is not a good place for winter travel, as the sky is often overcast and it can be very cold.

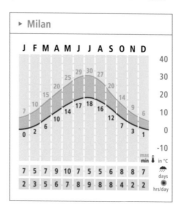

▶ Milan

	J	F	M	A	M	J	J	A	S	O	N	D	
max	7	10	15	20	25	29	30	27	20	14	9	6	in °C
min	0	2	6	10	14	17	18	16	12	7	3	1	
days	7	5	7	9	10	7	5	5	6	8	8	7	
hrs/day	2	3	5	6	7	8	9	8	8	4	2	2	

In the Alps the summer climate is usually extremely pleasant and not ◀ Mountain regions too hot; the dry autumn months are also a popular time for visits. In winter the **Alpine skiing resorts** attract many fans of winter sports. The spring is not the best season, as a good deal of rain and snow falls.

Tours

NOT SURE WHERE TO
GO? OUR SUGGESTIONS
WITH TIPS FOR
ESPECIALLY INTERESTING
ROUTES ARE SURE TO
HELP.

TOURS THROUGH LOMBARDY

If you still have no firm itinerary for your trip, our suggestions can help point you in the right direction. On the following pages we introduce three especially beautiful tours through Lombardy.

━━ **TOUR 1** **Pearls of Lombardy**
This tour takes in Lombardy's bustling capital Milan and the most important cultural centres of the region. ▶ **page 108**

━━ **TOUR 2** **Three-City Tour**
Tour 2 runs through the south-west of Lombardy with further treasures of art and architecture. ▶ **page 110**

━━ **TOUR 3** **The Edge of the Alps and the Lakes**
This tour covers Lakes di Como and Lake d'Iseo, and leads far into Lombardy's mountainous north. ▶ **page 111**

Gardesana Occidentale: spectacular coastal road on Lago di Garda

SWITZERLAND

✳ Chiavenna

Lago
di Como

✳ Sondrio

✳ Teglio

Lago
Maggiore

Lago
di Lugano

✳ Varenna   ✳ Valsassina   **TOUR 3**   ✳✳ Parco Nazionale delle
Incisioni Rupestri

✳ Lecco

©*Baedeker*   Lago d'Iseo   Lago d'Idro

▽   ✳ Iseo   Lago di Garda

✳ Monza   ✳✳ Bergamo   ✳✳ Brescia

◁   ✳✳ Milan

TOUR 1   ✳ Crema

✳✳ Certosa
di Pavia   ✳ Lodi   **TOUR 2**   ✳✳ Mantua

✳✳ Pavia   ✳✳ Cremona   ✳ San Benedetto (Po)

✳ Sabbioneta

*In the national park,
mysterious prehistoric
rock carvings have
been preserved*

*Mantua's wonderful
evening atmosphere*

*...ertosa di Pavia: the monastery is one
...˜ Lombardy's most important cultural
...onuments*

Travelling in Lombardy

The following suggested routes outline stretches through the loveliest and most important places in Lombardy. The **north Italian lakes** are featured in the descriptions of tours in the section Sights from A to Z, so the routes here focus on the southern part of the region. The lengths of the tours, given in kilometres and miles, do not include side trips. Although these routes are not overly long and can be covered quickly on major roads and motorways, several days should be set aside for each tour.

Mode of transport

The first choice for getting around is your **own vehicle**, be it a car, motorcycle or camper, especially for travellers who wish to be independent and spontaneous in planning their route and do not have much time on their hands. Those who do not take their own means of transport with them can rent a car or motorcycle in the larger cities. Another reason for taking your own vehicle is that **buses**, while they do stop at major destinations, only provide infrequent services to more remote places. As a result it can prove impossible to get away in the evening, meaning that visitors are compelled to make use of local accommodation – a situation that can often lead to unusual holiday experiences. Those getting around **by bike** or **on foot** are likely to get to know the country and its people even more intensively. The Grande Traversata delle Alpi (GTA), which runs from the Swiss border to the Mediterranean, is a famous long-distance route. In recent years, increasing numbers of routes for cyclists and mountain bikers have been signposted.

Where to stay

Visitors to major destinations are assured of finding a place to stay in guest houses and hotels. The alternatives in the countryside consist of the agriturismo accommodation offered on farms and wine-growing estates, an option that is particularly recommended for families with children.

Tour 1 Pearls of Lombardy

Start and finish: Milan   **Distance:** approx. 265km/165mi

This tour, which can easily be combined with tour 2, acquaints you with nearly all the larger and smaller towns and cities on the plain of the river Po. Take your time: set aside at least two days for Milan, a day for Bergamo and Brescia, and half a day for Cremona and Pavia.

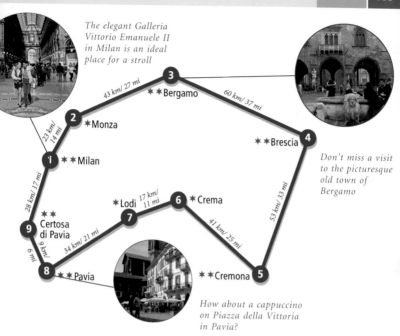

The elegant Galleria Vittorio Emanuele II in Milan is an ideal place for a stroll

3

43 km/ 27 mi ✳✳Bergamo 60 km/ 37 mi

2 ✳Monza

23 km/ 14 mi

✳✳Milan **1**

28 km/ 17 mi

✳Lodi 17 km/ 11 mi **6** ✳Crema

✳✳ Certosa di Pavia **9**

7

6 mi 9 km/

34 km/ 21 mi

8 ✳✳Pavia

4 ✳✳Brescia

Don't miss a visit to the picturesque old town of Bergamo

53 km/ 33 mi

41 km/ 25 mi

✳✳Cremona **5**

How about a cappuccino on Piazza della Vittoria in Pavia?

The bustling metropolis of ❶✳✳ **Milan** is a good place to start a journey through Lombardy. Cultural treasures and Lombard life are present in abundance here. Marked urban sprawl characterizes not only Milan and its surroundings but also ❷✳ **Monza**; for a pleasant change take a detour to the huge park of the Villa Reale north of Monza – though cars still play a role here in the Autodromo. From Monza, the E 64 motorway heads north-east and leads very quickly to ❸✳✳ **Bergamo**, where an evening in the enchanting *città alta* (upper town) is not to be missed. The next port of call is Brescia, approximately 48km/30mi southeast just off the E 64. ❹✳ **Brescia's** city centre, really quite sober in appearance, is full of cultural treasures for which time should be taken. There is a nice view of the city from the castle.

From Milan to Brescia

Once again, the next city on the route is quickly reached on the E 70 motorway or the parallel road (SS 45 bis): ❺✳✳ **Cremona** is the city of violin-making. The unique piazza is at its best in the evening. From Cremona, head along the SS 415 to ❻✳ **Crema**. Do not leave without having paid a short visit to the church of S. Maria della Croce on the northern edge of the city. Continue west on the SS 235 to ❼✳ **Lodi**. A detour to ✳ **Lodi Vecchio**, Lodi's predecessor, is

From Brescia via Cremona to Pavia

✔ **DON'T MISS**

- Milan: Lombardy's elegant and bustling capital
- The beautiful old town of Bergamo
- The splendid and important monastery complex of Certosa di Pavia

most rewarding. Leaving Lodi, continue further west on the SS 235. Pavia's cathedral dome – one of the largest in Italy – and its slim family towers announce your arrival there. The nicest route into ❽ ✷ ✷ **Pavia's** historic centre is along the bank of the Ticino within the city zone. On the way back to Milan stop off north of Pavia to view the splendid ❾ ✷ ✷ **Certosa di Pavia**, one of the most impressive experiences of this tour.

Tour 2 Three-City Tour

Start and finish: Brescia　　　　**Distance:** approx. 190km/120mi

This shorter tour is particularly interesting for its art-historical aspects; plan at least one full day for every city. The route combines well with tour 1.

From Brescia to Mantua　The starting point is ❶ ✷ ✷ **Brescia**, Lombardy's second-largest city, which does not seem especially appealing at first sight. The city centre, however, offers a broad range of worthwhile sights, dating from the period of Roman rule all the way to the 1930s central square. Take the SS 236 from Brescia and head south-east. From Castiglione delle Stiviere, with the church of S. Luigi, named after Luigi Gonzaga who was born here, continue towards Mantua.

 DON'T MISS

- The impressive cityscape of Mantua
- Enjoy the evening atmosphere on the piazza in Cremona.

To take a particularly impressive route into ❷ ✷ ✷ **Mantua,** turn off onto the SS 482 before reaching Mantua, skirt the north of the city and cross the bridge directly into the old town from the north-east – the beautiful panorama features the castle, medieval family towers, church spires and the dome of S. Andrea. One or two days are necessary to see the important sights of the city and to allow the lovely squares to work their magic at a leisurely pace.

For those who have time a detour south-east to ❸ ✷ **S. Benedetto Po** is recommended to view the Benedictine monastery. The SS 413 leads there from Mantua.

From Mantua via Sabbioneta to Cremona　Take the same route back, and west of Mantua turn onto the SS 420 in the direction of Sabbioneta. Another possibility here is to travel on the small roads heading directly west. At first there is a pretty stretch along the Po; passing Portiolo and Mottegiana, follow the

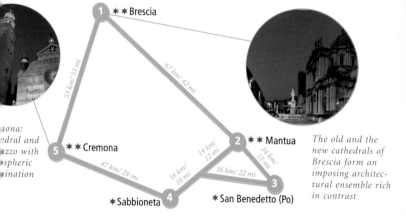

The old and the new cathedrals of Brescia form an imposing architectural ensemble rich in contrast

road west until Campitello and turn there onto the SS 420 to ❹ ✳ **Sabbioneta**, an »ideal city of the Renaissance«. From Sabbioneta continue on the SS 420 to Casalmaggiore, and here turn first onto the SS 343, then follow the signs in the direction of ❺ ✳✳ **Cremona**. If possible spend a night in Cremona, where the evening atmosphere on the illuminated piazza is a unique experience. Take the A 21 or the parallel SS 45 from Cremona to return quickly to **Brescia**.

Tour 3 The Edge of the Alps and the Lakes

Start and finish: Bergamo   **Distance:** approx. 260km/160mi

This route leads into the northern part of Lombardy, i.e. from the southern edge of the Alps into the north Italian lakes region and then up to the edge of the High Alps on the Swiss border. The route can be extended as desired, e.g. with a tour around one of the north Italian lakes. Tours around the lakes are described in the section »Sights from A to Z«. In addition, charming trips can be made into the lovely small side valleys.

Nowhere else is a location at the edge of the Alps more obvious than in ❶ ✳✳ **Bergamo**, with the *città bassa* at a lower level and the beautiful città alta higher up. A funicular leads up to the old town, and from here there is an extensive view south into the plain of the Po. Head west out of Bergamo and take the SS 342 to Lecco on ✳✳ **Lago di Como**. The plain is very quickly left behind and the

From Bergamo to Lecco

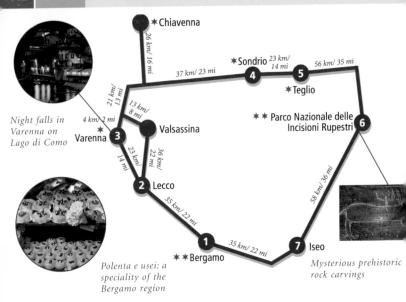

Night falls in Varenna on Lago di Como

Chiavenna

26 km/ 16 mi

37 km/ 23 mi

Sondrio 23 km/ 14 mi 5 56 km/ 35 mi

4

Teglio

21 km/ 13 mi

13 km/ 8 mi

**** Parco Nazionale delle Incisioni Rupestri** 6

4 km/ 2 mi

Varenna 3 **Valsassina**

14 mi 23 km/ 14 mi

36 km/ 22 mi

58 km/ 36 mi

2 **Lecco**

35 km/ 22 mi

1 35 km/ 22 mi 7 **Iseo**

**** Bergamo**

Polenta e usei: a speciality of the Bergamo region

Mysterious prehistoric rock carvings

route enters the region of the first mountains, which rise to almost 600m/2000ft. Near Cisano turn onto the SS 639 and follow the broad Adda valley. The river widens out to several lakes; passing first Lago di Olginate, continue along the shore of Lago di Garlate to **②Lecco**. The city in which Alessandro Manzoni set his novel *The Bethrothed* has few sights, but it is worth strolling through its small lively centre, and the surroundings are especially nice.

From Lecco to Varenna There are two possibilities for continuing the journey on leaving Lecco: the first is to take the road directly on the shore of Lago di Como. At the junction a good 6km/3.5mi north of Lecco, be sure to take the small coastal road in the direction of Varenna; the SS 36, which leads directly to Bellano, may be faster, but passes through a lot of tunnels. On the smaller road the route passes through towns that lie right on the lakeshore. Picturesque **③ ∗ Varenna** with its old villas and gardens is particularly worth seeing. From here **∗∗ Bellagio** is visible on a small tongue of land to the south, while **∗ Menaggio** lies on the western shore opposite.

The alternative is to travel from Lecco through **∗ Valsassina** and then pass by Bellano to reach the shore of Lago di Como. This option takes considerably longer as the road, though scenically very beautiful, is extremely winding. The mountains here reach elevations of over 2000m/6500ft. Pass the mountain townships Ballabio, Introbio, Primaluna and Cortenova. At Bellano continue on the smaller road along the shore. Pass through Dervio to eventually reach the northernmost part of Lago di Como near Colico.

Just beyond Colico the SS 36 leads north to ✳ **Chiavenna**. The road passes Lago di Mezzola and then follows the river bank into the town. Chiavenna is well known for its so-called »grotti« (the plural of grotto, or cave), generally simple, cosy beer gardens, some of which are built into the slope. The little town itself has a small, idyllic centre and several sights.

Side trip to Chiavenna

At the same junction at which the road to Chiavenna was taken, join the SS 38, which runs east through the entire ✳ **Valtellina** region. Those who want to travel through Valtellina at a more leisurely pace can switch to the small parallel roads at most points along the route. Morbegno is the entrance to the valley.

Through Valtellina

To the south and north-east it is possible to make the first detours into the side valleys of Valle del Bitto and Valmasino. About 25km/ 15mi beyond Morbegno lies ❹ ✳✳ **Sondrio**, the provincial capital. The peaks that rise around the small town are mostly snow-capped. Sondrio is comparatively untouristy, and it is worth stopping off here for a while. Piazza Garibaldi, the main square, is pretty, but the town's sights are not especially numerous.

Here, too, it is possible to take a detour into a side valley; to the north of Sondrio, Valmalenco extends directly into the high mountains. Heading east from Sondrio, be sure to take the Strada Panoramica dei Castelli. In good weather this is probably the most romantic part of the journey through Valtellina. Not only are there lovely views from the road, but the route also passes prettily situated churches and is lined by vine-covered slopes and little orchards. In ❺ ✳ **Teglio** take a look at Palazzo Besta, the cultural highlight of the region.

 DON'T MISS

- Bellagio: the »pearl of Lario« on Lago di Como with beautiful villas
- Valtellina: magnificent mountain landscapes
- Important prehistoric rock carvings in Valcamonica

From Teglio it is possible to extend the route along the Adda via Tirano and Grosio to ✳ **Bormio** or ✳ **Livigno**. Bormio is a pretty mountain town with an old centre. Beyond Bormio the road climbs to the famous Stelvio Pass (2757m/9046ft).

Side trips to Bormio and Livigno

Below Teglio the SS 39 leads up the slope in serpentine bends, and the route leaves Valtellina at the Passo di Aprica. Continue via Aprica and Edolo through the forested mountains and near Edolo turn onto the SS 42, which leads south through ✳ **Valcamonica**. It is immediately noticeable that Valcamonica is narrower and less populated than Valtellina. The valley has imposing scenery, and the mountain summits in the north are covered in snow all year round. A longer stay in the ❻ ✳✳ **Parco Nazionale delle Incisioni Rupestri**, where the famous rock carvings can be seen, is particularly recommended.

Through Valcamonica to Lago d'Iseo

Heading south towards Lago d'Iseo the valley widens somewhat. Just beyond Boario Terme there is a decision to be made: either follow the western shore of Lago d'Iseo or choose the route along the eastern shore.

✻ **Lago d'Iseo** is one of the most beautiful but unknown north Italian lakes. The towns on the eastern shore are quite noticeably spoiled by the road along the shore, which quickly leads to ❼ **Iseo**, one of the lake's two main tourist towns. Those with more time are better off taking the small SS 469 along the western shore. Passing first through the larger Lovere, the road leads through several unspoilt villages to end up in Sarnico at the south-western corner of the lake, the other main tourist spot. It is definitely worth taking a boat trip to ✻ **Monte Isola**, Europe's largest island in an inland lake. From Lago d'Iseo it is only about 20km/12mi to the busy conurbation of Bergamo.

← *Enchanting scenes, like this one on Lago di Orta,*
 are commonplace on the north Italian lakes

Sights from A to Z

THE RANGE OF THE REGION'S ATTRACTIONS IS BROAD: FROM ITS MEDITERRANEAN FLAIR AND THE SHOPS IN THE FASHION CAPITAL MILAN TO PREHISTORIC ROCK DRAWINGS.

★ ★ Ascona

E 4

Switzerland: Canton: Ticino/Tessin
Population: 4700

Altitude: 205m/673ft

Ascona extends picturesquely along the northern shore of ►Lago Maggiore, in a natural bay. At the beginning of the 20th century a group of intellectual idealists discovered what was then a quiet fishing village and settled down on Monte Verità (►Baedeker Special p.221). They were immediately followed by tourists also attracted by the exceedingly mild climate, the beautiful location and the Mediterranean vegetation, and Ascona developed into a chic health resort.

▶ VISITING ASCONA

INFORMATION
Ente Turistico Lago Maggiore
Viale Papio 5
CH-6612 Ascona
Tel. 0 91 7 91 00 91
Fax 7 85 19 41
www.ascona-locarno.com

FESTIVALS
The Settimane Musicali di Ascona, the music weeks, take place annually from the end of August to mid-October (www.settimane.musicali.ch). In addition puppeteers from all over the world meet in Ascona in mid-September for a traditional marionette festival.

WHERE TO EAT
▶ Expensive/Moderate
① **Da Ivo**
Via Collegio 7
Tel. 0 91 7 91 60 93
Restaurant in one of the old patrician houses in the old town with a large terrace, well known for its excellent food.

② **Grotto Baldoria**
Via S. Omobono 9
Tel. 0 91 7 91 32 98
Only a few steps from the esplanade – but in another world; diners do not place orders here, instead they eat whatever arrives at the table; quite good value for money.

WHERE TO STAY
▶ Mid-range
① **Albergo Carcani Mövenpick**
Piazza Motta
Tel. 0 91 7 85 17 17, fax 0 91 7 85 17 18
www.restaurants-moevenpick.com
This friendly hotel by the lake is part of a chain; centrally located but with a nice view.

② **Romantik Hotel Castello Seeschloss**
Piazza Motta
Tel. 0 91 7 91 01 61, fax 0 91 7 91 18 04
www.castello-seeschloss.ch
An 13th-century medieval castle has been converted into a hotel with the most modern of comforts. Located directly on the lake esplanade, in summer guests can eat on the terrace

The portrait painter is charmed by the seaside scenery too

Today an old, quite intact, car-free »borgo« (city centre) with charming burgher houses, galleries, boutiques and several art-historical sights awaits visitors to Ascona. The bustling **Piazza Motta**, the lovely shoreline esplanade, is a popular meeting place from spring to autumn and with its cosy cafes and restaurants is an inviting part of town in which to relax and be entertained.

Chic health resort

What to See in Ascona

The starting point of a tour of the town is the elegant Piazza Motta with its plane trees and palms. It is lined with splendid buildings decorated with loggias and arcades. The **town hall** with its portico was built in the 16th century.

Piazza Motta esplanade

Opposite to the west stands Casa Serodine, also known as Casa Borrani. Built in 1620, this was the **city palace of the Serodine family**, architects and artists to a man. The magnificent three-storey façade is decorated with Baroque stucco work (1587–1626) by Giovanni Battista Serodine, brother of the painter Giovanni Serodine (around 1594–1630); above the windows it is possible to make out the Madonna and Child (centre), Adam and Eve (left), and King David and Bathsheba (right). The stucco frieze running above tells the story of the two Old Testament couples.

★
Casa Serodine

Ascona *Map*

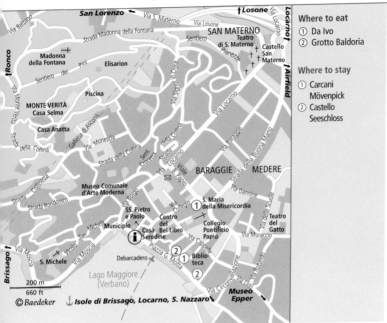

SS. Pietro e Paolo

On Piazza S. Pietro stands the church of SS. Pietro e Paolo, a **columned basilica** whose campanile is visible from quite a way off. First mentioned in 1264, it was fundamentally renewed from 1530 to 1535. The **interior** is decorated with three outstanding altar paintings by Giovanni Serodine, a *Coronation of the Virgin* (around 1623), *Christ in Emmaus* and *The Sons of Zebedee*. The vault frescoes (1783) are by Pietro Francesco Pancaldi-Mola. His brother Giovanni Battista created the tomb of the Vacchini brothers in the north aisle.

★
S. Maria della Misericordia

Narrow alleys lead east of the parish church to the church of S. Maria della Misericordia. It was built from 1399 to 1442. Its interior is decorated with the **most important late Gothic fresco cycle in Switzerland**. The wall paintings in the choir – scenes from the Old Testament on the north wall, from the New Testament on the south – were created in the early 15th century, while the frescoes in the nave date from the 16th century. The high altar polyptych with the Virgin of Mercy between St Dominic and St Peter Martyr at the centre was painted by the Asconese Giovanni Antonio de Lagaia in 1519. Take a look, too, at the fresco of the Madonna della Quercia (»Madonna of the Oak«), flanked by the plague saints Sebastian and Roch, on the southern wall of the nave (mid-16th century).

The Collegio Pontificio Papio, attached to the church, was founded by the patrician Bartolomeo Papio. It was built between 1585 and 1602 to plans by Pellegrino Tibaldi. The inner courtyard is especially beautiful with its two levels of arcades and Tuscan columns. Today the building houses a private school.

Collegio Pontificio Papio

Ascona has several museums. Along with temporary exhibitions, the **Museo Comunale d'Arte Moderna** (Via Borgo 34) shows modern art, in particular the works of the Russian Expressionist Marianne von Werefkin, who lived in Ascona for some years before her death in 1938. Opening times: March–Dec Tue–Sat 10am–noon, 3pm–6pm, Sun 4pm–6pm. In the **Museo Epper** (Via Albarelle 14), the extended former atelier of the artist couple Ignaz (1892–1969) and Mischa Epper (1901–78), wood carvings and paintings by the Swiss Expressionist and sculptures by his wife are shown. Opening times: Tue–Sat 10am–noon, 3pm–6pm.

Museums

Around Ascona

Take Via Borgo and Strada della Collina to reach the 321m/1053ft Monte Verità, the town's local mountain. In place of the utopians' former »light and air« huts, as they were called, the **Hotel Monte Verità**, built in 1927 in Bauhaus style by Emil Fahrenkamp, stands today; **Casa Anatta**, once the home of life-reforming idealists, is in the large park. In this, »Switzerland's most original wooden house«, the ideas and the history of the reform movement that started in and around Ascona in 1869 is documented (► Baedeker Special p.221). Two further buildings from the early days of the colony have been preserved: Casa Selma, built as a guest house around 1900, and a wooden pavilion in the style of 1900, where the panoramic painting *The Clear World of the Blessed*, created in 1923, is exhibited. Common opening times: April–Oct Tue–Sun 1.30pm–6.30pm, July–Aug until 7pm.

★
Monte Verità

A signposted path leads to the towerless pilgrimage church of Madonna della Fontana, built from 1617 to 1677 on the northern slope of Monte Verità over a spring. In the interior the walls are decorated by 17th-century frescoes. Legend has it that in the 15th century a young, dumb shepherdess discovered the spring and regained the power of speech. However the Celts probably already had a spring shrine here.

◄ Madonna della Fontana

North-west of Ascona extends the neighbouring municipality of Losone with its attractive granite houses, the 15th- to 18th-century *rustici*; a modern answer to them is provided by Casa Bianda (Via Ubrio 6), a cylindrical residence with a fortified look built in 1989 by the Ticino architect Mario Botta. The three local churches are worth a visit: S. Lorenzo was built in 1597, remodelled in Baroque style in 1776 and altered again in 1894. It has a notable altar (1751)

Losone

!   *Baedeker* TIP

Finest grappa
The best-known Ticino wine-grower, Angelo Delea, sells his wines, Ticino balsamico vinegar and mild grappa in Delea (Via Zandone 11, tel. 0 91/7 91 08, www.delea.ch) in Losone.

by Giuseppe Buzzi and paintings by Pancaldi and Orelli, as well as fine confessionals and a beautiful font (1580). The church of S. Giorgio, built in 1799 in the district of the same name, goes back to an 11th-century building from which the campanile and the choir have been preserved; in the interior are 14th- and 15th-century frescoes by Nicolao da Seregno and Antonio da Tradate. The interior of S. Rocco, built in 1584 and extended in the 19th century, was painted by Giovanni Antonio Vanoni in 1860. The painting of the Virgin with the plague saints Sebastian and Roch behind the altar is from 1614.

Arcegno To the west above Losone in the midst of chestnut forests lies the old mountain village of Arcegno (400m/1300ft) with its authentic, unspoilt houses. The 14th-century parish church of Sant' Antonio Abate, which was extended in the 17th century, has a painted 17th-century façade as well as remains of frescoes from the 14th to 16th centuries in the interior. On the road to Losone stands the Baroque chapel of **Madonna della Valle**, built around a wayside shrine from 1692; in the choir is a fresco dated to 1593 (Madonna and Child between St Anthony and St Roch).

Verscio Verscio, the small village 5km/3mi north of Ascona, possesses a cultural centre that is of international standard with a theatre and a school for physical theatre as well as the first Swiss »Museum of Comedy«. The whole thing is the work of a very special artiste: **Jakob Dimitri** is a Swiss clown and mime, a true all-round talent whose solo programmes, plays, directing work and paintings are celebrated on stages throughout the world. Opening times on performance days March–Nov 5pm–midnight; information: tel. 09 17 96 24 14, www.teatrodimitri.ch.

✴ ✴ Bergamo

L 6

Provincial capital
Population: 117,000

Altitude: 249–365m/817–1200ft

Bergamo, the capital of the province of the same name, lies out at the foot of the Bergamo Alps, where the two Alpine valleys of Brembo and Serio open out into the plain of the river Po. The city is a transport hub and centre of trade with large industrial zones.

▶ VISITING BERGAMO

Polenta e usei: a Bergamo speciality

INFORMATION

I. A. T.
Viale Aquila Nera
I-24100 Bergamo
Tel. 0 35 24 22 26
Fax 0 35 24 29 94
www.bergamotour.it

WHERE TO EAT

▶ Expensive

③ *Da Vittorio*
Brusporto, Via Cantalupa 17
Tel. 0 35 68 10 76
Closed Tue, Sun evening.
Enjoy outstanding food in this old
building in the upper town.

▶ Moderate

② *Osteria di Via Solata*
Via Solata 8
Tel. 0 35 27 19 93
www.osteriaviasolata.it
Closed Tue, Sun evening
This upper-town trattoria with a
pleasant atmosphere has been estab-
lished in a historical building.

▶ Budget

① *Da Franco*
Via Bartolomeo Colleoni 8
Tel. 0 35 23 85 65
www.dafrancobergamo.it
Crispy pizza and good, solid Bergamasque cooking are on the menu
here.

WHERE TO STAY

▶ Luxury

① *Excelsior San Marco*
Piazza Repubblica 6
Tel. 0 35 36 61 11
Fax 0 35 22 32 01
www.hotelsanmarco.com, 155 rooms
A very good hotel in a central location
near the funicular to the città alta;
lovely rooms, outstanding service,
large garage and car park; the extensive breakfast is served on the eighth
floor, from which diners have a
wonderful view over the towers of the
città alta.

▶ Mid-range

② *Il Gourmet*
Via S. Vigilio 1
Tel. 0 35 25 61 10
www.gourmet-bg.it, 11 rooms
Good hotel with a pleasant atmosphere and comfortably furnished
rooms; excellent cuisine served in the
restaurant.

▶ Budget

③ *Agnello d'Oro*
Via Gombito 22
Tel. 0 35 24 98 83
www.agnellodoro, 20 rooms
This simple hotel in a 17th-century
building lies directly in the centre of
the *città alta*; it can be rather noisy, especially at weekends, but the location
right in the middle of town makes up
for that; a restaurant is attached.

④ *Bed & Breakfast Villa Luna*
Via al Pianone 4
Tel. 0 35 2 45 54
www.bbvillaluna.it
Guests here stay in idyllic surround-
ings with a view of the countryside.

Two faces: the lower and upper towns

Bergamo is composed of two different municipal areas: on the plain extends the città bassa, the busy lower town, characterized by modern buildings and industrial activity. On a mountain ridge, about 120m/400ft above the river Serio, stretches the città alta, the upper town, which has remained distinctly medieval with its narrow, labyrinthine alleys and numerous art treasures.

History

When the Romans founded Municipium Bergomum in 2 BC, a Celtic settlement by the name of Berghem (mountain home) had already existed for over 300 years. In 575 the **Lombards** made the town a dukedom, and from 776 there followed the rule of Frankish kings and later the Holy Roman emperors. As early as 1098, lesser nobles, traders and guilds in Bergamo formed a rival government to the bishop, who was faithful to the emperor. The conflict reached its climax in 1165, when the residents took power from the bishop and proclaimed a city republic. The next two centuries were characterized by internal battles between the Ghibellines (on the side of the emperor) and the Guelphs (on the side of the pope). In 1295 Bergamo fell under the tyrannical rule of the Milanese Visconti family, from which it was liberated in 1428 when it subjugated itself to the Republic of Venice. In 1437 the Visconti tried to reconquer Bergamo, which lay just outside their gates. However Bartolomeo Colleoni, the condottiere in the service of Venice, inflicted a crushing defeat on them. As protection from further attempts at conquest the upper town was walled in as of 1561 and fortified with bastions. An economic and cultural flowering now followed. After Napoleon had dissolved the Republic of Venice, Bergamo fell to Austria in 1815, to the Kingdom of Sardinia in 1859 and to Italy in the course of the unification. Bergamo is the birthplace of the opera composer **Gaetano Donizetti** (►Famous People).

✷ ✷ Città Alta

Upper town

The old town of Bergamo has countless historic nooks and crannies, alleys and squares with beautiful old buildings. Inviting bars range from cosy to luxurious, and along with confectioner's shops and bakeries, from which seductive aromas emanate, ensure that visitors' creature comforts are well provided. The upper town is closed to traffic (though access to hotels is permitted). It is recommended to walk or go by bus to Viale Vittorio Emanuele, where the lower station of the funicolare di città alta, a **funicular** that has been in service since 1887, is to be found. From here the former marketplace, Mercato delle Scarpe, is just minutes away. Follow Via Gombito to **Piazza Vecchia**, the starting point of the route that will now be described. There is however also a regular bus service between the upper and the lower towns, and it is also possible to take the steps that begin immediately behind the lower station of the funicular (approx. 15 min).

Bergamo *Map*

1 Palazzo Nuovo Biblioteca
2 Torre del Comune
3 Palazzo d. Ragione
4 Battistero
5 Duomo
6 Capella Colleoni
7 S. Maria Maggiore
8 S. Croce
9 Museo Donizettiano

© Baedeker

Where to eat
① Da Franco
② Osteria di Via Solata
③ Da Vittorio

Where to stay
① Excelsior San Marco
② Il Gourmet
③ Agnello d'Oro
④ Villa Luna

Bergamo's città alta was fortified with an approximately 5km/3mi-long perimeter wall and 16 bastions between 1561 and 1590 on the orders of Venice. Many buildings had to be dismantled for the construction of the **best-preserved city fortification in Italy**. The four city gates still serve as gateways today.

Le Mura

Piazza Vecchia is the picturesque heart of the upper town

Piazza Vecchia ✱ Laid out between 1440 and 1493, Piazza Vecchia with its central fountain (1780) surrounded by stone lions and snakes forms the centre of the upper town along with the cathedral square.

Torre Civica ▶ The 54m/177ft-high city tower goes back to a 12th-century fortified tower of the Suardi family; the top section for bells was added in the 17th century. Those who are not put off by the idea of ascending 230 steps can enjoy a splendid view of the city and its surroundings. The only sight not visible from up here is the church of S. Maria Maggiore with its slate roof, which is hidden by several extensions. ⏱ Opening times: April – Oct Mon–Fri 9.30am–7pm, Sat, Sun until 9.30pm, other times Sat, Sun 9.30am–9.30pm.

Palazzo della Ragione ▶ ✱ The Palazzo della Ragione, the former town hall, occupies the south of the square. Today's building, with its open arcade on the ground floor, Venetian tracery and a relief of the lion of St Mark on the main façade, was constructed between 1538 and 1554. The covered outer steps from 1453 lead to the upper floor, in whose Salone delle Capriate precious 14th- to 16th-century frescoes can be seen – they were taken from other buildings and brought here.

Under the arcades of the palazzo there is an enormous **meridian** (1798) by Giovanni Albrici. A ray of sun shines through the disk (in the central arch of the south portico) and at midday over the period of a year it follows a curve marked on the floor. Outside the palace stands a statue of the poet Torquato Tasso (1681) by G. B. Vismara.

Biblioteca Civica ▶ The north of the square is occupied by the Biblioteca Civica, built in the style of the Renaissance by Vincenzo Scamozzi between 1611 and 1690, though its façade was only completed in 1919. The library's contents include several great works of manuscript illumination and calligraphy.

Walk through the arcades of the Palazzo della Ragione to reach the cathedral square, Bergamo's oldest core, also surrounded by important buildings. The cathedral with its Neoclassical façade (1886) stands here. It was built in 1207 as a Romanesque basilica, remodelled in the 15th century to plans by **A. Filarete** and eventually completed between 1680 and 1688 by C. Fontana. The church is furnished with numerous works dating from the 15th to 18th centuries. Of special note are the *Martyrdom of San Giovanni Battista* by Gian Battista Tiepolo (1743) in the apse and the 17th-century choir stalls by Giovanni A. Sanz.

★
Piazza del Duomo

◄ Cathedral of S. Vincenzo

The dominating building of the cathedral square is S. Maria Maggiore, onto which the Cappella Colleoni was built from 1472. The church, which has a nave and two aisles, was created in several phases (from 1137 to the 14th century). It has no façade as the episcopal palace adjoins its western side. On the east side, too, there is no open space in front of the church; the apse is adjoined by the Ateneo, built in classical style in 1810. Around 1350 the two entrances, one in the north and one in the south transept, were given Gothic-style porches with lions bearing the columns, a feature often seen in Lombardy. The baldachin architecture above the north doorway is striking: in the lower gallery an **equestrian statue of St Alexander** is framed by two saints; above them a **Madonna and Child** (1398) are enthroned, also between two saints.

★
S. Maria Maggiore

Apart from a few remains of 14th-century frescoes in the transept, among them *Scenes from the Life of St Eligius* and *The Last Supper* (just next to the north entrance), the interior furnishing dates from the 16th to 18th centuries. Note the Tuscan and Flemish 16th- and 17th-century **tapestries**, the **sepulchre of Cardinal Guglielmo Longhi** (around 1330; in the south aisle), the **monument for Gaetano Donizetti** (1855) by Vincenzo Vela next to it and the confessional by Andrea Fantoni (1704).

The treasures also include a 14th-century **wooden crucifix** and in particular the choir stalls, built from 1522 to 1555 by Gian Francesco Capoferro and Giovanni Belli. The front balustrades exhibit masterly marquetry (normally this is concealed behind decorated wooden boards and can only be viewed on Sundays). The scenes portrayed, modelled on earlier work by Lorenzo Lotto, are from the Old Testament: *The Passage through the Red Sea, The Flood, Noah's Ark, Judith and Holofernes* and *David and Goliath*.

★ ★
◄ Choir stalls

Next to the north porch of S. Maria Maggiore is the impressive Cappella Colleoni with its lavishly decorated Renaissance façade of black, white and red marble. In 1472 the condottiere (mercenary general) Bartolomeo Colleoni entrusted the sculptor and architect **Giovanni Antonio Amadeo** from Pavia with the construction of a family funerary chapel. The chapel was unfinished at the time of Colleoni's death in 1475, and work on the interior decoration continued until the

★
Cappella Colleoni

The architectural ensemble of S. Maria Maggiore

19th century, with the bronze grille in front not being installed until 1913. The façade sculpture, the deeds of Heracles in the plinth frieze, medallions with portraits of emperors and saints along the corner pillars, with fine ornamentation in between, was intended to glorify the deeds and the splendour of the Colleoni, successful commanders of old Bergamasque lineage in the service of Venice. Their tombs in the interior are also by Amadeo: four pillars resting on lions carry the large sarcophagus of Bartolomeo, which bears relief work; above it is a smaller sarcophagus in which his spouse was laid to rest, and a series of heroic statues stand in between. Above it all stands a gilded equestrian statue of the condottiere, a work by the Nuremberg woodcarver **Sixtus Frey** (1501); opposite in an alcove is the tomb of Medea Colleoni (died 1470) with a life-size recumbent figure of Bartolomeo's favourite daughter, also by Amadeo, from the Dominican church of S. Maria della Basella – which her father founded – near Urgnano. Note also the **frescoes** on the story of John the Baptist in the dome by G. B. Tiepolo (1733), the *Holy Family* (1789) by the Swiss painter Angelika Kauffmann and two choir benches by Giovanni A. Sanz with valuable marquetry (1780–85) by Giacomo Caniana.

To the right of the Cappella Colleoni stands the Battistero, built in 1340 by **Giovanni da Campione**. This marble octagon was originally in the church of S. Maria Maggiore. After baptisms were moved to the cathedral in 1660 the baptistery was dismantled and not rebuilt in its present position until 1898. The eight corners are emphasized by statues of the virtues; in the interior there is a font whose reliefs portray the life of Christ.

S. Croce

South-west of S. Maria Maggiore (left of its south porch) stands the 11th-century Romanesque chapel of S. Croce in a walled garden. It was moved here in 1885. Pass through the hall of the **Aula**, the former episcopal palace, which is decorated with 13th- and 14th-century frescoes, to return to Piazza Duomo.

Rocca

Take Via Gombito and Via San Lorenzo to reach the Rocca, the fortress. Building work began in 1331 under John of Luxemburg, Azzone Visconti completed it, and the Venetians reinforced the Rocca with a round tower. Further extensions followed in 1850 under the Austrians. Today the Museo del Risorgimento (which has been closed for some time) is here, as well as the small Parco delle Rimembranze. The view from the **tower** across Bergamo's upper and lower towns is marvellous. Opening times: Tue–Sun 9.30–1pm, 2pm–5.30pm; March–Sept to 7pm with no break.

The western continuation of Via Gombito is Via Colleoni. Near house no. 3 there is a passage into a courtyard in which a 16th-century column carries a lion standing up on its hind legs, the coat-of-arms of the Suardi; house no. 4 is the **Teatro Sociale**, designed by Ludwig Pollak in 1803 and opened in 1807. Once it accommodated audiences of more than 1300; today temporary exhibitions take place here (opening times: Tue–Sat 10am–1pm, 3pm–6.30pm, Sun 3pm–7pm). House no. 10 is **Casa Colleoni**, the first residence of the condottiere; here in 1466 he set up the Luogo Pio della Pietà, a foundation for impoverished girls. On the ground floor there are 15th-century frescoes and in a hall the *Portrait of Bartolomeo Colleoni* by G. Battista Moroni can be seen; there is a small collection on the life of Colleoni on the first floor.

Via Colleoni

From Piazza Mascheroni pass through the Torre della Campanella (1355; altered in the 19th century) to Piazza della Cittadella, the inner courtyard of the citadel built by the Visconti in 1355. There are museums inside: the **Museo Archeologico** exhibits prehistoric, early Christian and Lombard finds, including tools, ceramics and coins. (Opening times: Tue–Fri 9am–12.30pm, 2pm–6pm, Sat 9am–7pm). In the **Museo di Scienze Naturali E. Caffi**, a small natural history museum, there is a butterfly collection, a collection of herbs and the skeleton of a mammoth (opening times: Oct–March Tue–Sun 9am–12.30pm, 2.30pm–5.30pm; April–Sept Tue–Fri 9am–12.30pm, 2.30pm–6pm, Sat, Sun 9am–7.30pm).

Cittadella

Outside the Cittadella lies Colle Aperto, a large, lively square. From here it is just a few steps to the station of Bergamo's second funicular (funicolare), which runs up to San Vigilio. The old fortress, Castello di San Vigilio, is up here. It was first documented in 894, and building work on it continued into the 15th century. Originally it was connected to the città alta by means of an underground passage. There is a splendid view from San Vigilio over the city and its surroundings.

San Vigilio

Via Arena begins on the rear side of S. Maria Maggiore at the piazzetta of the same name. To the right stands the Palazzo della Misericordia. This accommodates the music school and the **Museo Donizettiano**. The life and work of composer Gaetano Donizetti (► Famous People) is documented here with several items of

★
Via Arena

memorabilia, including notes, letters, documents and pictures, as well as the grand piano on which many works were composed. Opening times: March–Oct Tue–Sat 9am–5pm, Sat also 2.30pm–5.30pm; Sun 10am–noon, 2pm–4pm. Opposite extends the complex of the **Benedictine nunnery of Santa Grata**, whose outer walls were originally covered with frescoes. At the end of Via Arena stands the **episcopal seminary of Giovanni XXIII**, built in 1819 and extended in 1965. It is dedicated to Pope John XXIII, born in 1881 in Sotto il Monte (15km/9.5mi west of Bergamo) as Angelo Giuseppe Roncalli. He attended the seminary as a pupil and was pope from 1958 until his death in 1963.

Via Donizetti

Casa dell'Arciprete ▶

In the beautiful Via Donizetti take a look at **Palazzo Scotti** (no. 1), where Gaetano Donizetti died in 1848, and the magnificent Renaissance palace Casa dell' Arciprete (no. 3), the »house of the archpriest«, built in 1520 to plans by Pietro Isabello. Continue along Via Porta Dipinta past the church of S. Michele al Pozzo Bianco (mid-12th century), whose frescoes date from the 15th and 16th centuries, to the **former S. Agostino monastery**. In the now deconsecrated church, which was consecrated in 1347 and extended in the 15th century, cultural events are staged today. Remains of 14th- and 15th-century frescoes are preserved in the interior; the two cloisters date back to the Renaissance.

Città Bassa

Around Piazza Matteotti

The focal point of the extremely busy lower town is Piazza Matteotti with its arcades housing luxury shops and the Teatro Donizetti. Via XX Settembre and Via Torquato Tasso are also ideal for a stroll. Set somewhat back from the road is the church of **SS. Bartolomeo e Stefano** (1604–42) on the corner of Largo Belotti and Via T. Tasso. Inside, a sacra conversazione, a beautiful Madonna and Child (1516) by Lorenzo Lotto, is behind the high altar. The city centre was built from 1914 to 1930 on the site of the **Sant'Alessandro fair**, one of Italy's oldest trade fairs, which has taken place every year in Bergamo since the 10th century (end of August to beginning of September). There are numerous shops in the surrounding area.

! **Baedeker TIP**

For lovers of piano music ...

... every year between the end of April and mid-June in Bergamo and Brescia the Festival Pianistico Benedetti Michelangeli takes place in the splendid rooms of the Teatro Donizetti. Information: tel. 0 30 29 30 22, www.festivalmichelangeli.it.

Via Pignolo

With its uniform 16th- and 17th-century buildings, Via Pignolo is a really interesting street. Once a forest path (»pignolo« means »pine cone«), it ran between Porta S. Antonio in the east, the former gate to the suburb of the same name, and the small Piazzetta del Delfino in the west. Just on the left (on the corner of Via T. Tasso) stands the church of **S. Spirito**, built around 1525 to designs by Pietro Cleris or Pietro Isabello and part of an old complex. It was vaulted around 1730, and the choir extended around 1850. Inside, note the high altar, a sacra conversazione by Lorenzo Lotto (1521) and the 15th-century sculptures of saints in the choir, probably once parts of a tomb. The beautiful Renaissance retable (1508) in the second chapel from the left is by Ambrogio da Fossano, known as Bergognone; in the fifth chapel lie the tombs of Domenico and Agostino Tasso, co-founders of the Thurn and Taxis postal organisation, which was successful across the whole of Europe in the 15th century. Via Pignolo climbs gently upward from here. In the small **church of S. Bernardino** (right) there is a panel from the famous high altar by L. Lotto (in the church of S. Spirito). The **Dolphin Fountain** stands at the point where the road opens into Via S. Tomaso; it was placed here in 1526. Follow Via S. Tomaso to reach the Accademia Carrara.

The Accademia Carrara (Piazza Carrara), a classical palazzo built in 1796 and remodelled in 1805 by Simone Elia, is one of the most important picture galleries in northern Italy. With the art collection of Count Giacomo Carrara at its core, it was expanded by later donations.

★ ★
Accademia Carrara

Italian painting is represented with outstanding works: Lombardy by the schools of Bergamo, Brescia, Cremona, Milan, Mantua and Ferrara; the Venetian schools by Bellini, Titian, Tintoretto, Tiepolo and others; the Florentine school by Fra Angelico, Botticelli etc.; and finally Tuscany and Umbria by Signorelli and Raphael. The treasures include the *Tarot Cards Madonna*a (around 1465), two Madonnas by Giovanni Bellini, of which the *Madonna di Alzano*most beautiful Renaissance pictures of the Virgin Mary, Titian's *Orpheus and Eurydice* (16th century), Pisanello's *Portrait of Lionello d'Este* (1441), and Sandro Botticelli's *Portrait of Giuliano de'Medici* (15th century). Opening times: June–Sept Tue–Fri 10am–9pm, Sat 10am–11pm; Oct–May Tue–Fri 9.30am–5.30pm, Sat 10am–6pm.

Opposite, a former monastery (Via S. Tomaso 53) is home to the Gallery of Modern and Contemporary Art, which contains works of the 20th century. It is planned to dedicate a hall to the Bergamasque sculptor Giacomo Manzù (1908–91). Opening times of the exhibitions: Tue–Fri 3pm–7pm, Thu 3pm–10pm, Sat, Sun 10am–7pm.

Galeria d'Arte Moderna

Around Bergamo

Bergamo is surrounded by various Alpine valleys to the north, hill country to the west and east and a small section of plain to the south. As such the two rivers flowing from the north, the Brembo and the Serio, have carved out two long, narrow **valleys**, Valle Brem-

Bergamasco

bana and Valle Seriana, which extend deep into the High Alps; the smaller valleys include Valle S. Martino, Valle Imagna, Val Taleggio – where the cheese of the same name is produced – and Val Cavallina. A visit to this region is worthwhile not only for its beautiful and in part unspoilt landscape but also for numerous art treasures.

Valle S. Martino

The small S. Martino valley extends between Bergamo and Lecco (►Lago di Como). In **Pontida**, about 17km/11mi north-west of Bergamo, Alberto da Prezzate founded a monastery that he passed on to the Burgundian Cluny Abbey in 1076. The abbey had its heyday in the 12th century, and, as was customary, its prior played a role as a mediator in political debates. Thus in Pontida in 1167 the free comuni of Bergamo, Brescia, Cremona, Mantua and Milan met and founded the **Lombard League** to oppose Emperor Frederick Barbarossa. The monastery's downfall came in the 13th century; in 1373 Bernabò Visconti destroyed the building. In 1798 the convent was dissolved and it was not reused until 1910, by Benedictine nuns. Today's church of S. Giacomo was built in 1310 and remodelled around 1500 and 1700. Its façade and the upper part of the bell tower date from the period between 1826 and 1832. In the southern wall of the choir are the remains of the sarcophagus of Alberto da Prezzate, and in the sacristy 16th-century frescoes of the Venetian-Lombard school have been preserved.

✳ Valle Brembana

Valle Brembana with its side valleys extends to the north of Bergamo for a length of 40km/25mi into the Bergamasche Alps, where the river Brembo, from which the valley gets its name, rises. The valley is bordered in the north-east by Pizzo del Diavolo (2914m/9560ft) and in the north-west by Pizzo dei Tre Signori (2554m/8379ft). At the end of the valley **Foppolo** (1508m/4948ft) offers very good opportunities for winter sports.

✳ S. Pellegrino Terme

The best-known place in Valle Brembana is without doubt S. Pellegrino Terme (358m/1175ft). This spa, with about 5500 inhabitants, seems to have seen better days. A couple of fine buildings now threatened by decay recall past greatness and exude a melancholy atmosphere. The elegant bathing resort developed at the beginning of the 19th century. The spa owes its reputation not only to the springs from which **allegedly the best mineral water in the world** bubbles, but also to a famous visitor: Queen Margherita, wife of Umberto I. She first came shortly after 1900 and attracted illustrious personages of the German, Italian, Russian and North

African nobility here. Today, S. Pellegrino is Europe's third-largest producer of mineral water. Directly on the bank of the Brembo stands the **Grand Hotel**, which though in need of renovation still hints at its former glory. Romolo Squadrelli and Luigi Mazzocchi

were the architects of the Art Nouveau building with its long façade. On the opposite side of the river is the spa quarter with gardens in which two buildings by the same architects stand: the **Palazzo della Fonte spa hall**, today attached to the Hotel Terme, and the casino. The spa hall is beautifully designed in Pompeian style. The famous water bubbles out of a rock at a rate of 225,000 litres (nearly 50,000 gallons) per hour at a constant temperature of 26°C/79°F. The Art Nouveau **casino** was opened in 1907, but as early as the First World War the gaming business was shut down and the beautiful building converted to accommodate a cultural and events centre; today it is used primarily for conferences and parties.

◄ Spa quarter

North-west of Bergamo begins Valle Imagna, a small valley between Adda and Brembo. On the way there those interested in art should consider a side trip to **Almenno S. Bartolomeo** . In the open country, about 1km/0.5mi east of the village, stands the small round church of S. Tomé in Lémine. It was built around 1140–50, and the choir followed between 1180 and 1200. The outer building is decorated with fine pilaster strips and semicolumns; the interior consists of a domed cylinder with two-storey ambulatories. The column capitals on the upper floor are from the 12th century, those on the lower floor probably somewhat older. Viewing: May–Sept Sat, Sun 2pm–5pm.

Valle Imagna

★

◄ S. Tomaso in Lémine

🕐

Above the right bank of the Brembo, about 3km/2mi outside the town, stands the Renaissance church of Madonna del Castello. There are 15th- and 16th-century wall frescoes inside. Note too the Renaissance tempietto above the altar (15th century). To its right is a Romanesque precursor building (around 1100) with an ambo on whose front side the evangelists' symbols are sculpted (12th century). Viewing: tel. 0 35 64 00 83.

◄ Madonna del Castello

S. Nicola, the church of an Augustine monastery that is now a restaurant, dates from the early 16th century; in the 17th and 18th centuries its interior was furnished in Baroque style with contributions from Giovanni A. Sanz, among others. Several of the original frescoes have however been preserved. As in many other churches, they were whitewashed during the plague of the 17th century for reasons of hygiene.

◄ S. Nicola

The river Serio rise north of Bergamo on Monte Torena and flows into the Adda near Montodino. The main town of the Serio valley is **Clusone** (34km/21mi from Bergamo). Its historic centre is Piazza dell' Orologio with loggias and the late Gothic town hall, the Palazzo Comunale, whose outer walls are still decorated with the remains of frescoes. The planetary clock that gave the square its name was made by Pietro Fanzago in 1583.

Valle Seriana

Somewhat above Clusone stands the Baroque **church of S. Maria Assunta**. The main sight is the funeral chapel Oratorio dei Disciplini

★

◄ Oratorio dei Disciplini

next to it with a famous fresco of the Dance of Death on the outer wall (1485) showing the triumph of death over all the dignitaries of late medieval society. The interior frescoes (1471) have scenes from the life and Passion of Christ as their theme, while a Majestas Domini and the Fathers of the Church are depicted in the choir. Finally, the carved Annunciation group is noteworthy.

Rovetta

A **reredos by Tiepolo** adorns the **parish church** of the neighbouring town of Rovetta. Casa Fantoni, in which the important Fantoni family of sculptors lived and worked from the 15th to the 19th century, is a museum today.

Val Cavallina

The Cavallina valley to the east of Bergamo extends between Bergamo and Lovere on ►Lago d'Iseo. Numerous castles once safeguarded the highway, a connection to ►Valcamonica. Right at the entrance to the valley stands the Cluniac monastery of **S. Paolo d'Argon**, founded in the 11th century but later completely remodelled. Thus the two cloisters with columned arcades date from the 16th century, and the monastery church of S. Paolo is a newer Baroque building from 1688. **Trescore Balneario**, a thermal spa, has a medieval centre. At the edge of the town, in the park of Villa Suardi (16th century), stands the small Renaissance church of S. Barbara. The Venetian painter Lorenzo Lotto painted its interior in 1524. Embedded in landscapes, towns and architecture, the legend of St Barbara is depicted on the north wall, the story of St Clare on the south wall.

Malpaga

Several miles south-east of Bergamo lies the little town of Malpaga. In 1456 Bartolomeo Colleoni, the condottiere from Bergamo, acquired this castle of the Visconti and converted it into a splendid residence. The square building is well preserved and can be viewed on the hour by arrangement (tel. 0 35 84 00 03, www.castellomalpaga.it). Some of the frescoes inside were commissioned by Colleoni (around 1470) as well as by order of the Martinengo family, who had taken over the castle after Colleoni's death and wanted to capture his deeds in wall paintings. One fresco depicts the visit of the Danish king Christian I in 1474.

In the neighbouring town of **Cavernago** stands Castello Martinengo, a late Gothic moated castle. In 1456 Colleoni acquired what had been a simple 14th-century fort. From 1597 its new owner, Count Martinengo, had it remodelled in Renaissance style. The inner courtyard with its two-storey arcades is in part painted; in the interior 17th-century frescoes are preserved.

! **Baedeker TIP**

Italy in miniature

Those wishing to walk from the Alps to Apulia in two shakes of a lamb's tail can do so in Fantasy World near Capriate (approx. 14km/9mi south-west of Bergamo). The whole of Italy is modelled here in miniature. Opening times: mid-March– late Oct daily 9.30am–7pm, tel. 02 90 9 01 69, www.leolandiapark.it

An outstanding example of Lombard industrial history is the town of Crespi d' Adda, 15km/9.5mi south-west of Bergamo. At the end of the 19th century, industrialist Cristoforo B. Crespi had a **workers' housing estate** built here based on British models. Designed to be people-friendly, it was built from brick in historicizing forms, including a domicile for the industrialist, houses for the workers, a theatre and sports field, as well as a church and cemetery. The last buildings were created in 1925, and in 1995 the settlement was added to the list of **UNESCO World Cultural Heritage sites**.

✴ **Crespi d' Adda**

✴ Brescia

07

Provincial capital
Population: 192,000

Altitude: 149m/489ft

Brescia is the capital of the eastern Lombard province of the same name, which at 4784 sq km/1847 sq mi is the largest in the region and takes up almost a quarter of Lombardy's total area. After Milan, Brescia is the second-largest Lombard city.

Brescia is the third most industrialized city in Italy after Milan and Turin. Because of its iron ore deposits, the province lives from the metal industry. Mechanical engineering and weapons production are the economic pillars of the city.

Industrial centre with historic core

The origins of Brescia are on Cidneo Hill, on which the castle stands today, in the north-east of the city centre. A first Ligurian settlement was probably established here as early as 1200 BC. In 4 BC the Celtic Cenomanes made this their main settlement. In AD 49 the town, now called Brixia (»brig« means »situated high up«), became a Roman colony and in the Roman Iron Age was an important centre of the Roman province of Gallia Cisalpina. In the 6th century the Lombards established a dukedom in Brescia. The period from 1100 into the 15th century was particularly turbulent. As a city of the Guelphs faithful to the pope, Brescia was a **member of the Lega Lombarda** and in the 12th century became involved in clashes with the neighbouring Ghibelline cities of Bergamo and Cremona.
In the 14th and 15th centuries the houses of Anjou, Visconti and Malatesta fought over the city. From 1428 to 1797 Brescia belonged to the Republic of Venice, afterwards to the Cisalpine Republic and the Napoleonic Kingdom of Italy. In the period of Austrian rule, which lasted from 1815 to 1859, a historic revolt took place in 1849.

History

The first impression of Brescia is shaped by industry and suburban settlements. In the Second World War the city was heavily bombed.

Cityscape

▶ VISITING BRESCIA

INFORMATION

Promozione Tourismo Provincia Brescia
Via Musei 32
I-25121 Brescia
Tel. 0 30 3 74 94 38, 30 3 74 99 16
Fax 0 30 3 74 99 82
www.provincia.brescia.it

WHERE TO EAT

▶ Moderate

① ***L'Osteria della Zia Gabri***
Via Gallo 17
Tel. 0 30 2 05 65 85, closed Mon, Sun evening
The pretty restaurant in an old house is centrally located. Good regional cooking.

② ***Al Frate***
Via dei Musei
Tel. 0 30 3 77 05 50
Modern-style restaurant; good wine selection; the Tartare di Manzo is a must!

WHERE TO STAY

▶ Luxury

① ***Hotel Vittoria***
Via X Giornate 20
Tel. 0 30 28 00 61
Fax 0 30 28 00 65
www.hotelvittoria.com, 65 rooms
The best hotel in Brescia and one of the few in the city centre; outstandingly furnished rooms and suites; a first-class restaurant is attached.

▶ Budget

② ***Igea***
Viale Stazione 15
Tel. 03 04 42 21
Fax 03 04 42 24
www.nh-hotels.com, 85 rooms
Relatively good value hotel in a convenient location on the edge of the centre of Brescia near the railway station. Car park.

It is all the more astonishing then that in the historic centre numerous monuments provide an almost uninterrupted testimony to about 2000 years of history. The most important sights are on Piazza Paolo VI, the adjacent Piazza della Loggia to the west and along Via dei Musei somewhat further east.

What to See in Brescia

Piazza Paolo VI   Piazza Paolo VI, named after the Brescia-born Pope Paul VI (1963–78), looks completely unspectacular in comparison to other central squares in Lombard cities. It took its present rectangular form in the 18th century. On the eastern side of the square the old cathedral, the new cathedral and the Broletto (old town hall) stand next to each other. The three buildings were created in different centuries and make a relatively heterogeneous overall impression. For a long time the piazza was Brescia's spiritual and communal focal point.

Brescia Map

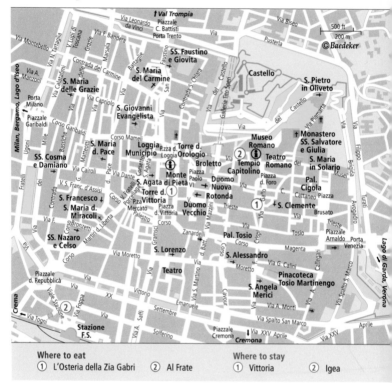

Where to eat
① L'Osteria della Zia Gabri   ② Al Frate

Where to stay
① Vittoria   ② Igea

The dominant building on the piazza is without doubt the Duomo Nuovo, the new cathedral, begun in 1604 to plans by **Giovanni Battista Lantana**. Under a variety of architects construction work continued into the 19th century. In the late 18th century the façade was installed, and in 1821 the **dome** was finally erected under the direction of Rodolfo Vantini. At a height of 80m/260ft, the dome is the **third-highest of its type in Italy**, after those of St Peter's in Rome and S. Maria del Fiore in Florence. In the Second World War it was destroyed in a bombing raid and subsequently rebuilt. In the interior, which takes the form of a Greek cross, there are numerous sculptures from six centuries. The modern 20th-century works are striking – such sculpture is very rarely seen in a Lombard church of this size.

Duomo Nuovo

Next to the Duomo Nuovo the old cathedral, the Duomo Vecchio, almost seems to disappear. However the Rotonda, as the church is also known, is actually the square's real gem. This Romanesque build-

★
Duomo Vecchio

Marked architectural contrasts: Duomo Nuovo and Duomo Vecchio

ing stands out for its simplicity and balanced composition and thus provides an architectural contrast to the neighbouring new cathedral. In the 12th century the walls were added on top of the existing remains of the early Christian 6th-century basilica of S. Maria Maggiore, and the Rotonda was roofed with a shallow dome. The Rotonda's outer walls have a sparing design employing a small number of windows and blind openings, as well as a frieze below the dome. The two doorways, which are on the level of the former Roman street, are striking.

Interior ▶ The interior is also effective, though its elevation appears more complicated because of its various levels at different heights. Several works of sculpture can be seen in the Rotonda. In the entrance area visitors first come across the **sarcophagus of Bishop Berardo Maggi**, on which the peace treaty between the Ghibellines and the Guelphs in 1298 is depicted – the bishop had a role in bringing about this agreement. Two **further bishops' sarcophagi** are set into wall niches on the opposite side: that of Domenico de Dominici from the late 15th century (left) and that of Lambertino Baldovino from the 14th century (right). In the 15th century the Rotonda was extended to the east with a main choir and in 1565 with two side choirs. The mosaics that are visible in the floor under glass come from the former basilica of S. Maria Maggiore. Under the choir lies the **Cripta di S. Filastrio**, built in the 9th century and remodelled into a hall crypt in the 12th century. Beautiful capitals from Roman times and the 9th century were integrated into the structure. Opening times: Mon–Sat noon–3pm, 7.30pm–midnight.

Adjoining the Duomo Nuovo to the north is the Broletto, the municipal centre. The building was erected in the 12th century, and the simple Torre del Popolo dates from this time, too. Large parts of the Broletto were first completed in the Gothic period (13th–14th centuries), and Venetian alteration work continued into the 18th century. The **brick-built church of S. Agostino** with a huge rose window was integrated into the northern block of the Broletto in the early 15th century.

Broletto

Immediately behind the Duomo Nuovo in Via Mazzini stands the Biblioteca Queriniana, an 18th-century building with beautifully designed reading rooms. The library has over 300,000 books and manuscripts. Opening times: Tue–Fri 8.45am–6pm, Sat 8.30am–12.30pm.

Biblioteca Queriniana

A second square worth taking a look at in the historic centre of Brescia is Piazza della Loggia, created from the end of the 15th century, i.e. at the time when Brescia was subject to the Republic of Venice. The square gives an impression of intimacy, and its eastern side in particular with arcades and a clock tower, the **Torre dell' Orologio** of 1595 with two figures that strike a bell, is clearly oriented to Venetian models. Piazza della Loggia serves as a meeting place, and cultural and political events take place here. A stele under the arcades of the eastern side recalls an **assassination** committed in 1974 during a trade union rally on the square, when a bomb explosion killed eight people. The most striking building on the square is the loggia, the massy Palazzo Nuovo del Comune on the western side. Building work began in the 15th century. The lower floor, built from 1492 to 1506 to plans by **Tommaso Formentone**, was created under the influence of the latest theories of the time espoused by the Florentine Leon Battista Alberti (1404–72). Jacopo Sansovino was among those who worked on the designs for the upper floor, probably along with Andrea Palladio – in any case, the latter at least took part in a competition. The original roof and three ceiling paintings by Titian were destroyed by fire in 1575. Today's domed roof was constructed only in 1914.

★
Piazza della Loggia

◄ Loggia

Monte di Pietà ▸ Above the southern side of the piazza stands the Monte di Pietà, the former pawnshop. The Renaissance façade with a double-arched loggia and a seven small arched windows above it is a 15th-century work by Antonio Zurlengo. Directly east adjoins the Monte Nuovo, created around 1600 to plans by **Pietro Maria Bagnadore**.

S. Agata On Corsetto di S. Agata behind the loggia to the west stands the late Gothic 15th-century hall church of S. Agata. The Baroque ceiling paintings (1683) with depictions of St Agatha and the Ascension of Christ are interesting. Quadratura painting creates the illusion of a space open at the top with a further columned storey from which smaller domes project.

Piazza della South of Piazza della Loggia lies Piazza della Vittoria, rebuilt under
Vittoria Mussolini in the 1930s with monumental architecture by Marcello Piacentini.

Corso Zanardelli Brescia's nicest shopping street is Corso Zanardelli, a pedestrian zone. The **Teatro Grande** here is relatively unprepossessing from the outside, but inside it is one of the most beautiful theatres in northern Italy. Its auditorium in Empire style has five circles, and frescoes adorn the foyer (1782).

Via dei Musei On the north-east corner of the Piazza della Loggia, pass through the Porta Bruciata (»Burnt Gate« – named after a fire in 1184), which remains from the old city fortifications, into Via dei Musei. This old road, which extends east beneath Cidneo Hill, led along the northern side of the forum in Roman times.

✳
Forum Excavations in the ancient forum began in 1823, and today **northern Italy's most important archaeological site** is here on Via dei Musei. The best-preserved building is the **Tempio Capitolino**, built by Vespasian in AD 73 on the narrow northern side of the forum. Parts of the temple were reconstructed in the 20th century. Three cells lie in a row behind the remains of the portico with Corinthian columns, most of them renewed; 2nd-century floor mosaics have been found here. It is thought that there were originally four cells, but that the eastern one fell victim to the construction of a theatre. The **Teatro Romano** immediately adjoining the temple building today still lies
🕐 partly underground, beneath Palazzo Gambara. Opening times: Tue–Sun 9am–7pm.

Museo Romano ▸ Follow Via dei Musei to reach the Museo Romano, in which archaeo-
🕐 logical finds such as busts, jewellery and glass are exhibited. Currently closed for renovations.

✳
Monastero di A little further east is the complex of San Salvatore e Santa Giulia. It
S. Salvatore e goes back to the 8th-century monastery of San Salvatore founded by
S. Giulia the Lombard king Desiderius. The original monastery was built on

Important excavation site: the ancient forum

the site of a private Roman house whose remains had just been discovered. According to legend Desiderius's daughter Ermengarda, whose marriage to Charlemagne ended in divorce, died here. Today the restored rooms house the **Santa Giulia Museo della Città**, in which the city's cultural treasures from two millennia can be found. The showpiece is the famous Vittoria, the Roman goddess of victory. This bronze statue was apparently reworked from a wingless statue of Venus after Vespasian's victory over Judea in AD 71 and today is Brescia's emblem. Further outstanding exhibits include a valuable cross, the 8th- or 9th-century **Croce di Desiderio**, richly set with precious stones and gems, and the 4th-century lipsanotheca, a reliquary made of ivory. The greatest treasure is the Purple Gospel Book, suspected to be part of a 6th-century manuscript commissioned by Emperor Theoderic in Ravenna. Opening times: Oct–May Tue–Sun 9.30amam–5.30pm; June–Sept Tue–Sun 10am–6pm.

In the convent church of S. Salvatore, which dates back to the time of the Lombards, the nave still contains remains of Carolingian paintings from the 9th century. At that time several friezes were painted on the walls showing scenes from the life of Christ. The capitals of the marble columns also date from the 9th century. An unusually finely worked 8th-century **relief** depicting a peacock is lovely. The two-storey Romanesque **chapel of S. Maria in Solario**, connected to S. Salvatore by means of two Renaissance cloisters, was built between 1150 and 1180 and served the nuns as an oratory. The monas-

✱
◄ Vittoria

✱ ✱
◄ Purple Gospel Book
🕐
◄ S. Salvatore

tery complex also includes the **church of S. Giulia**, built from 1466 to 1510 as the new monastery church and today the earliest example of Brescian Renaissance architecture.

Castello Colle Cidneo

In the 15th century, when Brescia was annexed to the Republic of Venice, the castello was built in the north-east of the city centre on Cidneo Hill, which commands extensive views. The name comes from the Ligurians, who named the small hill after the mythical god Cidno. Remains of a basilica are preserved from early Christian times, and the castle tower, the **Torre Mirabella**, dates from the 12th century. Opening times: daily 8am–8pm. The **Museo delle Armi Antiche** (Museum of Antique Weapons) in the castle has a collection of weapons dating from the 15th to the 18th centuries. The **Museo del Risorgimento** also housed here documents the fight for freedom in Italy in the 19th century with exhibits and pictures. Opening times: Oct–May Tue–Sun 9.30am–5pm, June–Sept 10am–5pm.

Pinacoteca Tosio-Martinengo

In the south-east of the city centre on Piazza Moretto stands the **Palazzo Martinengo da Barco**, a spacious early 16th-century city palace once owned by the Martinengo family, who played a dominant role in the city for centuries. Today, the Pinacoteca Tosio-Martinengo is housed in the palace. Its extensive collection of 13th- to 19th-century Italian painting focuses on the schools of Brescia and Venice. Opening times: Oct–May Tue–Sun 9.30am–5pm, June–Sept 10am–6pm.

Collezione d' Arte Contemporanea

The Collezione d' Arte Contemporanea (Via A. Monti 9) not far south of the Pinacoteca has received little recognition, although numerous works by international artists are on display. This comprehensive collection of modern art was donated to Brescia's Istituto Paolo VI by the Vatican in memory of the Brescian pope. Alongside well-known Italians, e.g. Fontana and De Chirico, artists such as Chagall, Dalí, Moore, Schmidt-Rottluff, Beckmann, Kokoschka and Giacometti are represented. Opening times: on appointment, tel. 0 30 3 75 30 02.

★ SS. Nazaro e Celso

Of all Brescia's churches, the church of SS. Nazaro e Celso am Corso Matteotti in the south-west of the old town is worth a visit. The classical 18th-century building is unspectacular, but its interior contains an important work of the Italian High Renaissance: **Titian's Resurrection Altar** (1522). The five paintings show the resurrection of Christ in the middle, saints Nazarus and Celsus below on the left, the martyrdom of St Sebastian below on the right and, above, the Annunciation with Gabriel (left) and Mary (right). As the church is normally closed, it is necessary to register for viewings in the nearby Chiesa S. Maria dei Miracoli on Corso Martiri d. Libertà.

S. Francesco

The church of S. Francesco on Via S. Francesco d' Assisi was built between 1254 and 1335 with late Romanesque and early Gothic elements for the Franciscan order. In the interior, take a look at the altarpiece by **Gerolamo Romanino** (around 1520), showing the Virgin and Child flanked by Franciscan monks. Romanino is considered to be one of the leading Brescian painters of the High Renaissance, who substantially oriented themselves on 16th-century Venetian painting. The attached cloister is beautiful.

S. Maria delle Grazie in the north-west of the old town, on Via delle Grazie, was built between 1522 and 1530 as a Renaissance church of the Hieronymites. The impression the interior today is shaped by the early Baroque decoration incorporated as of 1617. Note the fine stuc-

S. Maria delle Grazie

Oasis of peace and harmony: the beautiful cloister of San Francesco

co work, consisting of cherubs, heads and stylized floral elements, which cover arches, vaults and the domes in the side aisles. A santuario, rebuilt in 1876, is accessed via a small cloister.

S. Giovanni Evangelista

The church of S. Giovanni Evangelista (Contrada di S. Giovanni, side street of Corso G. Mameli) dates from the 15th century, but the interior was markedly altered in the 17th century. On the third side altar to the south is a famous depiction of the Massacre of the Innocents dating from around 1532.

The painting is a work of Alessandro Bonvicino, known as **Moretto**, who along with **Gerolamo Romanino** was Brescia's most important High Renaissance painter. Further works by Moretto can be seen in the right side of the sacrament chapel; the left side was painted by Romanino. The two painters worked on the decoration of the room at the same time during 1531.

SS. Faustino e Giovita

On Via S. Faustino north of Piazza della Loggia stands the Baroque church of SS. Faustino e Giovita, which goes back to a 6th-century building. Today's church was built between 1622 and 1698. St Faustino and St Giovita, after whom the church is named, are the city's patron saints: they are honoured as martyrs who successfully defended the city during an invasion. Their mortal remains are kept inside the church in the arca (1620–30) on the choir altar, a work by Antonio and Giovanni Carra.

S. Maria del Carmine

S. Maria del Carmine was built in the 15th century by Carmelites. In a chapel to the left of the chancel, part of the original late Gothic fresco painting can still be seen. In the 17th century the vault was installed in the interior and decorated with illusionist painting by Tommaso Sandrino. Note the dramatic late 15th-century *Mourning of Christ* by the sculptor Guido Mazzoni in terracotta.

Around Brescia

Monte Maddalena

East of the city centre a road leads in serpentine bends up to Monte Maddalena (874m/2867ft). There is a **splendid view** of Brescia from the road.

✳

Val Trompia

To the north of Brescia lies Val Trompia, which has always been known for its rich iron ore deposits. As the necessary water was also available, iron was already worked here in antiquity. Gardone Val Trompia has been famous for its weapons industry since the 16th century – and that is international fame, as for some years now even US cops have carried pistols made by the firm Beretta from the province of Brescia. The little town of **Concesio**, a few miles north of Brescia at the entrance to the valley, is famous for being the birthplace of Pope Paul VI. North of Gardone Val Trompia begins the more elevated and beautiful part of the valley with the pretty little villages of **Bovegno** and **Collio**, both of which attract tourists all year round.

Shaped by agriculture, the **Pianura Bresciana**, the »Brescian plain« extending to the south of the city, is not a tourist destination as such. Some things here are worth seeing, however, such as the small Museo della Donna (Via Mazzucchelli 2) in **Ciliverghe** east of Brescia (opening times: on appointment, tel. 0 30 2 12 09 75), the Romanesque 12th-century Chiesa di S. Pancrazio a little outside **Montichiari** south-east of Brescia, and the Santuario della Madonna in **Carpenedolo**, designed in the 18th century by Antonio Marchetti from Brescia. The agricultural centre south of Brescia is **Verolanuova**; in the town's parish church there are two paintings by Giovanni Battista Tiepolo (*The Sacrifice of Melchizedek* and *The Gathering of Manna*; c1738).

! **Baedeker** TIP

Men's fashion direct from the factory
Looking for a bargain? Northern Italy is a veritable treasure trove for fans of factory outlets. For example, Cesare Bruno in Castegnato (Via del Lavoro 47), north-west of Brescia, produces high-class men's fashion. Turn left on the large right-hand curve in the industrial area to reach his factory. Opening times: weekdays 9am–noon, 3pm–7pm.; tel. 0 30 2 14 80 14.

✶ Certosa di Pavia

G 9

Province: Pavia   **Altitude:** 90m/295ft

The Charterhouse of Pavia (9km/5.5mi north of Pavia) is one of Lombardy's most important cultural monuments and one of the best-known monasteries of the Carthusian Order.

The monumental architecture created here between the end of the 14th century and the mid-16th century testifies impressively to the mindset of the rulers of the time. Stylistically, the building exhibits predominantly late Gothic and Renaissance elements. In 1390 **Gian Galeazzo Visconti**, Duke of Milan, commissioned the design of a burial place for his dynasty. It was to be integrated into a monastery complex, which he wished to donate to the Carthusians. Building work on the church of Madonna delle Grazie began in 1396, but at first it proceeded slowly.

Only in 1450 was the building work given a decisive impetus by **Francesco Sforza**, the first ruler of the succeeding dynasty. He commissioned the architects of the cathedral of Milan, Giovanni and Guiniforte Solari, to continue the work; in addition Giovanni Antonio Amadeo, who had built the Cappella Colleoni in Bergamo, was also involved in the construction of the Certosa di Pavia. The com-

🕐
Opening hours:
Tue–Sun
9am–11.30am
2.30pm–5.30pm

CERTOSA DI PAVIA

✷✷ The Charterhouse building was commissioned by Gian Galeazzo Visconti, Duke of Milan, in 1390 as a burial place for his family. Work continued under the Sforza, who succeeded the Visconti as the ruling family in Milan. Today the Certosa di Pavia is one of Lombardy's most significant historical buildings.

🕐 Opening times:
Summer Tue–Sat 9am–11.30am, 2.30pm–6pm
Winter until 4.30pm only

① Illusionist painting
The illusionist paintings in the clerestory above the side chapel of the south transept are unique. For example two monks look out of windows into the interior and watch the goings-on in the church.

② Tomb of Moro/d'Este
A Renaissance masterpiece, the tomb of the ruler of Milan and his wife Beatrice d'Este, a highly educated woman who died at the age of 22. It was designed in 1497, after the death of Beatrice, by Christoforo Solari. The facial expressions of the couple are unusually well depicted. The clothes with their decorations are very realistic, and the recumbent bodies are apparent underneath.

③ Small Cloister
On the interesting terracotta arcades saints are depicted surrounded by putti and extensive plant decoration. The lavabo (a basin in which the priests wash their hands) on the south side of the cloister was worked by Giovanni Antonio Amadeo.

④ Grand Cloister
Here the typical cells on the side of the cloister can be viewed: the monks, who had taken a vow of silence, lived in a single cell all their lives.

Certosa di Pavia Plan

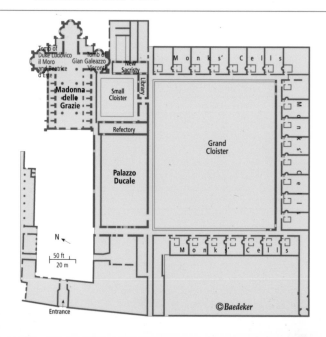

The Grand Cloister exudes an almost graphic effect

③

④

© *Baedeker*

Illusionist painting: who is that watching the visitors to the church?

he magnificently ainted choir

Tomb of Ludovico il Moro and Beatrice d'Este: an outstanding Renaissance work of art

plex was not completed until 1549 with the final work on the church façade, by which time the reign of both dynasties had long ceased. The Certosa was dissolved in 1782 and then used for a while by Carmelites. In 1968 it finally passed to the Cistercian order, whose monks farm the land.

★ ★ Monastery Buildings

Madonna delle Grazie

The church of Madonna delle Grazie is directly adjacent to the main entrance of the monastery complex. The church façade stands out thanks to its balanced proportions and the lavish Renaissance decoration of the masonry. The predominant decorative elements consist of incrustation work in multi-coloured marble, reliefs and marble figures. Christian and heathen, secular and spiritual themes are all depicted. They express the triumph of Christianity over heathenism: right down at the bottom are the figures of Roman and Eastern rulers, above them bas-reliefs of saints, apostles and prophets.

The design of the façade is by Giovanni Antonio Amadeo and by Cristoforo and Antonio Mantegazza.

Interior

In the interior the transition between Gothic and Renaissance is apparent. While the composition of the façade, built as of 1473, exhibits all elements of the Renaissance, the interior is still designed in late Gothic style. The narrow aisles are separated from the nave by massive compound piers. The choir and the two short transept arms end in three apses in a clover-leaf arrangement. Above the crossing is an octagonal tower – a work by Giovanni Solari – whose decorative effect is best appreciated from the Small Cloister. The frescoes were painted by Ambrogio Bergognone and others at the end of the 15th century. The west wall and several side chapels are decorated in Baroque style. Note the **illusionistically painted clerestory** above the side chapels. The choir stalls (1498) feature precious inlay work. A late Gothic ivory polyptych (around 1400) is kept in the old sacristy next to the choir. In the north transept, the tomb of Ludovico il Moro and his wife Beatrice d'Este, who died at the age of 22, is an outstanding example of Lombard sepulchral art. **Cristoforo Solari** created it in 1497, after Beatrice's death.

★ Tomb of Ludovico il Moro and Beatrice d'Este ►

On the opposite side in the south transept is the **tomb of Gian Galeazzo Visconti**, the founder of the monastery. Made by **Cristoforo Romano**, it was not begun until 1492, 90 years after the death of the duke, and the actual sarcophagus by Bernardo da Novate was not created until 1562.

Small Cloister

The south transept gives access to the smaller of the two cloisters, which was designed in the 15th century. The prettily decorated terracotta arcades, with depictions of various saints amongst extensive ornamentation featuring cherubs and floral elements, are very beautiful. The lavabo (a basin in which the priests wash their hands) on the south side was worked by **Giovanni Antonio Amadeo**. This is the best vantage point to see the crossing tower, designed by **Giovanni Solari**.

! **Baedeker** TIP

Lombard cooking

If you still have time after seeking spiritual nourishment at the monastery, indulge your worldly needs in Locanda Vecchia Pavia »al Mulino« (Via al Monumento 5), with highly recommended regional and fish specialties. Tel. 0 30-2 14 80 14, April–Oct closed Mon, Tues midday

The **refectory** adjoins the Small Cloister to the west. It was built in 1430, originally as a church, and the refectory was not set up here until 1497, though the Carthusians only dined together on holy days. Readings from the Bible were given from the pulpit during meals.

Grand Cloister

The Grand Cloister adjoining to the south is also furnished with terracotta arcades by **Rinaldo de Stauris**. The typical cells on the side of the cloister are interesting: the monks, who had taken a vow of silence, lived in a single cell all their lives.

Certosa di Pavia: the rich decoration of its façade is impressive

✴ Chiavenna

Province: Sondrio   **Altitude:** 33m/108ft
Population: 7300

Chiavenna extends north of Lago di Como in Valchiavenna, where the rivers Mera and Liro converge. To the north the SS 36 runs out of Lombardy over the Passo dello Spluga (2115m/6939ft) into Switzerland, in an easterly direction the SS 37 heads over the Passo del Maloja (1815m/5955ft) to St Moritz, also in Switzerland.

»Key« to the Alpine passes
The old Alpine passes Passo dello Spluga and Passo del Maloja have served to connect Italy and the neighbouring countries to the north since time immemorial – the **name of the town** comes from this key position (»chiave« means »key«). Because of this Chiavenna, located at the upper end of the Chiavenna plain, always had contact with a variety of cultures and rulers. A waystation was built here in Roman times.

✴ Townscape
Chiavenna is framed by high, somewhat dark mountains. The town itself, on the other hand, has an idyllic appearance, especially in the old centre along Via Dolzino and on the continuation of Via Pedretti with its narrow side alleys. From the bridge at the end of Via Pedretti there is a beautiful view of the Mera with old houses on its banks.

▶ VISITING CHIAVENNA

INFORMATION

I. A. T.
Piazzo Vittorio Emanuele
I-23022 Chiavenna
Tel./fax 03 43 3 53 27
www.valtellina.it

WHERE TO EAT

▶ **Inexpensive**
Ristorante Crotto Ombra
Viale Pratogiano 14
Tel. 03 43 3 34 03
www.crottoombra.com
In the Crotto Ombra – one of the cave restaurants, or crotti, characteristic of Chiavenna – the diners sit beneath cliffs. Gnocchetti alla chiavennasca and bresaola are prepared in a variety of ways. A large selection of reasonably priced set menus.

WHERE TO STAY

▶ **Mid-range**
Crimea
Via Pratogiano 16
Tel. 0 34 33 43 43
Fax 0 34 33 59 35
www.hotelcrimea.net, 30 rooms
Located in the central and quiet Crotti quarter of Chiavenna, this is a good, respectable hotel with a family atmosphere; pleasant and simply furnished rooms; the hotel has its own car park.

Chiavenna enjoys a wild and romantic location

What to See in and around Chiavenna

Several old palaces testify to an eventful past – Palazzo Pretorio on Piazza S. Pietro, for example, with 16th-century coats-of-arms that recall the Grigioni rulers. On Piazza Castello note the late Gothic Palazzo Balbiani (1477), built by the successors to the Visconti.

Palaces

On Via Picchi stands the collegiate church of S. Lorenzo, built in 1538 and markedly altered in the Baroque period. Opening times: March–May Sat, Sun 9am–noon, 2pm–5pm; June–Sept Tue–Sun 9am–noon, 2pm–6pm; Oct–Dec Sat 9am–noon, 2pm–5pm.

✱
Collegiata di S. Lorenzo
🕐

Attached is a **baptistery** that contains two outstanding artistic gems: the round Romanesque font (1156), a monolith, comes from the preceding church; a baptism scene has been carved out in half-relief. In addition the »Pace di Chiavenna«, the precious front cover of an 11th-century book of gospels, into which gold, enamel, 97 pearls and 94 different gemstones are worked, is kept here. The symbols of the four evangelists are arranged as gold reliefs around the cross – the angel for Matthew, the eagle for John, the lion for Mark and the ox for Luke. Opening times: Tue–Fri, Sun 3pm–6pm, Sat 10am–noon also.

🕐

Parco Botanico del Paradiso The entrance to Parco Botanico del Paradiso, in which exotic plants thrive, is on Via Quadrio. There are lovely views into the valley from the Paradiso and Belvedere hills. Attached is the **Museo della Valchiavenna** with exhibits on the history and archaeology of the region. Opening times: April–Oct Tue–Sat 2pm–5pm.

! **Baedeker TIP**

Experience the caves

A characteristic feature of Chiavenna are the grotti, natural rock caves in the mountain walls that ascend directly from the town. Typical products of the region are sold in these caves, and some have been fitted out as rustic bars – such as the Crotto Ombra, in which you can enjoy regional dishes beneath the cliffs.

Madesimo lies in a narrow valley on the stretch between Chiavenna and Passo dello Spluga at an elevation of 1534m/5032ft. To the east the mountain peaks of Monte Mater (3023m/9918ft) and Pizzo Groppera (2948m/9672ft) tower over the village. Until the construction of the reservoir, Lago di Montespluga was an established spa; today it is popular as a winter sports resort. In summer Madesimo is a popular starting point for trips to the surrounding lakes.

✴ Como

G 6

| **Provincial capital** | **Altitude:** 200m/656ft |
| **Population:** 83,000 | |

The provincial capital Como spreads out around the south-western end of the lake to which it gave its name. Como owes its prosperity to the textile and silk industry; it is the second-largest centre of silk processing after Japan.

City of silk The first mention of a manufactory that made »pura seta di Como« dates from 1510. Yet it was not until the 18th century that the planting of mulberry trees and silkworm breeding, whose secrets China had kept for centuries, began in the Brianza region. Meanwhile, however, most of the silk yarn comes from Asia, and is then further processed to make fabrics in the Como region.

✴ **Cityscape** Como has two different faces: approaching the city from the west or the south, a belt of ugly industrial buildings and residential estates serves as a reminder that this is a major industrial and trading centre. Coming from the north, either by water or on a road along the lakeshore, Como's charm is revealed, with its wonderful site on probably the most beautiful of the north Italian lakes. A city wall still largely encircles Como's old town, whose rectangular layout facing the lake goes back to a Roman encampment. Furthermore, the city possesses numerous important buildings.

In 196 BC the Romans conquered the old Celtic settlement of Como and founded Novum Comum as a border fortress. Thanks to its favourable location the town thrived. As events took their course the development of the town was determined by its **rivalry with mighty Milan**, whose trading routes north across the Alps led through a region controlled by Como. A war (1118–27) with this powerful neighbour led to the destruction of Como, whose people took their revenge when, on the side of Emperor Frederick Barbarossa, they conquered and completely devastated Milan in 1162. In 1335 Como fell to Milan and in 1521 to the Spanish Habsburgs, whose authoritarian rule lasted into the 18th century. Only later, under the Austrian Habsburgs, would the city experience a new upswing. Como's most famous sons were the physicist **Alessandro Volta** (1745–1827), the inventor of the battery, the Roman historian **Pliny the Elder** (AD 23/24–79), author of the 37-volume *Naturalis Historia* (both ►Famous People), and Pliny's nephew, the jurist Pliny the Younger (61/62–c111).

History

What to See in Como

The city tour begins on the cathedral square, which because of frequent flooding lies not on the lake but somewhat higher up in the city centre. To the east it is enclosed by the cathedral, the former town hall (Broletto) and the Torre Comunale. At their core, the city tower and Broletto with its open arcade on the lower floor date from the early 13th century.

★
Piazza del Duomo

Work on the cathedral of S. Maria Maggiore began in 1396 and lasted until 1744, making this place of worship one of the last important Gothic buildings in Italy. It is the masterpiece of the local school of stonemasons and sculptors, the **Maestri Comacini** (►Baedeker Special p.158), who for a millennium had a decisive influence on the architecture not just of northern and central Italy but also across the whole of Europe.

★ ★
Cathedral

The west façade, begun in 1457, is among the masterpieces of the Lombard early Renaissance. The works of the **Rodari brothers** include the relief *The Adoration of the Magi* in the wall section above the main doorway as well as the two seated figures to the left and right of the main doorway depicting Pliny the Elder and Pliny the Younger, a rare honouring of two »heathens« on a church. More extravagant still is the richly decorated Porta della Rana, the »Door of the Frog« in the north of the cathedral, which owes its name to a carved frog that these days is barely visible. In the interior the dark Gothic nave, the bright crossing in front of the Renaissance choir and the Baroque dome on a drum offer a lively contrast. The major-

◄ Interior

▶ VISITING COMO

INFORMATION

I. A. T.
Piazza Cavour 17
I-22100 Como
Tel. 0 31 3 30 01 28
Fax 0 31 24 01 11

WHERE TO EAT

▶ Moderate

① *L'Angelo del Silenzio*
Viale Lecco 25
Tel. 0 31 3 37 21 57
Closed Mon, Tue midday
This restaurant, one of the oldest in
the city, is also popular with the locals.
It serves very good Lombard cuisine at
moderate prices.

② *Le Colonne*
Piazza Mazzini 12
Tel. 0 31 26 61 66, closed Tue
Centrally located on a quiet square,
this pizzeria is always well visited.

WHERE TO STAY

▶ Luxury

① *Palace Hotel*
Lungolarion Trieste 16
Tel. 0 31 30 33 03
Fax 0 31 30 31 70
www.palacehotel.it, 99 rooms
Splendidly furnished hotel in a mar-
vellous location on the lake and in the
centre.

Silk products are still available in abundance in the so-called »city of silk«

► **Mid-range**

② *Firenze*

Piazza Volta 16
Tel. 0 31 30 03 33
Fax 0 31 30 01 01
www.albergofirenze.it
Classy hotel with a quiet and central location in a historic building on a pleasant square.

③ *Tre Re*

Piazza Boldoni 20
Tel. 0 31 26 53 74
Fax 0 31 24 13 49
www.hoteltrere.com, 41 rooms
Nice albergo with restaurant in the heart of the car-free city centre; nevertheless guests here get a good night's sleep and are a mere stone's throw from the shops.

ity of the furnishings date from the 17th century; highlights include the splendid 16th- and 17th-century **tapestries** from workshops in Ferrara, Florence and Flanders, a ***Descent from the Cross*** in the north aisle (1498), several **altarpieces**, including a *Flight into Egypt* by Gaudenzio Ferrari, an *Adoration of the Magi* and a *Madonna with St Jerome and St Ambrose* by Bernardino Luini (around 1500). The column-bearing lions of the two fonts in the nave date from the preceding building of the 11th century. Opening times: 7am–noon, 3pm–7pm. ⏲

Take Via Vittorio Emanuele II to the rear side of the church of S. Fedele, built in the 12th century on a ground plan in the shape of a four-leaf clover. The most interesting part is the apse, decorated with an elegant arcade. Note too the decorative **north doorway** and the **remains of frescoes** inside dating from the 12th and 13th centuries. The church stands on the beautiful **Piazza Fedele**, bordered to the west by two 16th-century half-timbered houses. On the first Saturday in the month a flea market is held on the square.

S. Fedele

Take a look, too, inside the city museum, located somewhat south on Via Vittorio Emanuele II. It has an impressive collection of archaeological, Roman and medieval exhibits. In the **picture gallery** works by Lombard artists of the 16th–18th centuries are on display.

Museo Civico

The history of the Italian unification movement is portrayed in the neighbouring Risorgimento Museum. Opening times for both museums: Tue–Sat 9am–12pm, 2pm–5pm, Sun 10am–1pm. ⏲

Museo del Risorgimento

Large parts of the 12th-century medieval fortifications still exist, including the three towers Torre di Porta Nuova, Torre di S. Vitale and the 40m/130ft-high Torre di Porta Vittoria at the end of Via Cantù.

Towers

From here it is not far to the church of S. Abbondio, which was consecrated in 1095. With a nave and four aisles, the church is among the most important sacred buildings of Lombard early Romanesque.

★
S. Abbondio

Como Map

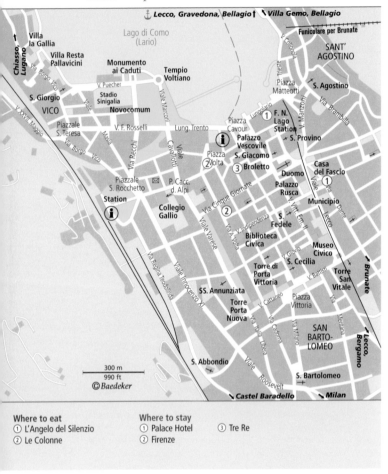

Where to eat
① L'Angelo del Silenzio
② Le Colonne

Where to stay
① Palace Hotel
② Firenze
③ Tre Re

The outside is structured by means of pilaster strips and round arch friezes. The **frescoes** in the apse in the interior, scenes from the life of Christ and the apostles Peter and Paul, were created by an unknown Sienese master around 1350. Adjoining to the north is a 16th-century cloister.

Shoreline esplanade

The shoreline esplanade that begins at Piazza Cavour leads towards Villa d'Olmo. Follow it to reach the classical **Tempio Voltiano** (1927). This temple houses a small **Science Museum**; dedicated to the physicist and discoverer **Alessandro Volta**, who was born in Co-

The cathedral took almost four centuries to build

mo in 1745, the museum tackles the subject of electricity. Opening times: April–Sept Tue–Sun 10am–noon, 3pm–6pm; Oct–March 10am–noon, 2pm–4pm.

Lavish villas line the western shore of the lake. The most famous is probably Villa d' Olmo. This classical building with a lovely park was created from 1782 to 1787 for **Marchese Innocenzo Odescalchi**. Today concerts, theatre performances and congresses are hosted in the extravagantly furnished rooms. Opening times: April–Oct Mon–Sat 9am–noon, 3pm–6pm.

There are two more villas in the neighbourhood: **Villa Gallia** was built as early as 1615 for Marco Gallio Tibaldi, the nephew of a cardinal. In the banqueting hall, original frescoes by Pier Francesco Morazzone have been preserved. The 18th-century **Villa Rotonda** is today the seat of the provincial government.

◄ Villa d' Olmo

◄ Further villas

Masterly sculpture by the Maestri Comacini on Como's cathedral

MIGRANT WORKERS FOR ART

They came from a remote valley between Lago di Como and Lago di Lugano. As stonemasons, master builders, plasterers and painters, the so-called Maestri Comacini or Comasques, the Maestri Intelvesi and Maestri Campionesi were in great demand and moved around Europe for centuries.

Between the 7th and 18th centuries, masters of the art of stonemasonry, named after their origins in Como, the Intelvi valley or Campione on Lago di Lugano, worked in closely organized masons' lodges. Knowledge and craftsmanship were handed down from father to son. In a period when Roman culture collapsed and much knowledge was lost through the upheaval of the age of migrations, they safeguarded the **knowledge of antiquity**.

From the 14th century the Maestri were migrant workers, moving from building site to building site. Everywhere they went, they learnt new building methods and styles. What appealed to them, they took on board. In this way they gathered immense knowledge. No-one understood better how to immortalize interlace-work, acanthus leaves, animal figures, human and demonic faces, worldly and mythological scenes in stone. They made their mark on numerous famous buildings: in Milan on the churches of S. Ambrogio and S. Maria delle Grazie, on the Certosa di Pavia,

in Como on S. Abbondio and on the cathedrals of Milan, Monza, Parma, Ferrara and Modena.

Their influence extended beyond Italy's borders. Indeed, the very word mason, from the French maçon, may derive from the Comacini. They worked in Lund in Sweden, where the **Comasque Donatus** built the cathedral. In Germany their work is preserved for posterity on the cathedrals of Mainz and Speyer, and a certain Quaglio from Laino in the Intelvi valley rebuilt the Bavarian Hohenschwangau in 1832 for Crown Prince Maximilian. Passau Cathedral was built by Carlo Antonio Carlone, whose family came from Scaria, just a few miles from Laino. The fresco painter **Carlo Carlone** was also active north of the Alps and left behind cycles of frescoes in Schloss Ludwigsburg in Germany and in Vienna. And were you aware of the fact that, under Ivan the Great in the 15th and 16th centuries, a certain Solari from Verna, a neighbouring village of Scaria, had a hand in the construction of the Kremlin?

Everything you ever wanted to know about the art of silk manufacturing is explained in the **Museo Didattico della Seta** (Via Castelnuovo 9) using original machines. Opening times: Tue–Fri 9am–noon, 3pm–6pm.

Brunate

A funicular runs from Piazza Funicolare in 10 minutes to the fine residential suburb of Brunate (716m/2349ft), to which a road also leads. There is a fine view over Como and the bay from here. An even more panoramic view can be enjoyed from the **S. Maurizio** district (906m/2972ft). A pleasant six-hour hike leads from Brunate to **Monte Boletto** (1234m/4049ft) and continues up to **Monte Palanzone** (1436m/4711ft).

◄ View

What style! – the classical Villa d'Olmo with its well-tended park

Castel Baradello About 3km/2mi outside the city centre to the south, on the 536m/1758ft-high Monte della Croce, the ruins of Castel Baradello still stand. The fortress was built in 1158 on the orders of **Emperor Frederick I Barbarossa** as protection against Milan; in 1527 it was destroyed. In 1277 Bishop Ottone Visconti, notorious for his cruelty, is said to have put his adversary Napo Torriani in a cage and hung it from the keep until he starved to death. Directions: from Piazza S. Rocco, cross the railway line and then follow the winding route upwards. Opening times: Thu, Sat, Sun 9.30am–5pm.

! *Baedeker* TIP

A stimulating break
In Caffè & Caffè (Via B. Luini 27) several types of tasty espresso coffee are on sale. You can also admire old espresso machines, and naturally down a cup or two of aromatic espresso.

S. Carpoforo At the foot of Monte della Croce stands S. Carpoforo, Como's first cathedral, which was probably founded in the 4th century. Today's structure was built as of 1025.

✳ Crema

L 8

Province: Cremona
Population: 33,000

Altitude: 79m/259ft

Crema, in a broad plain on the right bank of the river Serio, is a lively country town that hosts a lot of industry. The well-preserved and harmonious historic centre is enclosed by a medieval ring wall.

What to See in Crema

Piazza del Duomo Piazza del Duomo was always the religious and municipal centre of Crema. The piazza, dominated by the high walls of the cathedral, is not on the large scale of other Italian squares, but is distinguished by the harmony of its architecture. On the west side stands the 16th-century Palazzo del Comune. The town hall tower, known as the Torrazzo, was begun in the same time but not completed until the 17th century. The ensemble of buildings is rounded off by two palaces (1525): the Palazzo Pretorio adjoining the town hall to the north and the Palazzo Vescovile, the episcopal palace, to the east of the cathedral.

✳ Duomo S. Maria Assunta The Duomo S. Maria Assunta was built between 1284 and 1341 in the Lombard Gothic style. The raised main façade is striking stage-set architecture with a rose window, a dwarf gallery and wall openings, so that the sky is visible through it.

▶ VISITING CREMA

INFORMATION

I. A. T.
Via Racchetti 8
I-26013 Crema
Tel. 0 37 38 10 20, fax 0 37 3 25 57 28
www.prolococremona.it

WHERE TO EAT

▶ **Moderate**
Pata Negra
Via XI. Febbraio 38
Tel. 0 37 38 59 67
Closed Mon
Modern-looking restaurant on three levels; either eat a good substantial meal or just have a snack; small but well-chosen selection of wines.

WHERE TO STAY

▶ **Luxury**
Hotel Palace
Via Cresmero 10
Tel. 0 37 38 14 87
Fax 0 37 38 68 76
42 rooms
Set in a small park, this well-run hotel has rooms with air conditioning and a garage for hotel guests.

The interior, on a basilica plan, is distinguished by its amazing height, with massive compound pillars that separate the nave from the aisles. The oldest furnishings are a 14th-century **crucifix** and a Baroque altar painting of *Saint Mark in Prison, Visited by The Redeemer* by Guido Reni.

East of the cathedral square on Via Dante Alighieri are the monastery buildings of S. Agostino. The Augustine monastery was constructed as of the 15th century, and two cloisters and the refectory still exist. The Museo Civico, whose exhibits include an archaeological collection, is housed here. Opening times: Mon 2.30pm–6.30pm, Tue–Fri 9am– noon, 2.30pm–6.30pm, Sat, Sun 10am–noon, 4pm–7pm.

S. Agostino/ Museo Civico

North-east of the town centre stands Crema's main sight, the pilgrimage church of S. Maria della Croce. The founding of the church goes back to an apparition of the Virgin Mary. The Renaissance building was erected from 1490 to plans by **Giovanni Domenico Battagio**.
The octagonal brick-built rotunda towers between four chapels at half its height. Both Mannerist and Baroque paintings increase the ceremonial impression of the space.

★ ★ S. Maria della Croce

Around Crema

In the pretty country town of **Soncino**, about 20km/12mi north-east of Crema, the **Rocca**, one of Lombardy's most important and best-preserved castles, is worth a look. Built between 1473 and 1475 on a

The brick-built rotunda of S. Maria della Croce

🕐 square ground plan, it has several towers. Opening times: Tue–Fri 10am–noon, Sat, Sun 10am–12.30, 2.30pm–5.30pm; in summer until 7pm.

A visit to the **church of S. Maria delle Grazie**, located in the countryside about 1km/0.5mi south of Soncino, is rewarding. The church was built for the Carmelites between 1492 and 1528. Note especially the well-preserved Mannerist frescoes inside. Opening times: in summer 10am–noon, 4pm–7pm.

Caravaggio ✱ Caravaggio, 20km/12mi north of Crema, can pride itself on being the birthplace of the **painter Caravaggio**, actually Michelangelo Merisi, who was born here in 1573. Caravaggio is famous for the **Santuario della Madonna**, situated south-west of the town, to which 1.5 million pilgrims come every year. The church, to which a long avenue of chestnut trees leads, was built in 1451 on the site of an apparition of the Virgin Mary, and remodelled in the style of the late Renaissance in 1575. The high crossing tower is visible from a long distance away. The holy spring inside is said to have bubbled forth following the appearance of the Blessed Virgin.

Rivolta d'Adda The small village of Rivolta d'Adda (32km/19mi north-west of Crema) has a major Romanesque monument, S. Maria e S. Sigismondo.

The mighty defences of the Rocca of Soncino

This fortified brick church was built in the 11th century, remodelled in the Baroque period and then comprehensively reconstructed at the beginning of the 20th century. The imaginative **decorated capitals** and the **Romanesque frescoes** in both side apses date from the 12th century.

Parco della Preistoria in Rivolta d'Adda (25km/16mi north-west of Crema) is a joy for young and old alike, as here the evolution of the dinosaurs is shown using life-size models. There is also a botanical garden in the park. Opening times: high season daily 9am–6.30pm, otherwise 5/5.30pm; www.parcodellapreistoria.it.

Parco della Preistoria ⏱

★ Cremona

Provincial capital
Population: 72,800

Altitude: 47m/154ft

The city of Cremona on the river Po is well known as the cradle of violin-making – after all, the Amati, Guarneri, Bergonzi and Stradivari families all come from here (▶Baedeker Special p.169).

Cremona still has a well-known school of violin-making and numerous workshops, and every three years in October an **international**

City of violin-making

▶ VISITING CREMONA

INFORMATION

A. P. T.
Piazza del Comune 8
I-26100 Cremona
Tel. 03 72 40 75 84
Fax 03 72 40 70 35
www.turismo.commune.cremona.it

WHERE TO EAT

▶ Moderate

① *La Sosta*
Via Sicardo 9
Tel. 0 37 2 45 66 56
www.osteriasosta.it, closed Mon
This restaurant near to the central
piazza serves regional dishes and has a
well-stocked wine cellar.

WHERE TO STAY

▶ Mid-range

① *Continental*
Piazza della Libertà 26

Tel. 0 37 2 43 41 41
Fax 0 37 2 45 48 73
www.hotelcontinentalcremona.it
62 rooms
Very well-run hotel on the edge of the
historic centre; tasteful interior; well-
tended, nicely furnished rooms await
guests here, as well as a car park and a
large restaurant.

② *Duomo*
Via Gonfalonieri 13
Tel. 0 37 23 52 42
Fax 0 37 2 45 83 92
www.hotelduomocremona.com 23
rooms
This small, pleasant hotel, very prettily
located right in the city centre next to
the cathedral, exudes a friendly atmosphere; the good restaurant is also
popular with the locals.

---

triennial competition for stringed instruments takes place here. In
addition a varied concert programme throughout the year ensures
that the long tradition lives on. An important musician is associated
with the city: **Claudio Monteverdi** (▶Famous People) was born here
in 1565. Another outstanding person was born here around 1535:
the painter **Sofonisba Anguissola**. The city may have music in the
air, but it lives from agriculture – and it is not a bad living either: the
province of Cremona has one of the highest per-capita incomes in
Italy.

History   Initially a centre of the Celtic Cenomanes, in 218 BC Cremona became a Roman military colony. In 603 the Lombards invaded. In the
centuries that followed the city blossomed, traded by sea with Byzantium and in the late 11th century became a free comune. In the
clashes of the 12th and 13th centuries the city mostly took the side
of Emperor Frederick Barbarossa and Frederick II. In the 14th century the Visconti came to power, followed in 1441 by the Sforza
through the marriage of the 17-year-old Bianca Maria Visconti to
Francesco Sforza, who was 23 years older. At the time of Spanish rule
in the 16th century Cremona entered a period of cultural flowering.
The **first violin-making workshop** of the patrician Amati family was

Violin-making, which made Cremona famous, still takes place here

inaugurated; the Guarneri and Stradivari families followed suit. Painting, too, experienced an upswing: in the churches of the city, frescoes by several famous Cremonese painter families have been preserved from this time. From 1714 the city was subject to Austrian rule.

For all its great cultural past, Cremona rather gives the impression of being a quiet provincial town. However, the diminutive city– and this is less well known than its musical heritage – has several unusual architectural features that are well worth seeing. The ensemble of five buildings in the historic centre on Piazza del Comune is particularly impressive: cathedral, Torrazzo, baptistery, town hall and Loggia dei Militi.

Cityscape

✷ ✷

◀ Centro storico

What to See in Cremona

With its surprising size, clearly composed marble façade, immense campanile and two flanking brick-built towers, Cremona's cathedral is certainly conspicuous. It was begun in 1117 and consecrated as early as 1190. Only later were the Gothic transepts added, at first the north transept by 1288, then by 1342 the one to the south. The **west façade**, which faces the piazza, was built from 1180 to 1190 and cov-

✷ ✷

Duomo

Especially impressive: the cathedral and the Torrazzo are illuminated at night

ered in marble around 1500. Its dwarf galleries, large rose window and Porta Regia, the main doorway with its total of six column-bearing lions, catch the eye. Next to the figure of the Virgin Mary are the church's patron saints Imerio and Omobono (»the good man«). Above the rose window (1274) there are four figures of prophets: Jeremiah, Isaiah, Daniel and Ezechiel. The architectural connection to the campanile is an arcade passage, the **Portico della Bertazzola**, whose sculptures depict allegorical figures and saints. On the north façade the column-bearing lions at the doorway are again noteworthy. The depiction of Christ and the apostles dates from the earliest building phase (1130–40). Those who walk around the cathedral will notice the numerous slender decorative towers, which are concealed from the west side.

Interior ▶ The most impressive features of the interior are the fresco cycles in the nave on the themes of the life of Mary and the Passion of Christ by Biccaccio Boccaccino and others, who from 1514 created the superb Renaissance interior design in 15 years. The transept in contrast was first decorated in 1812. On some of the pillars hang Brussels tapestries (around 1685) depicting the story of Samson. In the

Cremona Map

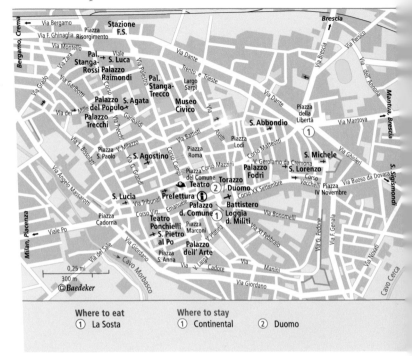

Where to eat
① La Sosta

Where to stay
① Continental   ② Duomo

long choir with its Baroque marble altar (1723) by G. B. Zaist the early Renaissance stalls with pretty inlay work stand out. Note the late 15th-century depictions of architecture, which include the west façade of the cathedral of the time as well as the river harbour. Opening times: daily 8am–noon and 4pm–7pm.

At 111m/364ft, this is the **highest bell tower in Italy** and the city's emblem. Known to the Cremonese people as the Torrazzo, the campanile was built in the mid-13th century on a four-sided ground plan. In the lower section, the walls – resembling those of a fortress – are sparingly punctuated by Gothic window openings, but moving up the structure to the octagonal tower the building gives an ever lighter, more transparent impression. A pointed cone roof forms the top of the tower. The real gem on the western side of the square is the large **Renaissance clock**, which formerly showed both the time and the date and in addition gave astronomical information. It is possible to climb up the Torrazzo and enjoy the superb view of the cathedral, whose size can only really be appreciated from this vantage point.

** **
Torrazzo

Battistero ✳ The baptistery, built on an octagonal ground plan, exhibits harmonious balance. Building began in the second half of the 12th century – as work on the cathedral was being continued. This brick-built octagon is topped by a dome with a lantern, which itself is crowned by a Gothic depiction of the archangel Gabriel (1370). On the baptistery, too, the marble covering is striking – it is incomplete and was carried out later in order to correspond to the marble-covered cathedral façade, also added later. The interior walls of the baptistery have columned arcades and galleries on different levels, and the sparing furnishings were made primarily in the Renaissance and Baroque periods. The 16th-century red marble font is superb.

Loggia dei Militi ✳ The two city palaces on the west side of Piazza del Commune are Gothic in style. The somewhat smaller Gothic Loggia dei Militi (1292) was the palace of the city militia. Above the half-open loggia is the assembly hall, made brighter by means of triforia.

Palazzo del Comune/ Sala dei Violini ✳ Next to it stands the town hall, which was built from 1204 to 1246 in the transitional style between Romanesque and Gothic, but remodelled and altered in the 16th and 19th centuries. The Palazzo del Comune is the musical heart of Cremona: the **Sala dei Violini**. The most famous violins are exhibited here – the small »il Cremonese«, which was made by Antonio Stradivari in 1715, »l' Hammerle« (1658) by Nicolò Amati, a violin for the French king Charles IX (1566) by Andrea Amati and one by Giuseppe Antonio Guarneri from 1734 that for a long time was played by Pinchas Zukerman. Opening times: Tue– Sat 9am– noon, 2pm–5pm.

North-east of the piazza on Corso Matteotti stands **Palazzo Fodri**, a typical city palace of the early Renaissance, built in 1490 for the wealthy merchant Benedetto Fodri. The **Cortile**, the two-storey inner courtyard, is a real gem – it is considered to be one of the most beautiful of its kind in Lombardy. Above the arcade passage and above the upper row of windows are two skilfully worked terracotta bands with depictions of battles.

Exhibited in lovely surroundings: violins in the museum

Monument to the man who made Cremona famous: the violin-maker Antonio Stradivari

VIOLIN HEAVEN

Was it the wood, the composition of the varnish or the small sound posts inserted between the back and the front of the violin? There are many theories, but no satisfactory explanation of how the fantastic tone of Stradivari violins was achieved.

The wood used for the front of the violin was soft pine or spruce with good vibration properties, while maple was used for the back. 150 to 180 man-hours were required to make a violin, which is composed of about 70 individual parts. When the back and the front – whose f-holes are extremely important for the tone of the instrument – have been connected by means of the ribs and finally the scroll has been inserted onto the fingerboard, the violins are hung on a line like washing and »ripened«. 602 genuine Stradivari instruments are still in existence: 540 violins, 12 violas and 50 cellos. Who was this **Antonio Stradivari**, to whom 1200 instruments have been ascribed? He was born around 1644, was married twice and had eleven children, but we do not know much more. He was obviously aware of the high quality of his work, because he demanded a lot of money for his instruments.

Stradivari was without doubt the greatest violin maker in Cremona, but he was not the first. Abut 100 years before Stradivari was born, **Andrea Amati** already had a violin-making workshop in the town. His grandchild Nicolò Amati was the teacher of **Andrea Guarneri** and Antonio Stradivari. The Amati, the Guarneri, the Stradivari and the Bergonzi built veritable dynasties. They passed their knowledge down from generation to generation, constantly refining their methods as time went on.

With Stradivari, violin-making attained its pinnacle. For a long time afterwards there was no instrument production in the town to speak of – until the occasion of the 200th anniversary of Stradivari's death in 1937, when an international violin-making school was opened. And it really is international – the students come from all over the world. Today almost all Stradivari instruments still in existence are in the hands of museums, musicians or collectors. Owners of Stradivaris include the violin virtuosos Anne-Sophie Mutter and the violinist Itzhak Perlman, whose instrument was previously played by Yehudi Menuhin, and the cellist Yo-Yo Ma.

S. Michele

The church of S. Michele at the end of Via Gerolamo da Cremona was founded in the 7th century and extended in the 12th century. While the façade is a historicizing creation of the 19th century, the interior has retained its Gothic appearance of the late 12th century with the remains of frescoes.

✱ **Piazza Roma**

The extensive Piazza Roma, a nice green space with high trees, herbaceous borders and benches, is an ideal place to have a break. In the front part a small, weathered flagstone carries the inscription: »Sepolcro di Antonio Stradivari e suoi eredi anno 1729« – the memorial slab has survived from a Stradivari family tomb, which is the reason why the year given is not the year of the famous Stradivari's death; the tomb was previously in a Dominican church that stood here. The Inquisition once had its headquarters in the Dominican monastery, an unpopular building that was torn down in the 19th century to create this open space.

✱ **Museo Civico, Museo Stradivariano**

Head along the busy shopping street Corso Campi and turn into Via Palestro, on which Palazzo Affaitati, a 16th-century patrician's palace, stands. There are two museums here: in the Museo Civico (entrance on Via Ugolani Dati 4) works of local 16th-century painters are on display. The Stradivari Museum, though in the same building, is accessed at Via Palestro 17. Visitors can see valuable documents, tools, designs and models from the Stradivari workshop as well as a range of stringed instruments by various instrument makers. Opening times: Tue–Sat 9am–6pm, Sun 10am–6pm.
In the immediate vicinity there are several violin workshops (liuterie): at Via Palestro 25 and Corso Garibaldi 45 and 95.

Palazzo del Popolo

Once, Palazzo del Popolo (1256) on Corso Garibaldi was home to the **assembly rooms of the Guelphs**, who were the opposition at the time – in the Palazzo Comunale, the seat of government, sat the Ghibellines.

✱ **S. Agata**

Opposite the Palazzo del Popolo stands the 15th-century church of S. Agata; today's classical façade was added in the mid-19th century. An important work is kept inside the church: the icon-like **Tavola di S. Agata**, considered to be among the most important late 13th-century panels in Lombardy. It was painted by an unknown artist and shows scenes from the life of St Agatha.

Palazzo Raimondi

Palazzo Raimondi at Corso Garibaldi 178 was built in 1496 by Bernardino de Lera. Cremona's **school of violin-making** occupies the building.

On the corner of Corso Garibaldi and Viale Trento e Trieste stands the brick-built church of S. Luca, which dates from the 13th century, i.e. the early Gothic period. In 1471 it was remodelled and today's façade put up. The domed octagon next to the façade is unusual – also by Bernardino de Lera, it was built in the 16th century on the occasion of the town surviving an epidemic.

S. Luca

Of all the small churches in Cremona, S. Agostino on the piazza of the same name must be the prettiest. It was built in the 14th century and altered in the 15th and 16th centuries; the campanile was added in 1461. In the interior take a look at the frescoes (around 1452) by Bonifacio Bembo in the chapel to the right of the choir. They show a large number of scenes from the life of St Augustine.

S. Agostino

S. Sigismondo, east of the actual city centre, is described as **one of Lombardy's most important Renaissance buildings designed in the time before Bramante**. The church, which unfortunately is often closed, was founded by Bianca Maria Visconti and Francesco Sforza, who were married in a smaller preceding church on this site. Construction began in 1463.
The interior, a barrel-vaulted cross, is covered with wonderful frescoes by the famous Cremonese painters of the 16th century. A door leads through to the Renaissance cloister.

★
S. Sigismondo

★ Lago di Como · Lake Como

G–J 3–6

Region: Lombardy
Altitude of lake: 198m/650ft

Provinces: Como and Lecco
Area: 146 sq km/56 sq mi

Lago di Como – also known as Lario due to its Roman name of Lacus Larius – stretches between the Luganese and the Bergamasche Alps. It is 50km/30mi long and up to 4km/2.5mi wide.

Lago di Como is for many **northern Italy's most beautiful lake**; at any rate, at a depth of 410m/1345ft, it is one of the **deepest lakes in Europe**. It owes its beauty on the one hand to the backdrop of surrounding mountains, on the other to the Mediterranean flora. Thanks to a mild climate jasmine, oleander, cypresses and fig trees thrive on the lake's shores; wine and olives are grown on the mountain slopes, which were formed into terraces back in Roman times. The western shore enjoys the mildest climate and has the lushest vegetation. The section between Menaggio and Cernobbio, framed by gentle mountain slopes, is especially beautiful, as is the peninsula of Bellagio. As early as the 19th century, this section of the lake often played host to visitors. The northern part, surrounded only by mountain foothills and therefore quieter, is well known as Lago di

Landscape

VISITING LAGO DI COMO

INFORMATION

I.A.T. Menaggio
Piazza Garibaldi 8
Tel. 0 34 43 29 24

I.A.T. Cernobbio
Villa Erba, Via Regina 23
Tel./fax 03 1 51 01 98

A.P.T. Como
Piazzo Cavour 17
Tel. 03 1 33 00 11 12, fax 03 1 26 97 11

Pro Loco Varenna
Piazza Venini 1
Tel./fax 03 41 83 03 67
www.comersee-info.de

I.A.T. Bellagio
Piazza della Chiesa
Tel./fax 0 31 95 02 04

WHERE TO EAT

► Moderate

Bilacus
Via Serbelloni 30/32
Bellagio
Tel. 0 31 95 04 80
Out of season closed Mon
This local restaurant is somewhat higher up than the esplanade in a stepped alley; diners eat international cuisine on a roof terrace; very popular, with Italians too.

La Darsena
Via al Porto
Bellagio-Loppia
Tel. 0 31 4 45 11 02
Closed Tue
This modern restaurant with a small terrace has found its ideal home in Loppia.

Vecchia Varenna
Contrada Scoscesa 10
Varenna
Tel. 03 41 83 07 93
Closed Mon
Diners must eat with a view of the lake – and deliciously prepared fish from its waters is on the menu.

WHERE TO STAY

► Luxury

Grand Hotel Menaggio
Via IV Novembre 69
Menaggio
Tel. 0 34 43 06 40
Fax 0 34 43 06 19
www.grandhotelmenaggio.com, 87 rooms
Outstanding hotel on the western shore of the lake; prettily furnished rooms, excellent service, garage for hotel guests.

Grand Hotel Villa d'Este
Via Regina 40
Cernobbio
Tel. 0 31 34 81, fax 0 31 34 88 73
www.villadeste.it, 156 rooms
This legendary luxury hotel in a famous historical villa is uniquely situated – beach and park are part of the package, naturally.

Grand Hotel Villa Serbelloni
Via Roma 1
Bellagio
Tel. 0 31 95 02 16
Fax 0 31 95 15 29
www.villaserbelloni.com, 86 rooms
The traditional hotel of Lago di Como in an old villa on the shore oozes splendour and charm; many greats of politics and the silver screen have stayed here; restaurant on the terrace out front; it is possible to swim in both the swimming pool and the lake.

Royal Victoria
Piazza S. Giorgio 2
Varenna
Tel. 03 41 81 51 11
Fax 03 41 83 07 22
www.centrohotelslagocomo.it, 43 rooms
No less a guest than Queen Victoria of England stayed here, and allegedly longer than planned; the buildings and garden extend down to the lake in terraces; the well-kept rooms enjoy a view either of the lake or of the pretty village square. Restaurant with terrace and a view of the lake; car park.

▶ Mid-range
Albergo Lenno
Via Lomazzi 23
Lenno
Tel. 03 44 5 70 51
Fax 03 44 5 70 55
www.albergolenno.com
In the quiet town of Lenno, located directly next to the moorings; it is definitely worth asking for a room with a view of the lake.

Belvedere
Via Valsassina 31
Bellagio
Tel. 0 31 95 04 10
Fax 0 31 95 01 02
www.belvederebellagio.com, 58 rooms
Very popular hotel with a pleasant atmosphere and a view of the eastern arm of Lago di Como; extensive grounds with lawn and swimming pool; restaurant with a view of the lake.

Villa Cipressi
Via IV. Novembre 18
Varenna
Tel. 03 41 83 01 13
Fax 03 41 83 04 01
www.hotelvillacipressi.it, 21 rooms
A lovely 16th-century villa in a park with old trees that stretches down to the water; terrace with a view of the lake.

▶ Budget
Albergo Olivedo
Piazza Martiri 4
Varenna
Tel./fax 03 41 83 01 15
www.olivedo.it
Probably Italy's narrowest hotel, the Albergo Olivedo is located next to the moorings and full of old furniture; not all rooms have a bathroom, but no. 15, with both a bathroom and a balcony overlooking the lake, is recommended.

La Pergola
Piazza del Porto 4
Bellagio
Tel. 0 31 95 02 63
Fax 0 31 95 02 53, 10 rooms
Very simple but extremely pretty hotel in the harbour bay on the east side of Bellagio; a restaurant with lakeside terrace is attached.

Albergo Fioroni
Carate Urio
Tel. 0 31 40 01 49
Fax 0 31 40 00 37
www.hotelfioroni.it
Pretty hotel with recommendable annexe next door; good value for money; restaurant with lakeside terrace.

Highlights Lago di Como

Villa Carlotta
This villa near Tremezzo is primarily worth visiting for its magnificent park.
► page 177

Bellagio
Bellagio, the most chic holiday resort on Lago di Como, is known as the »pearl of Lario«.
► page 181

Villa Melzi
Villa Melzi in Bellagio also has a wonderful park.
► page 183

Como's **surfing area**. Lago di Lecco, above which tower the steep slopes of Grigne (2410m/7907ft), extends to the south-east and is less marked by tourism.

History Wealthy Romans built the first splendid villas on the shores of Lacus Larius as early as the 2nd century AD. As the Teuton attacks from the north became more frequent, Via Regia was built along the western shore of the lake. The military road led from Milan via Como and Chiavenna into Gallic Raetia. In the 18th and 19th centuries Lario was a favoured summer residence for the nobility and the wealthy. Today, **numerous grand villas** in paradisiacal gardens recall the era when the owners arrived here with clothes trunks, hatboxes and servants to hold court for weeks on end. They were followed by less well-to-do guests whose names are nevertheless rather more stimulating to the intellect, such as Goethe, Flaubert, Stendhal, Bellini, Liszt and many others, all of whom extolled the area's beauty and enthused about this dramatic »Shakespearean landscape«, as Flaubert called it.

Today the inhabitants of Lago di Como live predominantly from growing wine and olives, fishing and industry, mainly textiles and silk processing. **Tourism** also plays a role, though only 5% of the region's income derives from this source. The extensive range of activities for visitors includes water sports, hiking and climbing, as well as winter sports on Grigna. In addition there is a varied cultural life.

✶ ✶ Western Shore

Como ►Como

Cernobbio
✶
Villa d' Este ►

Following the western shore north from Como leads first to the classy holiday resort of Cernobbio, which has now almost merged with Como. The famous Villa d' Este was built here in 1568 to plans by **Pellegrino Tibaldi**. The client was Cardinal Tolomeo Gallio, who also commissioned the construction of many other villas on Lago di Como. After his death the villa changed hands frequently. In the early 19th century Caroline of Brunswick, wife of the English prince regent (the future George IV), had the palatial building converted in the style of the time. Since 1873 the villa, which stands in a magnificent Baroque garden, has been the **most famous hotel on Lago di Como**. It is accessible only to hotel guests.

> **!** *Baedeker* TIP
>
> **Lovely views from the lake**
>
> The ship tours on Lago di Como are a nice experience. Many run between the western and eastern shores, frequently providing the most beautiful views of villas and gardens. For information call tel. 8 00 55 18 01 and see www.navigazionelaghi.it.

16km/10mi further on, the small, winding road ascends **Monte Bisbino** (1325m/4347ft) to a fine view and pilgrimage church. Continuing on the old Strada Regina, the road along the shore to Torrigia, the route passes small villages, beautiful villas, parks and small harbours. Those in more of a hurry can take the S 340 national road lower down.

From Argegno a funicular takes a few minutes to reach the top of **Pigra** at an elevation of 870m/2854ft. Argegno is also the point of departure for a side trip into Valle d'Intelvi and on to ►Lago di Lugano.

Argegno

Situated between the Como and Lugano lakes, the Intelvi valley is not merely scenically very beautiful. From the 7th to the 18th century it was also home to the **Maestri Intelvesi** (►Baedeker Special p.158), important stonemasons and master builders. The most famous masters from the Intelvi valley are the Carloni from Scaria, the Solari from Verna, and the Bregno from Osteno. Beautiful examples of their work include the Oratorio della Madonna del Restello in **Castiglione d'Intelvi**, the church of S. Antonio in **S. Fedele Intelvi**, the church of S. Lorenzo in **Laino** and the parish church of **Scaria**. A splendid view of Lago di Lugano can be enjoyed from the 1300m/4265ft **Sighignola**, a mountain ridge near Lanzo.

✸ Valle d'Intelvi

Between Sala Comacina and Ossuccio near to the road along the shore lies the only island in the lake; there are boat connections from both places. For centuries the small island played an important role as a military base. In the Middle Ages there was a settlement here with a castle and five churches. The island was on the side of anti-imperial Milan, and during a clash with Frederick Barbarossa it was destroyed completely and abandoned »as a punishment«. The foundation walls, including the 11th-century church of S. Eufemia dell'Isola and the 16th-century church of S. Giovanni, are still preserved.

Isola Comacina

Villa Carlotta's beautiful terraced garden is laid out in Italian style

Ossuccio In Ossuccio, or more precisely in the Ospedaletto district, stands the Romanesque church of **S. Maria Maddalena**. Its striking belfry storey was added to the campanile in the 14th century. Above Ospedaletto about 3km/2mi to the north-east stands the 16th-century pilgrimage church of **Madonna del Soccorso**; Via Crucis, built in 1635, leads past 14 Baroque chapels. In the Romanesque church of **S. Giacomo** in the district of Spurano a number of Romanesque and Gothic frescoes have been preserved. Like Lenno, Ossuccio is a starting point for a hike into **Val Perlana**; one possible destination is the 11th-century Romanesque church of S. Benedetto, which can be reached on foot in about an hour. The tours to **Monti di Tremezzo** (1700m/5577ft), **Monte di Lenno** (1589m/5213ft) and **Calbiga** (1698m/5571ft) are tiring, but the views are magnificent.

★
Villa del Balbianello Between Ossuccio and Lenno the forested **peninsula of Punta di Lavedo** projects far out into the lake. The picturesque Villa del Balbianello at its tip can only be reached by boat from Ossuccio. In the 16th century Cardinal Tolomeo Gallio commissioned the construc-

tion of Villa Arconati Visconti here. In the 18th century it was acquired by Cardinal Angelo Maria Durini, a man in love with life, who ordered major alterations and renamed it Villa del Balbianello. The park, accessible from mid-March to mid-November, is worth seeing. Opening times: Tue, Thu–Sun 10am–6pm.

North of the Balbianello promontory lies Lenno, whose name recalls the Greek colonists from the island of Lemnos who were resettled here under Caesar. The church of **S. Stefano** was built in 1593, though it did not receive its illusionist painting until 1750. Like the baptistery next door, the hall crypt underneath the church belongs to an earlier building from the 11th century. Above Lenno stands the **Abbazia dell' Acquafredda** abbey with three paintings (around 1620) by Giovanni Mauro della Rovere, known as Fiammenghino.
Near Giulino di Mezzegra (about 200m/650ft up the road from the lake) a cross marks the place at which Benito **Mussolini** and his mistress Clara Petacci were shot by partisans on 28 April 1945 as they tried to flee into Switzerland.

Lenno

Tremezzo lies about halfway between Como and Sorico. Along with the Bellagio peninsula, the section of shore that now follows, extending to Cadenabbia, is **the most beautiful part of Lago di Como** and is also dubbed the Riviera Tremezzina.
There are little villages here as well as some of the loveliest villas, among them Villa Carlotta at the edge of Tremezzo. It was built in 1747 for Giorgio Clerici, a field marshal in the service of Maria Theresia of Austria, then remodelled in classical style around 1800 and named after its new owner, the Prussian Princess Charlotte von Sachsen-Meiningen, in 1850. The Italian-style terraced garden and the English park are worth a visit, especially in April and May when the rhododendrons and azaleas are in bloom. In the prestigious villa, today a museum, furniture, clocks, paintings and sculptures are on display. Along with the wall frieze *The Entrance of Alexander the Great into Babylon* (around 1800) by Berthel Thorwaldsen there are sculptures by Antonio Canova, although *Amor and Psyche* is a copy. Opening times: mid to late March, April–mid-Oct 9am–6pm; mid-Oct–mid-Nov 10am–4pm. The neighbouring town of Cadenabbia gives a more worldly impression. Verdi composed his opera *La Traviata* in **Villa Margherita-Ricordi** around 1853. In **Villa La Collina** German chancellor **Konrad Adenauer** spent his summer holidays until 1966; it now belongs to the Konrad Adenauer Foundation.

✱ Riviera Tremezzina

✱ ◄ Villa Carlotta

◄ Cadenabbia

On a small spit of land, Menaggio is the **economic and tourist centre on the western shore** of Lago di Como. Its attractions are an old centre and its flower-bedecked shoreline esplanade. Beyond Menaggio the country becomes more mountainous. Simple houses instead of villas mark the scene; instead of grand hotels there are camping sites and holiday homes. Windsurfers find good conditions here.

✱ Menaggio

Dongo
Dongo's 12th-century Romanesque church of **S. Maria in Martinico** is worthy of mention; the lavish decoration of the Baroque church of **S. Stefano** was done by the masters of the Intelvi valley.

Gravedona
Gravedona is the historic centre of northern Lario. In the Middle Ages it was temporarily an independent city republic. The 12th-century Romanesque church of **S. Maria del Tiglio** on the southern edge of the town dates from this time; the crucifix on the main apse and the remains of the wall frescoes are from the 13th–15th centuries. Standing directly on the lake, the church of **S. Vincenzo** was built in 1072 in place its early Christian predecessor. The hall crypt, which remains from the earlier church, is worth a look. The church itself was remodelled in Baroque style in the 17th and 18th centuries. Also right on the water is the castle-like **Palazzo Gallio**, built in 1583 to plans by Pellegrino Tibaldi for Cardinal Tolomeo Gallio.

✴ Eastern Shore

Colico
The little town of Colico owes its great appeal to its location: to the north rise the mountains of Chiavenna, to the east the mighty Monte Legnone (2609m/8560ft).

✴ Abbazia di Piona
In Olgiasca, nearly 6km/3.5mi south of Colico, a small road, offering copious views, branches off in the direction of the lake. It leads first high above the water through a residential area and then through a wood down to a former Benedictine, now Cistercian, monastery and

its church of S. Nicolò. There is a view from the mooring (directly beneath the church) of Gravedona on the opposite shore. The monastery was founded by Bishop Agrippino of Como in the 7th century. Today's buildings were created later, however. The church was consecrated in 1138, and the choir still has 13th-century frescoes. The small cloister was added between 1252 and 1257. The Cistercians of the abbey sell products they make themselves: honey, liqueurs and handmade articles.

Place of peace: Abbazia di Piona

Halfway between Colico and Bellano lies **Corenno Plinio**, a small medieval village that extends down to the lake. The fortress was built in the 14th century as a residence for the counts Andreani; it is in ruins today. The industrial town of **Dervio** lies at the entrance to Valvarrone, where iron was mined from the 15th to the 17th century. The road ends in Premana, a small holiday resort. There is a spectacular panorama from **Monte Legnone** (2609m/8560ft), the ascent of which takes about four hours.

Bellano's old quarter extends up the mountain behind the shoreline esplanade. The parish church of SS. Nazaro e Celso, built between 1342 and 1350, stands here. A ten-minute walk from the church in an easterly direction along a signposted path leads to the **Orrido**. This spectacular gorge was carved out by the Pioverna river, which emerges here from Valsassina and can be approached on footbridges. There is a splendid view of the small town and the lake from the cemetery above.

Bellano

Bellano is the starting point for an approximately 40km/25mi-long side trip into Val Muggiasca and further into Valsassina. The first section is especially steep but has lovely views; just outside Taceno the route turns onto the road to Cortenova. From here it ascends gradually, passing through the townships of Cortabbio and Primaluna to **Introbio** (550m/1804ft), the centre of local cheese production. After a side trip to Baiedo and Pasturo, continue beyond Colle di Balisio (723m/2372ft) to **Ballabio**, a municipality popular with tourists and also known for its cheese, which is ripened in caves. Lecco is another 8km/5mi away.

★
Side trip into Valsassina

Varenna lies at the place where the lake is at its widest (5km/3mi). The old centre extends up the mountain and the church of S. Giorgio (1300; remodelled in the 17th and 18th century) towers over it. Above the lake stands the 16th- to 19th-century **Villa Cipressi** – today a hotel – in a garden accessible from May to October (opening times: daily 9am–6pm; June–Aug until 7pm). There are regular ferries to Bellagio and Menaggio from the small harbour. At the southern end of the resort stands the long, narrow Villa Monastero, which goes back to a nunnery founded in 1208. After it was dissolved in 1567 the grounds were acquired by an aristocrat from Valsassina who had the marvellous gardens laid out and erected the buildings seen today. After several changes in ownership, since 1953 the villa has belonged to the Italian state, which holds conferences and congresses here. The rooms are furnished with original furniture and works of art. Opening times: Mar–May, Sept–Nov Sat, Sun, holidays 9am–1pm, 2pm–6pm; June–Aug Mon– Fri 9am–7pm.
The terraced park is considered the most beautiful along the eastern shore and is accessible to visitors. Opening times: April–Oct daily 9am–7pm. www.villamonastero.it

Varenna

🕐

◀ Villa Monastero

★
◀ Park
🕐

The route to Lecco is now primarily characterized by industrial plants. Mandello del Lario, at the foot of the jagged Grigna Meridionale (2184m/7165ft), is the headquarters of the legendary Moto Guzzi motorcycle works, founded in 1921.

Mandello del Lario

Lecco and its surroundings Lecco, the provincial capital, extends along the lake of the same name. It is surrounded by the S. Martino (1046m/3432ft) and Resegone (1875m/6152ft) mountains as well as the Grigne massif. Industrial works (iron, steel and cement works, silk industry) and new buildings characterize the cityscape. In the Middle Ages Lecco was allied with Milan and developed early into an important trading centre. The Torre del Castello tower, fortified with battlements, goes back to the Visconti; it stands on **Piazza XX Settembre**, on which a colourful market is held on Wednesdays and Saturdays. The remains of a 15th-century Visconti fortress are today home to the **Museo del Risorgimento** e della Resistenza, with documents on the unification movement and both World Wars. Azzone Visconti built the eleven-arched bridge that is named after him and spans the Adda back in the 14th century.

! **Baedeker TIP**

On the trail of the betrothed

Lecco and its countryside were granted literary immortality through the descriptions in the novel *I promessi sposi* (*The Betrothed*), an exciting tale of two lovers in the 17th century by Alessandro Manzoni (1785–1873). A tour follows in the footsteps of the betrothed; a map with the route is available in the tourist office.

Villa Manzoni ► In the district of Caleotto stands Villa Manzoni (18th century; Via Guanella 1); on the ground floor is an exhibition dedicated to the author Alessandro Manzoni, who spent his youth here; on the upper floor a collection of paintings is on display in the Galleria Comunale. In the 18th-century **Palazzo Belgioioso**, in the Castello district (Corso Matteotti 32), fossils and prehistoric and Roman archaeological finds are exhibited. Opening times of all museums in Lecco: Tue–Sun 9am–2pm.

The surroundings of Lecco are extremely beautiful: the up to 2400m/7874ft-high **Grigna** massif is a popular area for hiking trips. Rising to the east and north respectively, **Piani d'Erna** (1329m/4360ft) and **Piani di Resinelli** (1276m/4186ft), from which Grigna Meridionale (2184m/7165ft) can be ascended in three hours, can be reached either by cable railway or on a winding road via Ballabio.

Civate Civate lies on the northern shore of Lago di Annone south-west of Lecco. For confirmed fans of Romanesque church architecture and painting the somewhat difficult task of making the pilgrimage up to the **church of S. Pietro al Monte** is recommended. The church lies on a mountain slope above Civate and is only accessible on foot. S. Pietro al Monte originally consisted of a nave with three apses. Because the oratory of S. Benedetto lies somewhat below the choir and it was decided to create direct access, the main apse was opened up and a new entrance was installed here. A new choir was built on the opposite side. The frescoes (around 1100), created under the influence of Byzantine art, are especially fine. Their theme is the Last Judgement. The stucco reliefs are also worth taking a look at. Figures of saints are depicted on the frescoes in the oratory of S. Benedetto.

Varenna's peaceful evening atmosphere

In the »Triangle« of Lago di Como

The point of departure is again ►Como. The first town reached on the S 583 along the shore is Torno, which has a splendid location on a rocky ledge. Among the numerous villas, **Villa Pliniana**, in a concealed position and only visible from the water, stands out despite the fact that it is not one of the two villas owned by Pliny the Younger. It was built in 1575 for Giovanni Anguissola. In its grounds however is the spring mentioned by Pliny in a letter to his friend Licinius that changes its water level on a daily basis. In the old centre of Torno stands the 12th-century Romanesque **church of S. Giovanni**, altered in the 15th century and in the Baroque period.

Torno

The narrow road along the shore now leads past picturesque villages to Bellagio.

Bellagio, the »pearl of Lario«, occupies the point of the narrow peninsula that divides Lago di Como into its two southern arms, Lago di Como and Lago di Lecco. There is a magnificent view from here of all three arms of the lake as well as their Alpine perimeter. There are

**✷ ✷
Bellagio**

ferry connections to Menaggio and Varenna. The Romans recognized the favourable location and founded the settlement of Bilacus (»double lake«) here. In the 19th century the small fishing village was discovered by wealthy summer holidaymakers. Within a short time magnificent villas and palaces of the nobility were built along both lakeshores. Because of this, today Bellagio is not only the lake's highest-class tourist destination, but also a highlight for both scenery and art. **Borgo** (the town centre) on the western side of the peninsula has retained its medieval townscape; stepped alleys lead up to the 12th-century Romanesque **basilica of S. Giacomo**, which was remodelled in the 17th century and possesses an altarpiece (around 1500) ascribed to Perugino. The tourist information office is housed in the tower.

★

Villa Serbelloni ►

Villa Serbelloni stands above the town. The core of the building goes back to a Renaissance palace built in 1492 by the fabulously wealthy noble Stanga family from Cremona. Today the villa is the elegant **Grand Hotel Villa Serbelloni** with a wonderful garden (guided tours, information tel. 0 31 95 02 16).

Also on the eastern shore is **Villa Giulia**, once the residence of King Leopold I of Belgium and still in private ownership.

Bellagio: the undisputed »pearl of Lario«, as the lake is also called

A second large villa lies on the western shore in the district of Loppia, on the road to Como. Villa Melzi was built with a magnificent garden from 1808 to 1815 to plans by Giocondo Albertolli. It was commissioned by Francesco Melzi d' Eril, who under Napoleon was leader of the Cisalpine Republic for a short time. The park, a mixture of an Italian and English garden, is furnished with statues and artificial caves. One of the many romantic stories centring on the villas of Lago di Como took place in Villa Melzi. The composer **Franz Liszt** and the married **Countess d' Agoult** spent some months here, and in 1837 their daughter Cosima was born, later the wife of the composer Richard Wagner. Opening times: March–Oct daily 9am–6.30pm.

★
◄ Villa Melzi

🕑

Villa Trivulzio, on whose grounds the 11th-century Romanesque **church of S. Maria di Loppia** stands, is also on the same side of the lake; the campanile dates from the 12th century.

From Bellagio it is possible to continue on to Erba (23km/14mi). The winding road passes through a valley of the Alpine foothills, Vallassina, as Bellagio's hinterland is known. The route passes the small holiday resort of Civenna (623m/2044ft) and near Magrelio the chapel of **Madonna del Ghisallo** (755m/2477ft), the patron saint of cyclists. In the chapel hang racing bikes, jerseys and pictures of cycling greats such as Eddy Merckx and Fausto Coppi. Passing through Asso, from which the whole valley gets its name, and Canzo the route continues to the industrial town of Erba, from where it is 17km/11mi to Lecco (see above) and 15km/9.5mi to ►Como.

Vallassina

★ Lago di Garda · Lake Garda

Regions: Lombardy, Veneto, Trentino - Alto Adige
Area: 370 sq km/230 sq mi

Altitude of lake: 65m/213ft

Population: 160,000

This area was described by the Venetians as »magnifica patria« (»wonderful fatherland«), by Goethe as »a delightful spectacle«, and by the Roman poet Catullus as »a star for the eye«: Lago di Garda, known as Benaco in Latin. Here, in the foothills of the Alps near the Italian border, northern Europeans find the fulfilment of their dreams about the radiant light of the south.

With an area of 370 sq km/145 sq mi, Lago di Garda is the largest and probably the most diverse of Italy's lakes. In the ice ages great glaciers gouged out its bed, which is 52km/32mi long, between 2km and 17km (1–10mi) wide and up to 346m/1135ft deep. The Marmitte dei Giganti, famous glacial cauldrons near Nago (see below, Torbole), remain from this era. Every year five million visitors, half of them from Germany but many from the UK, come to Lago di

Italy's largest lake

▶ VISITING LAGO DI GARDA

INFORMATION

Garda
I AT
Lungolago Regina Adelaide 13
Tel. 0 45 6 27 03 84
Fax 0 45 7 25 67 20
www.garda.com

Gargnano
Consorzio Riviera dei Limoni
Via Oliva 32
Tel. 03 65 79 11 72
Fax 03 65 79 14 84
www.rivieradeilimoni.it

Riva
I.A.T.
Via Verdi 1
Tel. 0 18 54 5 70 11
Fax 0 18 54 5 95 75
www.turismoinliguria.it

BOATS

As many of the places on the lake look their best from the water, a boat trip is one of the highlights of a trip to Lago di Garda. Ferries connect all the important places on the lake, with a choice between the faster jetfoils (aliscafi) and the more leisurely steamers. In July and August daily lake cruises operate.

WHERE TO EAT

▶ Moderate

Agli Angeli
Via Dosso 7
Gardone Riviera
Tel. 03 65 2 08 32
www.agliangeli.com, closed Mon
Cosy trattoria in the centre of Gardone; reservation recommended, especially if you want to sit outside.

La Forgia
Via Calle 1
Lazise
Tel. 04 57 58 02 87
A restaurant particularly known for its fish dishes, in the old quarter near the lakeside promenade. The young waiters are quick and friendly.

Miralago
Piazza Cozzaglio
Pieve
Tel. 03 65 95 30 01
In this restaurant the view is so spectacular that you could almost forget your food: Miralago lies in Pieve on the Tremosine plateau on the edge of a rocky precipice.

Trattoria Antica Contrada
Via Colombare 23
Sirmione
Tel. 03 09 90 43 69
Closed Mon, Tue midday
Restaurant in the upper price
bracket. International dishes, but
also outstandingly cooked lake fish.
Varied wine list, menus between
25 and 40 €.

La Campagnola
Via Brunati 11
Salò
Tel. 0 36 52 21 53
Closed Mon, Tue midday
Try the Campagnola's fish from
Lago di Garda: trout, tench, pike or
whitefish. There is also a wide
selection of meat dishes and vegeta-
bles, all cooked using the excellent
local olive oil.

WHERE TO STAY
► Luxury
Palace Hotel Villa Cortine
Via Grotte 6
Sirmione
Tel. 03 09 90 58 90
Fax 03 09 1 63 90, 55 rooms
www.palacehotelvillacortine.it
Luxury hotel in an old villa set in a
park full of beautiful trees; the main
building dates from 1957; exclusive
furnishings, excellent service. Swimming pool, tennis court and private
beach.

► Mid-range
Duomo
Lungolago Zanardelli 63
Salò
Tel. 03 65 2 10 26
Fax 03 65 2 10 27, 22 rooms
www.hotelduomosalo.it
Well-run hotel on the shores of the
lake; prettily furnished rooms,
good service, restaurant.

Flaminia
Piazza Flaminia 8
Tel. 03 09 1 60 78
Fax 03 09 1 61 93, 45 rooms
This well-kept hotel with a lovely
sunny terrace is in the middle of the
old quarter right by the lake.

Montefiori
Via dei Lauri 8, Morgnaga
Gardone Riviera
Tel. 03 65 29 02 35
Fax 03 65 2 14 88
www.hotelvillemontefiori.it, 31 rooms
This hotel in a historic building has a
particularly fine setting and a lake
view; park, swimming pool, restau-
rant.

Villa Paradiso
Via Zanardelli 254, Gardone Riviera
Tel. 0 36 52 18 83
Fax 0 36 52 9 48 11, 36 rooms
www.villaparadiso.com
Centrally located, very pretty hotel
with a little park, swimming pool and
its own parking spaces.

Villa Sofia
Via Cornella 9, Gardone Riviera
Tel. 03 65 2 27 29
Fax 03 65 2 23 69
www.savoypalace.it, 30 rooms
One of the newest additions to the
hotel scene on the lake, in an old villa
with magnificent grounds and a view
to die for from the upper floors.

► Budget
Panoramica
Via del Panorama 28, Salò
Tel. 03 65 4 14 35/6
Fax 03 65 52 12 10, 20 rooms
www.panoramica.org
This reasonably priced hotel enjoys an
elevated location outside Salò, from
where there is a beautiful view of the
lake; gardens and parking.

Garda. In the summer months mass tourism makes its mark here more than on any of the other Italian lakes. It is the clear, pure lake water that holds the attraction for many visitors. The section between Riva and Torbole draws **windsurfers and sailors**, as the winds are ideal here: from midnight to midday the mountain wind, called »sover« or »tramontana«, blows from Riva towards the south; in the afternoon it gives way to the stronger »ora«, a southerly wind. The surrounding hills and mountains constitute excellent terrain for hiking and biking.

✶ ✶
Scenery

The distinctive charm of Lago di Garda results from its location on the borders of the Alps, its markedly mild climate and variety of vegetation, which gives a first taste of Mediterranean flora. The narrow northern part of the lake thrusts like a fjord between the steep rocky walls of the Monte Baldo massif (2218m/7277ft) to the east and the Brescian Alps to the west. The **most northerly olive trees in Italy** grow here. To the south, the lake broadens to a small sea and extends far into the plain of the river Po. Fig trees and vines cover the flatter and more densely populated western and southern lakeshores. Lemons were once cultivated here on a large scale (▶ Baedeker Special p.79). Oleander, mimosa, acacia, hibiscus, bougainvillaea and palms also flourish.

The villas and gardens that grace the other north Italian lakes are less in evidence on Lago di Garda. This is partly because the terrain on the banks of the lake is not suitable for large villas. A further reason is that cardinals preferred to build their country residences on the shores of Lago di Como, land ruled by the conservative Spanish Habsburgs, rather than on more liberal Venetian territory. The untouched scenery of Lago di Garda elicited the enthusiasm of travellers such as **Goethe**, who praised it as a magnificent natural spectacle on his Italian journey in September 1786. He was not the only famous person who was attracted to the shores of the lake: Dante, Franz Kafka, Rainer Maria Rilke, André Gide, Stendhal and the controversial Gabriele d'Annunzio, whose Vittoriale in Gardone is open to visitors (▶ Baedeker Special p.202), also found inspiration here.

? DID YOU KNOW …?

■ In 1432 the Venetians made enormous efforts to improve the defences of Lago di Garda: in the space of two weeks, 2000 oxen pulled a naval force up the river Adige and then overland up to the Nago Pass. The six galleys and 25 smaller warships were then rolled down to the shore at Torbole on thousands of logs.

The oldest traces of human settlement are the remains of prehistoric houses built on stilts between Desenzano and Lonato and on Lago di Ledro, and rock carvings on the slopes of Monte Baldo near Torri del Benaco. From the 2nd century BC the **Romans** systematically cultivated the area. In 1405 **Venice** took control of Lago di Garda and Verona, ruling there until 1797, when Napoleon conquered Lom-

The scenery of Lago di Garda has a beguiling Mediterranean character

bardy and Venetia. From now on the fate of Lago di Garda was tied to that of the rest of northern Italy. In 1866 Lombardy and Veneto became part of the newly founded Kingdom of Italy, but Trentino and Riva remained part of Austria until the end of the First World War.

Benito Mussolini, il Duce, gave the little town of Salò a place in the history books during the Second World War, when he proclaimed the Repubblica Sociale Italiana there in 1943. In 1945 he was shot by partisans on Lago di Como while fleeing towards Switzerland. When Italy became a republic in 1946, Lago di Garda was divided into three regions: the northern part (Torbole and Riva) belongs to Trentino - Alto Adige, the Brescian shore between Limone and Sirmione to Lombardy and the Veronese shore (from Peschiera to Malcesine and far beyond) to Veneto.

Highlights Lago di Garda

Sirmione
Don't miss the picturesque old quarter and above all the Rocca Scaligera, the finest waterside castle in northern Italy.
▶ page 193

Monte Baldo
A hike up Monte Baldo, which can also be reached by cable car from Malcesine, is

rewarding not just for the wonderful view, but also for the rare mountain flora.
▶ page 189

Gardone Riviera
The most elegant resort on the lake has a remarkable attraction: the home of the eccentric Gabriele d'Annunzio.
▶ page 200

Eastern Shore · Gardesana Orientale

Riva

Riva, a town that was settled in Roman times, and neighbouring Torbole lie sheltered from the wind in a bay at the north end of Lago di Garda. It is overshadowed by the 374m/1227ft Monte Brione. Thanks to its strategically important location as a trading post on the route to the Alpine passes, the town was much contested in the Middle Ages and underwent frequent changes of ownership. With the northern part of the lake, it did not become part of the Kingdom of Italy until 1919. Today Riva with its 13,000 inhabitants is the second-largest town on the lake and a centre of tourism. Despite being extended and rebuilt many times, the little town has retained its medieval core with alleys and squares adorned by arcades. The borgo centres around **Piazza III. Novembre**, which is bordered to the east by the 13th-century Torre Apponale and to the west by Palazzo Pretorio (c1370) and the Palazzo Municipale (1475–82). Further east is the moated castle built in the 12th century by the della Scala family. Today it is home to the **Museo Civico** (municipal museum; opening times: Tue–Sun 10am–12.30pm, 1.30pm–6pm, July–Sept also Mondays).

It is also worth visiting the domed church **dell' Inviolata**, which was built in 1603 to plans by a Portuguese architect (at the end of Viale Roma on the road to Arco). The interior is extravagantly decorated with stucco and frescoes. From here it is about 3km/2mi (signposted) to the Cascata Varone, a waterfall that drops almost 100m/330ft through a rock funnel. Opening times: Jan, Feb, Nov, Dec daily 10am–5pm, March, April, Sept, Oct daily 9am–5pm, May–Aug 9am–7pm.

Cascata Varone ▶

Nago-Torbole

Riva's neighbour, Nago-Torbole, a town at the mouth of the river Sarca, is the **European windsurfing capital** thanks to the favourable winds that blow there. The **parish church of S. Andrea** stands on elevated ground. The beautiful painting on the high altar, *The Martyrdom of St Andrew*, is a work of Giambettino Cignaroli.

Torbole lies sheltered from the wind at the north end of the lake

From Torbole a trip to the Marmitte dei Giganti, »giants' cauldrons«, is recommended. These enormous holes in the steep rocks can be found about 3km/2mi from Torbole on the road to Nago, surrounded by olive trees. They were formed in the ice age when rubble that was pushed along by glaciers hollowed out the rock.

◀ Marmitte dei Giganti

A few miles further south lies the Riviera degli Ulivi, a section of the lakeshore known as the »Olive Riviera«. The picturesque resort Malcesine grew up under the crenellated walls of a castle of the della Scala family. The fortification crowns a rocky promontory that falls steeply to the lake. The **Castello Scaligero** was constructed in the 13th and 14th centuries, and extended in the 17th century. It consists of a lower and an upper residence and three courtyards, and is home to a small **museum** with collections on natural history and fishing (opening times: April–Sept 9.30am–8pm). Until the end of Venetian rule in 1797 the 16th-century **Palazzo dei Capitani** on the harbour was the seat of the capitano, the leader of the league of lake communities and Venetian governor.

✱ **Malcesine**

⊕

It is worth making a trip up Monte Baldo to see rare plants which grow nowhere else. From Malcesine a cable car goes up to the summit from April to October. In the botanical garden below the summit at a height of 1200m/3950ft some 600 different Alpine plants can be admired.

✱ **Monte Baldo**

The little harbour town of Torri del Benaco, which takes its name from the Latin word for Lago di Garda, is situated on a particularly

Torri del Benaco

beautiful stretch of the Riviera degli Ulivi opposite Maderno. In summer a car ferry operates between the two towns daily from 8am to 7pm. The powerful battlemented **castle** was built in 1383 by the della Scala family to protect the harbour. The little **museum** in the castle presents the history of fishing on Lago di Garda and the processing of olives (opening times: daily 9.30am–6.30pm). One of the last limonaie, hothouses for growing lemons, is by the south wall of the castello (►Baedeker Special p.78). At the centre of Torri del Benaco lies the pretty harbour, framed by typical old fishermen's houses and the little church, Chiesa della Trinità, which has 14th-century frescoes and is now a war memorial. At the edge of the town the **Torre di Berengario** commemorates Berengar I (murdered in 924), who was styled »king of Italy«.

The beauty of the Punta S. Vigilio, a outlying ridge of Monte Baldo that forms a little peninsula near Garda, is best appreciated from the lake. The exclusive **Hotel San Vigilio** has had such eminent guests as Winston Churchill and Prince Charles. The privately owned Villa Guarienti and its lovely park occupy the tip of the peninsula. The villa was built in about 1540 by Michele Sanmicheli for Agostino di Brenzone.

★
Punta S. Vigilio

Garda, a town on a site that was already settled in the Stone Age and has given its name to the lake, lies in a broad bay surrounded by mountain slopes and groves of cypress and olive trees. Its landmark is the 294m/965ft-high **Rocca di Garda**, on which Theoderic, king of the Ostrogoths, is thought to have built a castle in the 5th century. With its medieval town centre and long lakeside promenade, Garda attracts many visitors. On pretty Piazza Catullo stands the **Palazzo dei Capitani**, built in the 13th and 14th centuries in the Venetian style.

Garda

The parish church, **S. Maria Maggiore**, in the southern part of the town dates from the 16th century, but its campanile is older. The adjacent cloister originally belonged to the 14th-century monastery Chiostro della Pieve. It is worth driving on from here to the **pilgrimage church Madonna della Corona**, which seems to cling to a rock 600m/2000ft above the valley of the Adige.

Bardolino is an attractive holiday resort and the centre of the wine region of the same name. The main types of grape used for dry, ruby-red Bardolino are Corvina, Rondinella and Molinara (up to 20%), from which the better-known Valpolicella is made. The well-marked **Strada del Vino** (»wine route«) leads to about 50 wine estates in the hinterland. Information is available in the tourist office. Bardolino possesses two significant churches: **S. Severo**, a Romanesque basilica, is in the town centre. Its east end with three apses is

★
Bardolino

← *Windsurfers love Lago di Garda*

A good harvest ensures that the next wine festival in Bardolino will be a success

especially impressive. The church was built in the 12th century, and the crypt that has been excavated behind the altar dates from the 9th century. Higher up, within a courtyard is **S. Zeno** church. This small barrel-vaulted building was erected in the 9th century under Carolingian rule on a cross-shaped ground plan; remains of the old frescoes can still be seen on the walls.

In **Cisano** (about 2km/1mi south) the **Museo dell'Olio** (»oil museum«) is devoted to the processing of olives and sells olive oil. Opening times: Mon–Sat 9am–12.30pm, 2.30pm–7pm, Sun 9am–12.30pm.

Lazise

Lazise, a holiday resort at the southern end of the Riviera degli Ulivi, has an extremely charming medieval town centre and a **picturesque harbour** lined by restaurants. Here are the 12th-century Romanesque **church of S. Nicolò** and the **Dogana**, the former Venetian customs house dating from the 16th century, now used for exhibitions and concerts. The magnificent 15th-century **Castello Scaligero** is a short distance away.

✷ Canevaworld ►

Canevaworld (3km/2mi south of Lazise), one of the largest water parks in Italy, ensures that all members of the family enjoy their holiday. The big attraction, apart from the wave pool and diving towers, are the gigantic water slides. The Movie Studios with various shows are part of the complex. Internet: www.canevaworld.it

Parco Natura Viva

Parco Natura Viva (8km/5mi south-east of Lazise) is actually two parks with separate entrances. In the **Safari Park**, where visitors must stay in their cars, giraffes, zebras and rhinoceros roam free. The second park, **Parco Faunistico**, can be explored on foot. It is a zoological garden with kangaroos, monkeys, hippos, birds and life-size replicas of dinosaurs. Opening times: Feb–Nov 9am–6pm. Internet: www.parconaturaviva.it

✷ Gardaland

Gardaland, a large and popular amusement park between Lazise and Peschiera, is the **»little brother« of Disney World**. Its attractions include a large dolphin pool, acrobatic performances and adventures such as a pirate ship, a Wild West village and a Valley of the Kings in the style of ancient Egypt. There are also a roller coaster, carousels, water rides and sports. Opening times: high season daily 10am–6pm; summer until 11pm.

A strong 16th-century fortress with bastions and moats dominates Peschiera, a site settled from early times at the south-east end of Lago di Garda, where the Mincio flows out of the lake. On Mondays a market is held in the old quarter.

Peschiera

The narrow Sirmione peninsula projects 4km/2.5mi into the lake between the Gulf of Desenzano and Peschiera. Colombare, Lugana and Rovizza on the main banks of the lake also belong to Sirmione, but

★ ★
Sirmione

Sirmione: romantic backdrop for a stroll through the old quarter

ROCCA SCALIGERA IN SIRMIONE

✶ ✶ This mighty castle built by the della Scala dynasty around the year 1300 is the emblem of the town and at the same time the entrance defending the old quarter. The lakeside castle is the best example of the art of military architecture on Lago di Garda. The castle does not show its age – the centuries seem to have passed without leaving a mark on it.

⏰ Opening times:
Apr–Sept Tue–Sun 8.30am–7pm
Nov–March Tue–Sun 8.30am–4.30pm

① Castle walls
The construction techniques used on the castle are remarkable, as the walls consist both of bricks, which were manufactured locally, and stone quarried nearby on Cortine hill.

② Gate and drawbridge
The drawbridge that was once installed on the castle gateway has now been replaced by a fixed bridge. However, the ingenious method of raising the drawbridge by means of levers can still be clearly seen on the gateway. When it was closed the long levers were retracted into recesses that look like embrasures and are visible above the gate. The fulcrum of the levers was within the recesses, and at the ends they were attached to the bridge with chains. Thus the inner end of the lever was pulled downwards, and the bridge was raised.

③ Inner courtyard
The courtyard has a somewhat gloomy appearance, as it is completely enclosed by massive walls.

④ Tower complex
The corner towers of the castle are linked by battlements that are reached by climbing steps. From here there is access to the 47m/154ft-high main tower, the Masti, from where there is a superb view of the southern end of the lake.

⑤ Harbour
The massive walled and crenellated castle harbour is unique in all of Europe as a feature of a fortification. It once served to defend and provision the town, but is now a tranquil place where water lilies grow.

Today thousands of tourists cross the bridge to the castle, a site once defended

From the Mastio, the 47m/
154ft-high tower, there is a fine
view of Sirmione and the
Grotte di Catullo (shown here)

© Baedeker

A romantic scene
ke this makes for
pleasant evening

The method of raising the drawbridge by means of levers can clearly be seen on the castle gateway

its picturesque historic centre lies at the very tip of the peninsula, where up to 10,000 visitors per day have to be handled in summer and at weekends. The only cars that are permitted to pass the gate of the borgo are those of the locals and of visitors who have booked an overnight stay within the walls of the old quarter.

✱ ✱
◀ Rocca Scaligera

The della Scala family used this strategically favourable site to build the Rocca Scaligera castle here in about 1250. It is considered to be the **most beautiful waterside castle in northern Italy**. Drawbridges in the south and west give access. Visitors can view local finds from the Roman and medieval periods in a little **museum** and walk around the surprisingly dark castle interior with its stairways, towers, courtyards and battlements. The harbour, which is almost completely encircled by walls, was the eastern harbour of Sirmione in Roman times. The della Scala family integrated it into the fortress. A superb view is the reward for climbing up the 47m/ 154ft main tower. Opening times: Apr–Sept Tue–Sun 8.30am–7pm, Nov–March Tue–Sun 8.30am–4.30pm.

Somewhat north of the Rocca Scaligera stands the 15th-century church of **S. Maria Maggiore**, which has frescoes from the same period. The Boiola spring, from which sulphurous water flows at a temperature of 69°C/156°F, was known in antiquity. The **thermal baths** are housed in a plain modern building on the west side of the peninsula.

Grotte di Catullo

The Grotte di Catullo, an archaeological attraction at the end of the Sirmione peninsula, can be reached either with a tourist mini-train that departs from the thermal baths or on foot. On the way there don't miss a visit to the little church of **S. Pietro in Mavino**, which was mentioned as early as 760. It is hidden in an olive grove between the town and the archaeological zone. The bulky ruin of the Grotte di Catullo stands among fine old olive trees at the extreme tip of the peninsula. It has not been fully excavated, and according to tradition is the country house of the **Roman poet Catullus** (c87–54 BC). Archaeologists, however, put a date 200 years later on the remains of these buildings, which occupy a wonderful site on white cliffs above the lake. The enormous size of the complex, over 20,000 sq m/215,000 sq ft, makes it the largest of its kind in all of Italy.

It was built around the year AD 150 and probably collapsed in the 4th century. Including the northern and southern parts attached to the villa, it is a rectangular site measuring 167m x 105m (183yd x 115yd). As the complex was built on uneven ground, lower floors were built or cut into the rock in places. It is essentially these lower storeys that the visitor sees today, as nothing remains of the two floors above with their rooms of state. Lead pipes laid on the lake

A thoroughly Italian sight: the Porto Vecchio of Desenzano, →
lined by old palazzi

bed supplied a large swimming pool with sulphurous water from the Boiola spring. A small **museum** at the entrance to the building displays the remains of pediments and frescoes, as well as drawings reconstructing the villa. There is a particularly good view from here of the southern half of the lake, but to get the best all-round view of the ruins, take a boat trip around the peninsula. Opening times: March–Oct Tue–Sun 9am–7pm.

Western Shore · Gardesana Occidentale

Desenzano

Desenzano, with 20,000 residents **the largest town on Lago di Garda**, was a significant centre of trade from Roman times and bears the marks of tourism much less than the neighbouring towns Sirmione and Salò. Its large modern harbour is the base for the big ferries that sail to Riva at the north end of the lake. There is also a pretty little old harbour, beyond which the historic quarter with its merchants' houses rises up the slope. Above it are the remains of a castle dating from the 14th and 15th centuries. The parish church of **S. Maria Maddalena** was built in about 1586; a *Last Supper* by Giovanni Domenico Tiepolo (around 1760) adorns its Chapel of the Sacrament. The **Villa Romana** in Via degli Scavi to the north-west of the harbour is a reminder of the foundation of the town in Roman times. It was constructed in the 4th century AD on the walls of an older building and is famous for its floor mosaics, some of which are very well preserved and show geometric ornamentation, hunting scenes and mythological motifs. Further finds are on display in a small museum. Opening times: early March–late Oct Tue–Sun 8.30am– 7pm, early Nov–late Feb Sat 8.30am–5pm.

! **Baedeker TIP**

Lakeside market

Looking around a market is always a pleasure. In Desenzano a market is held on the lakeshore promenade on Tuesdays. All manner of goods are on sale – not just food, but also clothes.

Side trip to the south
Solferino

»In Solferino the idea of the **Red Cross** was born«, proclaim the place-name signs of this village, 18km/11mi from Desenzano. In 1859 a battle took place here between the Italians, French and Austrians, at the end of which over 40,000 dead and wounded were left to their fate. **Henri Dunant**, a Swiss citizen, was staying in the region at that time. The appalling plight of the victims gave him the idea, for which he received the Nobel Prize for Peace in 1901, of founding an organization to help them. Later the international Red Cross emerged from it. In the centre of Solferino the **Museo Storico Risorgimentale** takes the war of 1859 as its theme (closed for renovations). From here an avenue of cypresses leads to the **Chiesa Ossario**, a charnel house in which 1413 skulls and the bones of about 7000 more victims of the war are kept. There is a fine view from **Piazza Castello**, where a square medieval tower, the rocca, rises to a height of 23m/75ft. The parish church of **S. Nicola** (1572) lies just outside the village.

The Valtenesi to the north of Desenzano is fertile, hilly country where olives and grapes are cultivated. While **Chiaretto** is a lively cherry-red summer wine, the ruby-red **Groppello**, which can mature for several years, is a wine of character. On many of the hills, fortifications or the remains of them testify to a turbulent history. This region is densely populated. Between Desenzano and Salò the main road no longer runs along the shore of Lago di Garda; instead the holiday resorts on the lake are reached via small roads running down to its banks. From **Punta Belvedere** there is a good view of the little islands S. Biagio and Conigli, as well as the bay of **S. Felice del Benaco**, a town devoted to tourism and agriculture which is the centre of the S. Fermo peninsula and has formed a single township with Portese since 1928.

* **Valtenesi**

Close to the S. Fermo lies the Isola di Garda, with a length of 1km/0.5mi the **largest island in Lago di Garda**. Complete with a stately villa built in the late 19th century and a lush park, the island belongs to the Borghese family.

Isola di Garda

The busy little town of Salò is situated at the end of a deep bay at the foot of Monte S. Bartolomeo (568m/1864ft). Under Venetian rule it was the political centre of the western shore. The town made headlines between 1943 and 1945 when it was the seat of the Repubblica Sociale, a German-backed regime led by the dictator Benito Mussolini, who had been forced out of Rome.

* **Salò**

The huge cathedral of S. Maria Annunziata, which was built between 1453 and 1502, is the **most significant example of late Gothic architecture on Lago di Garda**. Its façade (1506–09) remained incomplete. Antonio della Porta and Gaspare da Cairano from Ticino were responsible for the beautiful entrance adorned with figures. The interior was the work of artists from Brescia and Venice, and the illusionist painting of the nave is by Tommaso Sandrino.

* ◄ **S. Maria Annunziata**

In 1901 the town was severely damaged by an earthquake, after which the broad lakeshore promenade Lungolago Zanardelli was built. It is the site of the 14th-century town hall, **Palazzo della Podestà**, which is joined by an arcade to the **Palazzo della Magnifica Patria**, a 16th-century structure that houses the **Museo Civico** and its archaeological collection (opening times: Tue–Sun 10am–noon, 5pm–7pm). The old quarter lies behind Piazza della Vittoria. In Barbarano, 2km/1mi to the north-east of the centre, stands the magnificent **Palazzo Martinengo**, which was built in 1577 for the Marchese Sforza Pallavicino. It is visible only from the lake.

☉

The section of lake just beyond Salò and extending as far as Gargnano is known as the »Brescia Riviera«. The mountains close in on the

* **Riviera Bresciana**

Kings and emperors spent the summer in Gardone, one of the most exclusive places on Lago di Garda since the late 19th century

shore and the road again runs right by the lake amid luxuriant tropical and subtropical vegetation. In the late 19th century wealthy travellers discovered this part of the lake, as a number of palatial hotels, fine villas and exotically planted gardens and parks still show.

✷ Gardone Riviera

High-class palatial hotels such as the venerable Grand Hotel with its large terrace on the lake and splendid villas give Gardone its reputation as the **most elegant resort on Lago di Garda**, a place that has played host to such notables as King Farouk of Egypt, Emperor Wilhelm II of Germany and Empress Elisabeth of Austria. Fine hotels, aristocratic summer residences and magnificent villas still mark the appearance of Gardone. The historic centre, Gardone Sopra, nestles on green slope above the Gardesana (Corso Zanardelli). The mountains shelter the town from the cool tramontana winds and give it the **Mediterranean climate** that made it possible to establish a unique botanical garden here. To the south Gardone and Salò almost merge: concealed behind palms, cypresses and oleanders, palazzi form a link between the two towns. The main attraction of Gardone Sopra, however, is the Vittoriale degli Italiani, the »Victory Monument of the Italians«. This is the last **residence of Gabriele d'Annunzio** (1863–1938, ► Baedeker Special p.202), a poet, »war hero« and supporter of Mussolini who bought Villa Cargnacco in 1921. He bequeathed the complex consisting of a villa and park to his »beloved Italy« under the name »Vittoriale«.

✷ Vittoriale degli Italiani ►

The main house, today a museum, contains a host of mementoes to the controversial and eccentric d'Annunzio, who owed his fame in part to a liaison with the actress Eleonora Duse (►Famous People). The Vittoriale is also home to a small open-air theatre that is used in summer. At the highest point in the park stands a mausoleum containing the sarcophagus of d'Annunzio in the circle of his legionaries from Fiume. A domed building houses the biplane in which he flew to Vienna in 1918 in a daring stunt to scatter anti-Austrian leaflets over the city. Cypresses surround an unusual monument: the bows of the cruiser *Puglia*. In 1919 some of its crew were killed in an operation near Fiume (today called Rijeka). The front part of the war ship was detached and embedded in a wall of the Vittoriale. D'Annunzio's **house**, known as the Priora, can be visited only as part of a tour. Expect to spend some time in a queue, but the strangeness of the experience makes it worthwhile. Every room has its own name (Study of the Maimed, Globe Room, etc) and individual furnishings. The gloomy interior is crammed with an array of furniture, statues, pictures, cushions, aircraft propellers and much more. Opening times: Vittoriale Apr–Sept daily 8.30am–8pm, Oct–March daily 9am–5pm; guided tours of d'Annunzio's house and Museo della Guerra: Apr–Sept Tue–Sun 9.30am–7pm, Oct–March 9am–1pm, 2pm–5pm; www.vittoriale.it.

Lower down the slope from the Vittoriale and a few minutes' walk away, the Giardino Botanico is a quite different kind of idyll. It was initiated by the Austrian doctor **Artur Hruska**, who began to lay out ponds and watercourses in 1910. He planted trees and many botanical souvenirs that he brought back from numerous trips around the world. For decades the garden was neglected and largely overgrown, but in the 1980s the Viennese artist **André Heller** took over the garden and breathed new life into it. Today sculptures from Heller's private collection have been placed among a great variety of subtropical, tropical and alpine plants. Opening times: March–Oct daily 9am–7pm.

★
◄ Giardino Botanico

The twin municipality of Toscolano-Maderno lies at the foot of the 1582m/5191ft Monte Pizzocolo on the delta of the Fiume Toscolano, which supplied the water for the local paper industry right into the 20th century. In Maderno the Romanesque church of S. Andrea, built around 1130, has a late Gothic campanile (1469) and an impressive doorway with elaborate sculptural decoration. A Renaissance choir replaced the apse in the 16th century. Inside the church the capitals of the massive piers are also masterpieces of Lombard sculpture; the murals date from about 1500.

Toscolano-Maderno

★
◄ S. Andrea

The neighbouring parish church of **S. Ercolano** was built in the 18th century. The church of **SS. Pietro e Paolo** in Toscolano (1584) has beautiful 17th-century frescoes by the Venetian artist Andrea Celesti.

Gargnano is a quiet little town. A number of cannonballs now embedded in the façades of palazzi on the harbour are a reminder of the bombardment of Gargnano by Austrian gunboats in 1866 during

Gargnano

ECCENTRIC AND DRAMATIC

Who was Gabriele d'Annunzio, the man whose mausoleum still attracts 300,000 visitors each year and who gave names such as Study of the Maimed and Leper's Room to the rooms of his villa?

To set the record straight: the man who owned this villa saw himself as a leper in the medieval sense of the word, as one who had been »touched by God«, i.e. a holy person. He was an incomparably **eccentric man**, possessed by an unquenchable thirst for life, with a liking for opium and beautiful women and, moreover, was endlessly self-regarding and vain. Gabriele d'Annunzio (1863–1938) was a major Italian poet with a powerful gift of expression, a »war hero« and a successful Don Juan. He described himself as an »interpreter of human madness«. Visitors to his famous residence on Lago di Garda, the Vittoriale degli Italiani in Gardone Riviera, can hardly fail to ask themselves whether he was not merely an interpreter, but instead a representative of human madness. From 1921 until his death d'Annunzio inhabited this strange villa in the company of his wife and several mistresses. When he had had enough of himself, he retreated to the Leper's Room and engaged in ascetic meditation. A few days before buying the villa he had ended a 16-month occupation of Fiume (now Rijeka) which he undertook on his own responsibility: in 1919, in contravention of the armistice agreement, he occupied the town, which had been awarded to Yugoslavia, with a small group of armed men in order to reclaim it for Italy. He had carried out another crazy military adventure on 9 August 1918, when he flew his biplane over the enemy city of Vienna and scattered anti-Austrian pamphlets.

One-of-a-kind eccentric, war hero or major poet? D'Annunzio polarizes opinion.

Vittoriale degli Italiani

»Life is very boring without war fever«, wrote d'Annunzio, and showed his nationalist fighting credentials by filling the house and gardens of his »Vittoriale« with mi-

Self-dramatization, even in death: the poet's grandiose tomb

litary equipment. The strangest memorial there is probably the bows of the warship xxxPugliayy, which he once commanded. The pinnacle of his self-dramatization, however, is the villa, into which he crammed an unbelievable quantity of extraordinary works of art, knick-knacks and appalling kitsch. In the Chamber of Relics, for example, he kept not only countless statues of various saints, prophets and gods but also the dented steering-wheel of a motorboat in which a friend met his death. His »workshop«, i.e. his poet's study, can be entered only with a bow, as the doorway is so low: a measure to enforce awe in the face of his work. The Labyrinth Corridor holds 2000 books from his library of 30,000 volumes. Amongst all these dark, mostly wood-panelled rooms, the only one that makes a friendlier impression is the dining room (Cheli Room), which is designed in Art Deco style with a heavenlike ceiling in blue and gold and wall decorations in red, black and gold. The name Cheli commemorates d'Annunzio's large deceased tortoise, a replica of which with its genuine shell stands on the dining table.

The most disconcerting testimony to his self-glorification is the **marble mausoleum** in the park. At the centre of a viewing terrace stands a majestic sarcophagus, with the marble caskets of his war comrades from Fiume radiating out from it. This strange shrine to death is a sight strongly reminiscent of fascist architecture, an impression that is not deceptive: in political terms, too, d'Annunzio felt drawn to Mussolini even at a time when the later Duce was an unknown socialist.

Literary works

D'Annunzio's association with fascism, his dissolute and unconventional lifestyle and egocentric nature brought his significant body of work as a poet into discredit. He published his first book of poetry at the age of just 16. He later worked as an editor of *La Tribuna*, published short prose works, hymns and elegies that were suffused with pathos and in 1889 wrote a novel entitled *Il Piacere* (translated as *The Child of Pleasure*) that was influenced by Nietzsche and made him famous. He also wrote plays, for example *Città Morta* (*The Dead City*). One of d'Annunzio's strengths was his receptiveness to the literary trends of the period, especially French Symbolism. He also espoused a pagan cult of beauty and the senses, and was one of Italy's most controversial poets. To this day he polarizes opinion: was he a gifted poet, a fascist, a vain libertine, a saint, or even a leper, as he described himself?

the struggle for Italian unification. **Palazzo Feltrinelli** north of the harbour was the seat of Mussolini's »Republic of Salò« from 1943 to 1945; Milan University now holds summer schools here. **Villa Feltrinelli** (1km/0.5mi north), now the Grand Hotel, accommodated the Duce. In the district of S. Francesco in the south of the town a visit to the church of the same name, built in 1289 by Franciscan monks, is recommended. In the 17th and 18th centuries it underwent a Baroque makeover, with the exception of the façade; the pretty adjacent cloister was not altered, however. The distinctive feature of the church are its sculpted capitals portraying the leaves and fruit of the lemon and orange trees that were once cultivated here. Opening times: end of July to end of August daily 10am–1pm, 3pm–7pm, rest of year 9am–6pm.

Villa Bettoni ▶

Villa Bettoni in Bogliaco, a southern district of Gargnano, was built in about 1750 and modelled on Schönbrunn Palace in Vienna. Its show façade can unfortunately only be seen from the water. The large and elegant gardens, however, separated from the villa by the main road, can be enjoyed by everyone. They were laid out between 1764 and 1767 to designs by the Tuscan architect **Amerigo Vincenzo Pierallini**.

Gardesana Occidentale

The Brescian Riviera ends just beyond Gargnano. From this point the lakeside road, the famous Gardesana Occidentale, runs along the slopes above the lake at an elevation until it reaches Riva. Built in 1931, the road is a daring feat of engineering that is very narrow and curving in places.

Side trip into the hinterland

A side trip into the extensive hinterland of Lago di Garda is extremely rewarding here. North of Gargnano a very steep side road branches off to the **plateau of Tignale**. Close to Gardola the pilgrimage chapel **Madonna di Monte Castello** stands majestically on a rocky outcrop. .It originated in the 13th and 14th centuries and was later remodelled in Baroque style. Late Gothic frescoes remain inside. North of Campione a mountain road turns off and leads through a narrow gorge to the pretty village of **Pieve**. This is an attractive hiking area where the views of the lake are vertiginous in places.

Limone

Stay on the main lakeside road to reach Limone, which occupies a sheltered bay below steep cliffs (► Baedeker Special p.78). In the summer months the old quarter here is hopelessly overcrowded. Beyond Limone is the border between Lombardy and Trentino, which belonged to Austria until 1919.

✳ Lago d'Idro

Highest lake in Lombardy

Between Lago d'Iseo and Lago di Garda lies the highest lake in Lombardy, the south Alpine Lago d' Idro, at an altitude of 368m/1207ft. It is only around 2km/0.5mi wide, up to 122m/400ft deep and

Gardesana Occidentale: a spectacular road along the lake with breathtaking views

10km/6mi long. Its long, narrow shape and the surrounding mountains give it the appearance of a fjord. In a few spots on the northern and eastern banks flat beaches offer good places to swim, although the water is colder than that of the less elevated Lago di Garda. Lago d'Idro is a popular destination thanks to its **facilities for water sports and day trips**, but it lacks the southern European mood and romantic atmosphere that make the larger lakes nearby so famous. Apart from a few camp sites there is little tourist infrastructure. The through road heads north on the western bank, with wonderful views, past Idro and Anfo to the town of Ponte Cafarro/Lodron. On the eastern bank it is possible to drive from Vantone to Vesta, but cliffs make the north-eastern bank of the lake impassable.

✳ Bagolino

The trip to the mountain village of Bagolino, 8km/5mi north-west of Lago d' Idro at 778m/2553ft, is worthwhile. Bagolino, which has been inhabited since the 10th century, has a very attractive historic centre and is famous for its **carnival**, which involves dances according to an ancient traditional ritual. The church of **S. Rocco** has a 15th-century cycle of frescoes. High above the centre of the village stands the 17th-century church of **S. Giorgio**.

✳ Lago d' Iseo · Lake Iseo

M/N 6/7

Provinces: Brescia and Bergamo   **Altitude of lake:** 185m/607ft
Area: 65 sq km/25 sq mi

Lago d' Iseo – also known as Sebino in Italian, from the Latin term Sebinus Lacus – nestles in the slopes of the southern Alpine foothills. The seventh-largest lake in Italy is about 25km/16mi long, on average 3km/2mi wide and up to 251m/824ft deep.

✳ Small lake with a large island

The neighbouring ►Valcamonica to the north-east and Lago d' Iseo form a single geographical unit. The foremost attraction of the lake is **Monte Isola**, an almost rectangular island which with an area of 4 sq km/1.5 sq mi and a circumference of some 8km/5mi is the largest island on any European lake.

✳ Scenery

The scenery on Lago d' Iseo is extremely varied. While the northern end of the lake extends into the Alpine region where the highest summit in the background is usually covered in snow, the southern shore is gently rolling country and in places actually completely flat. Here wine production is possible in the pleasantly mild climate. Fruit trees and olive groves grow on the less steep slopes.

Tourism is the most important source of income around the lake. Iseo and Sarnico are the main towns for holidaymakers. Monte Isola is busy with day trippers, but there are also a few hotels on the island for those who want to stay longer. Sailing and windsurfing are the principal sports on offer. Although the water quality in the lake is good and it is well stocked with fish, **swimming** in the inviting turquoise water is only possible in a few places, as the banks of the lake are mostly too steep.

Tour of the Lake

✳ Iseo

A tour of the lake begins in Iseo on the southern shore. This little town was protected by a wall in the Middle Ages and expanded in the 14th century. In the picturesque historic town centre, which is particularly lively at weekends, **Piazza Garibaldi** is bordered by arcaded walks. The 18th-century **S. Maria del Mercato**, which resulted

▶ VISITING LAGO D'ISEO

INFORMATION
Agaenzia Territoriale per il Turismo
Lungolago Marconi 2
I-25049 Iseo
Tel. 0 30 98 02 09, fax 0 30 98 13 61
www.commune.iseo.brescia.it

BOATS
A regular service connects all the towns on the banks of Lago d'Iseo and also runs to Monte Isola.

WHERE TO EAT
▶ Moderate
Trattoria Al Castello
Via Mirolte 53
Tel./fax 0 30 98 12 85
www.trattoriaalcastello.it
closed Mon evening, Tue
The entrance to the restaurant is from an inner courtyard, partly hidden and thus mainly used by the locals; the seating areas both inside and outside in a little garden are extremely pleasant; delicious food and a wide range of good Franciacorta wines.

Il Gabbiano
Via Muciano 2
Predore
Tel. 0 35 93 84 81, closed Mon
The »Seagull« has an attractive little terrace right on the lake; it is worth making the trip to remote Predore just to pay a visit to this idyllic little spot. Along with meat dishes the menu includes fish from both the lake and the sea.

WHERE TO STAY
▶ Luxury
L'Alberta
Via V. Emanuele II 23
Erbusco
Tel. 03 07 76 05 50, fax 03 07 76 05 73
www.albereta.it, 42 rooms
A luxury hotel amid the outstanding scenery of the Franciacorta wine region between Brescia and Bergamo south of Lago d'Iseo; large rooms in country house style, some of them with a fireplace; guests also have use of a tennis court and swimming pool.

▶ Mid-range
I due Roccoli
Via S. Bonomelli
Loc. Invino
Iseo
Tel. 03 09 82 29 77, fax 03 09 82 29 80
www.idueroccoli.com
13 rooms
Small country hotel in a park above Lago d'Iseo; there is a wonderful view of the lake and mountains from the pretty rooms; the facilities include a swimming pool, tennis court and restaurant.

Villa Kinzica
Via Provinciale 1
Sale Marasino
Tel. 03 09 82 09 75, fax 03 09 82 09 90
www.villakinzica.it
This small hotel in country house style is situated above the east shore of the lake and is furnished with great elegance: a salon with a fireplace and a reading room with a view of the lake.

▶ Budget
Ambra
Via Porto G. Rosa 2
Iseo
Tel. 0 30 98 01 30, fax 03 09 82 13 61
www.ambrahoteliseo.it, 29 rooms
A good, reasonably priced hotel in Iseo directly by the little harbour; many rooms have a balcony and lake view; parking next to the hotel.

from the rebuilding of a 14th-century church, is set back from the piazza. Late Gothic frescoes that have survived from the first church can be seen inside. **Piazza Gabriele Rosa** has a completely different character, as it opens to the lake and has a touch of harbour atmosphere. Boats for excursions and the regular scheduled services put in here, and a few cafes with a lake view make for a pleasant break. On Piazza del Sagrato stands the 12th-century church of **Pieve di S. Andrea**. Its interior was adorned in a variety of styles in the following centuries. **Castello degli Oldofredi**, which was constructed by a noble family in the 11th century, today houses an arts centre. There is also a war museum. Opening times: 9am–noon.

Riserva Naturale delle Torbiere del Sebino

To the south-west of Iseo lies a **marshy area** that formed over a long period from peat diggings and is now a nature reserve in easy walking distance of Iseo. A distinctive flora and fauna has evolved here on an area of about 2 sq km/500 acres. The **monastery of S. Pietro in Lamosa**, situated some way above Torbiere, was founded in the 11th century by Cluniac monks and has 16th-century frescoes. It has a good view of the nature reserve. Viewing on appointment, tel. 0 39 9 29 21 00.

Peschiera on Monte Isola is a pretty place

The best way to reach Monte Isola is to take the ferry from Sulzano (5km/3mi north-east of Iseo). The island and its villages can be explored on foot or by bus. The main town is **Peschiera Maraglio** in the south-east, where the bus departs directly opposite the quay. Settlement on Monte Isola goes back to Roman times, and the island has a long history as a destination for travellers. The Visconti came here to take part in hunts. Although Monte Isola is small, about 2000 people live in its eleven villages. These include the picturesque fishermen's villages Peschiera, Maraglio and **Sensole**; **Menzino** with its 15th-century watchtower; **Siviano**, where there is another medieval fortified tower on the piazza; and **Carzano**, the starting point for a walk uphill to the 16th-century chapel of Madonna della Ceriola in **Cure**, the highest village on the island. Two privately owned islets lie close to Monte Isola: Isoletta di Loreto to the north, on which a convent of the Poor Clares can be discerned, and Isola di S. Paolo to the south.

★ ★
Monte Isola

The SS 510 runs along the eastern shore through Pilzone, Sulzano, Sale Marasino and Marone. With the exception of **Marone**, where the lakeside area is pretty, all of these places have been spoiled by the busy road and are not much worth visiting. Near Marone a detour east into the mountains towards Zone leads to imposing rock formations in the shape of pointed, tower-like pyramids which have been created by thousands of years of erosion.

Eastern shore

Pisogne at the end of the eastern shore lay on the Via Valeriana, a Roman road that connected Brescia with Valcamonica. Three remaining town gates testify to the medieval period, when Pisogne was fortified. The most interesting building here is the 15th-century church Madonna della Neve with its cycle of frescoes dating from the 16th century.

The principal town on Lago d'Iseo is lively **Lovere** at the far north end of the western shore. From the long lakeside promenade there are fine views across the lake to Valcamonica and the snow-covered mountains in the distance. Palazzo Tadini, right by the lake in Lovere, houses an **art collection** including works by Venetian and Lombard painters, porcelain, Flemish tapestries and archaeological finds. Luigi Tadini built the palazzo in 1828 as a home for the Accademia Tadini. His grave is in the adjoining chapel. Opening times: March–Sept Tue–Sat 3pm–7pm, Sun, holidays 10am–noon, 3pm–7pm; Apr–Oct .

Western shore

🕐

From Lovere continue to **Riva di Solto**, an idyllic little place with a pretty lakeside promenade. It is worth making a detour up to **Solto Collina**, as the panorama of the lake from the road is wonderful. From Riva di Solto the narrow road right on the bank of the lake leads on to **Tavernola Bergamasca**, where there is a yacht marina with cafes and restaurants. Part of this village was destroyed by a landslip in 1906. Around **Predore** the countryside is prettier, the

Franciacorte is known for its sparkling wines

mountains retreat and the road passes little olive groves and orchards. Predore itself is a charming village. Here Palazzo Mezzatorre, right by the quay, originated in a 15th-century castle.

Sarnico, a settlement going back to Roman times, lies at the southwestern end of Lago d' Iseo. It is a holiday resort with excellent water sports facilities. The sights here, in addition to the historic centre with the 15th-century church of **S. Paolo** and a pretty clock tower, are the Baroque **church of S. Martino di Tours** and, directly on the lakeshore on the edge of the town, **Villa Faccanoni**, built in 1912 in Art Nouveau style.

Franciacorta The hilly countryside of Franciacorta with its vineyards extends south of Lago d' Iseo. This region was once known for its rustic red wine, but in recent decades has acquired a reputation as a miniature version of Champagne, as most Italian sparking wine made according to the classic method comes from here.

✷✷ Lago di Lugano · Lake Lugano

F/G 4/5

Switzerland: Ticino/Tessin Canton
Provinces: Como and Varese
Area: 51 sq km/20 sq mi

Italy: Lombardy
Altitude of lake: 271m/890ft

The many-branched Lago di Lugano is surrounded by forested mountain ridges. It thrusts its arms like fjords into the hills and mountains, while bays and necks of land make for varied scenery. The lake, which takes its name from the best-known town on its shores but is also known to the locals as Lago Ceresio (from the Celtic word »keresios« meaning »horn«), occupies a sheltered site among the southern foothills of the Swiss Alps.

A little gem Lago di Lugano has an area of just 51 sq km/20 sq mi, which makes it smaller than Lago d'Iseo; its depth is up to 288m/945ft. Most of it is on Swiss territory, and only the eastern arm, the western bank between Ponte Tresa and Porto Ceresio and the enclave of Campione

▶ VISITING LAGO DI LUGANO

INFORMATION

Ente Turistico del Mendrisiotto e Basso Ceresio
Via Angelo Maspoli 15 (next to the motorway exit)
I-6850 Mendrisio
Tel. 09 16 46 57 61
Fax 09 16 46 33 48
www.mendrisiotourism.ch

BOATS

A boat trip on the lake is one of the great treats in this area. Ships operate regularly from Lugano, including its districts of Paradiso and Castagnola, and from Gandria and Melide. Round trips of the lake run from June to September.

WHERE TO EAT

▶ Moderate
Risorgimento
Via Vanetti 16
Porlezza
Tel. 0 34 46 11 22
www.hotelrisorgimento.com
Mid-scale restaurant serving international and regional cuisine; good meat dishes.

▶ Inexpensive
Grotto Pojane
Via Pojana 63
Riva San Vitale
Tel. 09 16 49 74 31
Closed midday Tue and Wed
International and regional cuisine; good meat dishes.

WHERE TO STAY

▶ Mid-range
Art Deco Hotel Dellago
Melide
Tel. 09 19 49 70 41
Fax 09 19 49 89 15
www.hotel-dellago.ch

Modern design with warm colours and a wonderful view of the lake.

Elvezia al Lago
Sentiero di Gandria 21
Castagnola
Tel. 09 19 71 44 51
Fax 09 19 72 78 40
www.elvezialago.ch
A family-run hotel with a superb location right on the lake and a private beach.

Regina
Via Lungolago Matteotti 11
Porlezza
Tel. 0 34 46 12 28
Fax 0 34 47 20 31
www.hregina.com, 23 rooms
Almost next door to the Hotel Europa is the Hotel Regina, which is somewhat more expensive; simple decor but friendly atmosphere.

▶ Budget
Europa
Lungolago Matteotti 19
Porlezza
Tel. 0 34 46 11 42
Fax 0 34 47 22 56
www.hoteleuropaitaly.com, 35 rooms
Beautiful location, rooms of a reasonable standard, gardens and garage.

d' Italia belong to Italy. Two glaciers were responsible for the formation of the lake during the ice ages: the Ticino glacier from the north and the Adda glacier from the west. The deep green, sometimes opaque colour of the lake water derives from the large number of algae. The shores of the lake were already settled by the Etruscans and Celts, but more testimonies to the past have survived from the Roman, Lombard and Frankish periods. In the Middle Ages the region was often drawn into the conflicts between Milan and Como, and much of it fell under Swiss rule in 1512. Except on the eastern bank north of Campione, **scenic lakeside roads** run all around Lago di Lugano. A causeway at Melide (Ponte-Diga) crosses the middle section of the lake.

What to See on Lago di Lugano

Ceresio   The spit of land that stretches far into the lake between Lugano in the east and Agno in the west is called Ceresio. Its eastern part is a mountain ridge extending from **Monte S. Salvatore** (912m/2992ft)

The view from Monte S. Salvatore extends far beyond the lake to the Alps of Valais

to Monte Arbostora (822m/2697ft); its western part is the lovely Collina d' Oro, the »Golden Hill« (Monte Croce 654m/2146ft). This area has attracted many artists.

Gentilino

The first village on the peninsula, Gentilino, is surrounded by chestnut woods. It is an old village, its buildings decorated with sgraffiti. In solitary eminence above the village stands the church of S. Abbondio, which was built in the 16th century and remodelled in Baroque style in 1658. The impressive stucco ceiling survives from this time. The ossuary was added in 1723. The cemetery opposite is the last resting place of the writer **Hermann Hesse**, the Dadaists **Hugo Ball** and **Emmy Ball-Hennings** and the conductor **Bruno Walter**.

The famous poet and novelist **Hermann Hesse** made **Montagnola** his home in 1919. At first he occupied a wing of the palace-like Casa Camuzzi, which he described as an »imitation of a Baroque hunting lodge«. The little **Hesse Museum** displays the writer's travel gear, manuscripts and watercolours (Ra Cürta 2; opening times: March to Oct daily 10am–6.30pm, Nov–Feb Sat, Sun 10am–5.30pm). In 1931 Hesse moved to the nearby house of his friend Hans Bodmer on the road to Agra and stayed there until his death in 1962.

Baedeker TIP

In Hermann Hesse's footsteps
A marked trail follows the footsteps of the world famous poet: from the houses where he lived to his grave. Information: tel. 09 19 93 37 70, www.hessemontagnola.ch.

Carona

Carona, perched high above Lago di Lugano on a terrace between Monte S. Salvatore and Monte Arbostora, has retained its late medieval appearance with fine burghers' houses. Famous families of artists and architects lived here and established the prosperity of the village, which is evident to this day. The parish church of S. Giorgio (1598) possesses interesting frescoes and copies of famous works. From the tower of the church the two-storey Loggia del Comune (1591) leads across to the priest's house. Late Gothic frescoes can be admired in the **church of S. Marta**, which lies above the village. It was originally Romanesque, but was extended in the 17th century. Take a forest path lined by the stations of the cross south-west of the village to the 18th-century **pilgrimage church of S. Maria d' Ongero**. Inside are magnificent stucco work, sculptural decoration and paintings. From the square in front of the church, which has a beautiful view of the lake, **S. Maria Assunta di Torello**, a 13th-century monastery church, can be reached.

Morcote

Morcote at the foot of Monte Arbostora (south side) has preserved its historic appearance, especially in the centre, and is one of the most popular destinations in Ceresio for excursions. 408 steps lead to the pilgrimage church of **S. Maria del Sasso** with its free-standing campanile, which was first built in the 13th century and altered several times. It contains outstanding 16th-century frescoes. At the other end of the square is the chapel of S. Antonio di Padova, and it is also worth visiting the **cemetery** of Morcote, where the composer Eugen d'Albert (1864–1932) and the playwright Georg Kaiser (1878–1945) are buried.

◀ Parco Scherrer

Not far away Arthur Scherrer (1881–1956), who made his fortune in textiles, created a »magic garden« and filled it with everything that he brought back from his long journeys abroad. Among lovingly planted palms and flowering shrubs, fountains and sequestered paths, are such items as a copy of the Erechtheion from the acropolis in Athens, a Moorish sun temple and a tastefully furnished Siamese tea house. At the entrance is a 14th-century house which Scherrer moved here from Lugano to serve as his dwelling. Opening times: mid-March–late Oct daily 9am–5pm, July, Aug until 6pm.

! **Baedeker TIP**

Switzerland in miniature

The great attraction in Melide, halfway between Lugano and Morcote, is Swissminiatur (Via Cantonale), which displays small-scale models of the main sights of Switzerland. Opening times: mid-March to Oct 9am–6pm; www.swissminiatur.ch.

Riva S. Vitale nestles between Lago di Lugano and Monte S. Giorgio (1100m/3610ft). The striking tower and elegant dome of the church of S. Croce can be seen from afar.

Riva S. Vitale is famous for the baptistery of S. Giovanni on the south side of the medieval centre. It dates from the 5th–6th centuries, and is the **oldest surviving church in Switzerland**. It stands next to the parish church of S. Vitale, which dates from the 10th century and was remodelled between 1756 and 1759. The octagonal core of the baptistery was built of squared masonry in the 5th–6th centuries, as was the baptismal font sunk into the floor, in which adult converts could be completely immersed. When the custom changed to baptism by sprinkling with water in the early Middle Ages, a round monolithic font was placed above the earlier basin. The fragments of frescoes on the walls of the east apse date from the 10th century, those in the niches at the sides from the 12th century. The floor with geometric inlaid patterns is also noteworthy.

◀ Baptistery

◀ S. Croce

To the north of the old village centre, S. Croce (1588–94), **one of the most significant Renaissance churches in Switzerland**, glows yellow and white. The architect was Giovanni Antonio Piotti, also known as **Vacallo**. Eight large columns bear a high drum dome. The murals are attributed to the Pozzi brothers (1592), the altarpieces to Camillo Procaccini.

The woods conceal a work of contemporary architecture: **Casa Bianchi**, designed in 1973 (Via Fomeggie 6) by the famous Ticino architect Mario Botta. The **Casa Comunale** and **Palazzo della Croce** from the Renaissance are also worthy of note.

Charming villages on the banks of the lake

From Riva San Vitale a lakeside road leads to Brusino-Arsizio, a fishing village in an idyllic setting at the foot of the wooded Monte S. Giorgio. In the **church of S. Michele** (16th–17th century) is a fresco attributed to Seregnesi which once adorned the wall of a house. To get a magnificent view take the cable car from Brusino-Arsizio up to the climatic spa **Serpiano** (650m/2133ft). On account of its unique geological treasures – countless rare fossils of marine dinosaurs and fish have been found here – **Monte San Giorgio** (1096m/3596ft) was included on the Unesco list of World Natural Heritage in 2003.

Brusino-Arsizio and surroundings

The »head of the lake«, to translate the Italian name, is at the southern end of Lago di Lugano, next to Riva S. Vitale, at the foot of Monte Generoso. Supporters of the Risorgimento printed their writings opposing Austrian rule at the »Tipografia Elvetica« here between 1830 and 1856.

Capolago is best known for its rack-and-pinion railway. The journey up to Monte Generoso (1704m/5590ft) takes 40 minutes. From the summit the fantastic view takes in the Alps and the Lombard plain all the way to Milan. For refreshments try the **Grotto Eremo S. Nicolao**, about 1km/0.5mi from the summit terminus.

Capolago

✳ ✳
◀ Monte Generoso

Capolago is a base for a trip into charming hilly country, known after its main town Mendrisio as **Mendrisiotto**, or »Swiss Tuscany«. This wedge of land points from Lago di Lugano into Italy. Despite insensitive development, Mendrisio has preserved its historic centre, where several fine town residences and churches can be seen. The Easter processions that have taken place here since the 16th century

Mendrisio

Baedeker TIP

Regional wines

Wines from Ticino are available at Vinattiari Ticinesi in Ligornetto or via the homepage. Tel. 0 91 6 47 33 33; www.zanini.ch.

are famous far and wide. The canton art gallery **Pinacotheca Giovanni Züst** in Rancate (4km/2.5mi west of Mendrisio) and the **Museo Vela** in neighbouring Ligornetto, home of the Vela family of artists, are also worth a visit. Museo Vela exhibits sculptures by Vincenzo Vela (1820–91). Opening times: mid-Aug–Sept Tue–Sun 10am–6pm, Oct–Dec until 5pm. In **Stabio** stands the **Casa Rotonda**, built in 1981 and designed by **Mario Botta** (Via Pietane 12).

Campione d'Italia

Midway along the eastern bank the **Italian enclave** Campione d'Italia lies on Swiss territory, though no border checks are made. The »Italian Las Vegas« owes its name to the lakeside casino and numerous nightclubs. Here, too, the well-known contemporary architect **Mario Botta** created a huge landmark with the **new casino**. It is impossible to overlook this golden-yellow palace of glass with a panorama restaurant, which rises to the sky on the banks of the lake. The political status of Campione d'Italia goes back to 777, when the territory was donated to the Milanese monastery S. Ambrogio. In 1797 Napoleon handed over Campione to the Cisalpine Republic, with which it later passed to Austria. Since 1860 Campione has belonged to Italy. In the Middle Ages the **»Maestri Campionesi«** were famous architects, sculptors and painters who worked all over Lombardy.

S. Maria dei Ghirli ►

The pilgrimage church of S. Maria dei Ghirli, south of the town on a terrace above the lake, is not well known (keys to the church are available in the priest's house opposite). The present church was constructed in the 13th and 14th centuries and remodelled in Baroque style in the 17th century. In 1740 the porch on the lake side and the monumental flight of steps were added. The church has outstanding murals. The **frescoes** on the southern external wall, a representation of the Last Judgement, are by Lanfranco de Veris and his son Filippolo (1400). The cycle on the south and rear wall is even older. It depicts scenes from the life of John the Baptist, painted by an unknown Lombard master from the school of Giotto in the 14th century. The paintings in the choir are by Isidoro Bianchi from Campione (1634).

Porlezza and surroundings

Porlezza, a little fishing town at the east end of the lake, is the largest place on the Italian arm of Lago di Lugano and a good base for trips into the mountainous hinterland, the beautiful **Val Rezzo** and **Val Cavargna**. It is also convenient for an excursion to Menaggio on the western bank of ►Lago di Como, passing a smaller lake, Lago di Piano. Above Carlazzo looms **Monte Grona** (1736m/5696ft), and on the right **Monte Tremezzo** (1700m/5578ft). There are also good views from Sasso di S. Martino (862m/2828ft) and Crocetta a Specchi (505m/1657ft), which is reached from Croce.

✳ Lago Maggiore · Lake Maggiore

C – F 3 – 6

Switzerland: Canton: Ticino/Tessin
Provinces: Varese and Novara
Area: 212 sq km/82 sq mi

Italy: Lombardy and Piedmont
Altitude of lake: 194m/636ft

Lago Maggiore – also known in Italy as Verbano, a name deriving from a Celtic water deity called Verbeia – is the second largest of the north Italian lakes after Lago di Garda and the one with the most islands. The northern tip of the lake belongs to the Swiss canton Ticino. Of the Italian part, the western shore belongs to Piedmont, the eastern shore to Lombardy.

Lago Maggiore, like the other north Italian lakes, was created during the ice ages when glaciers hollowed out its bed. It is 65km/40mi long and 2–11km/1–7mi wide. At its deepest point, between Ghiffa and Porto Valtravaglia, its depth is 372m/1221ft. Tourism is the main source of income here. The parts that receive most visitors are the Swiss areas around Locarno, Ascona and Brissago, and on the Italian side the western bay between Pallanza and Stresa, where the wonderful **Borromean Islands** with their subtropical parks are the main attraction.

Lake with international border

The northern shores are enclosed by high, largely wooded hills, with the Ticino and Valais Alps as a backdrop. In the south the country flattens out towards the Lombard plain. The western shore is particularly favoured in terms of both scenery and climate. Here the principal spas and holiday resorts have developed, and magnificent villas and gardens extend over the slopes of the hills. The eastern shore, sometimes pityingly referred to as »the poor side«, has a more natural appearance. The banks of the lake are steep and wooded on this side. There are also unspoiled stretches of shore where tourism has had little impact.

✱ ✱
Scenery

Thanks to the mild climate, the vegetation of Lago Maggiore is luxuriant. Close to the lake subtropical plants flower splendidly. In the hilly hinterland and higher mountains this gives way to a subalpine and alpine flora. This means that a small area is home not only to Mediterranean and many exotic plants such as fig, olive, pomegranate, almond, lemon and orange trees, mimosas, camellias and eucalyptus trees, sago palms, carob trees and cork oaks, but also to alpine roses, saxifrages and gentians.

◄ *Flora*

✳ Western Bank

The principal places on Lago Maggiore are described here as a tour around the lake in an anticlockwise direction. The starting and finishing point is Locarno.

▶ VISITING LAGO MAGGIORE

INFORMATION

Lago Maggiore
Piazza Marconi 16
I-28838 Stresa
Tel. 03 23 3 01 50
Fax 03 23 3 13 08
www.distrettolaghi.it

IAT Verbania
Via delle Magnolie 1
I-28922 Verbania Pallanza
Tel. 03 23 35 76 76
Fax 03 23 50 77 22
www.distrettolaghi.eu

IAT Luino
Via Piero Chiara 1
I-21016 Luino

Tel. 03 31 53 00 19
www.vareselandoftourism.it

BOATS AND FERRIES

The boat trip (in operation all year)
between Locarno and Arona is
strongly recommended. In summer
aliscafi (jetfoils) operate, stopping
alternately on the western and eastern
bank of the lake. There is a car ferry
between Intra and Laveno.

WHERE TO EAT

▶ Moderate
Due Scale
Piazza Libertà 28-30, Luino
Tel. 03 32 53 11 75
Closed Mon

Grand Hôtel des Iles Borromées

Frescoes decorate the walls and ceiling of this house, the birthplace of the writer Piero Chiara; high-class cuisine and an enoteca in the cellar vaults.

Internazionale
Piazza Marconi 18
Luino
Tel. 03 32 53 00 37
Closed Tue
Good cooking of regional and international dishes, wide choice of wines.

Osteria del Castello
Piazza Castello 9
Intra
Tel. 03 32 51 65 79
Closed Sun
This little osteria is hidden away in the centre of town; there are tables on the leafy terrace and in the rustic-style interior; wide range of open wines, many of them from Piedmont.

► Inexpensive
Taverna Antico Agnello
Via Olina 18
Orta S. Giulio
Tel. 03 32 9 02 59
Closed Tue
Attractive osteria with international and regional dishes, including delicious fish from Lago di Orta; good wine list.

Orient Express
Piazzale Stazione 8
Stresa
Tel. 03 23 93 43 65
Closed Mon
Locals say this place has the best pizza in town.

WHERE TO STAY
► Luxury
Grand Hôtel des Iles Borromées
Corso Umberto I. 67
Stresa

Tel. 03 23 93 89 38
Fax 03 23 3 24 05
www.borromees.it
The grand hotel par excellence on the lake, opened in 1863; royalty and high society have stayed here; obviously the luxury comes at a price.

► Mid-range
Leon d'Oro
Piazza Motta 42
Orta S. Giulio
Tel. 0 32 2 91 19 91
Fax 0 32 29 03 03, 38 rooms
In Orta, centrally located right on Piazza Motta on the lake with a view of Isola S. Giulio; modern, prettily furnished rooms; good restaurant with lakeside terrace.

Il Monterosso
Loc. Cima Monterosso
Tel. 03 23 55 65 10
Fax 03 23 51 97 06
Old, beautifully restored stone house the hill with a fantastic view; apartments available; excellent cooking.

► Budget
Meublé Tilde
Via V. Veneto 63
Verbania
Tel. 03 23 50 38 05
Between Pallanza and Intra; a charming old villa with a wonderful garden and a view to die for.

Dei Tigli
Via Paletta 20
Angera
Tel. 03 31 93 08 36
Fax 03 31 96 03 33
www.hoteldeitigli.com, 28 rooms
The best hotel in Angera, but reasonably priced; central location, adequate facilities and parking spaces by the hotel.

Highlights Lago Maggiore

Boat trip
The best view of the fine lakeshore villas is from the water.
► page 218

Isole Borromee
Follow poets' footsteps in beautiful Baroque gardens.
► page 225

Isole di Brissago
A peaceful island with a botanical garden that harbours many species
► page 222

S. Caterina del Sasso
The most photogenic church on the lake in an impressive setting
► page 228

Locarno ►Locarno

Ascona ►Ascona

Ronco
The road along the western bank first leads to the little holiday resort of Ronco, 4km/2.5mi south-west of Ascona on the eastern slopes of Corona dei Pinci. The 15th-century parish church of **S. Martino** dominates the village. Its slender campanile dates from 1860. In the choir the late Gothic frescoes (1492) and an altarpiece by Antonio Ciseri are notable. Opposite the church, **Casa Ciseri** (originally 17th century) is the house in which the painter of the same name (1821–91) was born and lived. Above the parish church lies the rather plain Baroque chapel of **S. Maria delle Grazie** with its pretty porch (1712). The frescoes of the choir dome are by Giuseppe Antonio Felice Orelli (c1730). There is a wonderful view from the piazza. A steep path with 800 steps, known as »Heaven's Ladder«, leads down to **Porto Ronco**, the harbour on the lakeside road, from where boats run to the Isole di Brissago. The **Corona dei Pinci** (1293m/4242ft), an outlying summit of the great Gridone massif, towers above Ronco. The rewarding ascent takes about four hours. From the top there is a magnificent view down to Lago Maggiore and the Isole di Brissago, north-west to Centovalli, and across the Onsernone valley to Val di Vergeletto.

Panorama ►

Fontana Martina
Fontana Martina, about 2km/1mi south-west of Ronco, is a picturesque mountain village. In 1923 the Swiss printer Fritz Jordi bought the abandoned village in order to establish an **artists' colony**. To finance the scheme he founded a pottery, which is still in business. The products are on sale in the attached shop. The artists' community has now become a popular holiday village.

Brissago
Brissago, at the foot of the 2189m/7182ft Monte Limidario, is known to cigar smokers for the long, thin **Virginia cigar »Brissago«**, which

»Searchers for truth« on Monte Verità

A WORLD FOR DREAMERS

Some people called her a crank – and she was certainly an unusual woman: Antoinette de Saint-Léger (1856–1948), the wife of Richard Flemyng Saint-Léger from Kingstown in Ireland. In 1885 she and her husband settled on the Isole di Brissago in Lago Maggiore.

The couple transformed the stony fields of the islands into a luxuriant garden. They planted rare trees, shrubs and flowers which they had brought back with them from extended journeys and which flourished in the warm, humid climate. Baron Saint-Léger left his wife in 1897, but she remained on the islands and invited artists, writers, poets and scholars to join her. The »Lady of the Lake« gradually became impoverished. In 1927 she was forced to sell the islands, and in 1948 she died in the poor-house of Intragna.

The new owner, a **Hamburg merchant named Max Emden**, tore down the villa and built a neo-classical palazzo in its place. In 1950 the Swiss canton of Ticino bought the islands and established the Parco Botanico del Cantone di Ticino, in which 1800 different plants now thrive. The Italian-speaking canton owed its emergence as a tourist destination to early **drop-outs**. The opening of the St Gotthard railway tunnel in 1882 allowed individual travellers to discover this beautiful region for themselves. In 1901 Henri Oedenkoven, a Belgian industrialist, and his mistress, the German pianist Ida Hofmann, arrived in Ancona, where they bought a large estate on Monti Monescia. They renamed it Monte Verità (»Mountain of Truth«) and founded there a »**cooperative vegetarian colony**«, practising nudism, free love and rejection of private property. They sewed their own clothes, grew their own food and engaged in a search for truth through meditation and discussion in the hope of solving the problems of society. »Back to nature« appealed to many who wished to escape the petrified conventions of bourgeois society: artists and writers, psychologists and political refugees and many others flocked to the colony. Among those who came were James Joyce, Carl Jung, **Hermann Hesse**, Paul Klee, Gustav Stresemann and Isadora Duncan. Some stayed only a short time but others, including Hesse and the artist Jean Arp, settled in the area for good. Daphne du Maurier's short story »Monte Verità« (published in *The Birds and Other Stories*) is a fictionalized account of the colony.

has been made here for over 100 years. The parish church of SS. Pietro e Paolo (1526–1610), surrounded by 600-year-old cypresses, is the focal point of the village. From here a little alley leads to the Baroque **Casa Branca**, which has a richly decorated façade facing the lake with a loggia of five arches on the upper floor. It is also worth taking a look at **Casa Borrani**, a patrician villa formed by combining several 17th-century buildings. On the lakeshore at the south end of the village stands the church of **S. Maria di Ponte** (1526–46) with a tall, freestanding campanile that can be seen from afar. Close by is the **Fabbrica Tabacchi Brissago**, founded in 1847 and thus the oldest factory in Ticino. Since 1999 the building, which has an octagonal dome and a gallery of columns, has been a cultural centre, the Centro Dannenmann. Well-known modern architects such as Snozzi and **Aurelio Galfetti** have made their mark in Brissago. The latter built Villa Bianca, luxurious apartments with their own moorings.

◄ Surroundings

A number of typical mountain villages are situated above Brissago: **Cadogno**, Porta, **Incella** and **Piodina**, with Renaissance and Baroque houses, some of them decorated with frescoes. To reach the pilgrimage chapel **Sacro Monte dell'Addolorato** above Brissago take the way of the cross through Valle del Sacro Monte. Its stations are decorated with frescoes.

Isole di Brissago

The two elongated islands known as the Isole di Brissago, **Isola Grande** and **Isolino** (»small island«) are just under 2km (about 1 mile) from Brissago. The fastest crossing to the larger of the two (the only one open to the public) is from Porto Ronco. Boats also leave from Brissago, Ascona and Locarno. In the 13th century a religious order dedicated to poverty and an ascetic life settled on the islands. Three centuries later the monks left and the monastery buildings fell into decay. The islands were used for hunting and by fishermen as a place of refuge. In 1885 Baronessa Antoinette de Saint-Léger bought both islands and made her dreams reality (►Baedeker Special p.221). In 1950 the Parco Botanico del Cantone Ticino opened on Isola Grande. It is remarkable for the variety of its species: over 1800 have been arranged here in groups according to their place of origin. The villa is used for art exhibitions. Visiting times: mid-March to late Oct daily 9am–6pm; www.isolebrissago.ch.

✳
Botanical garden ►
🕐

✳
Cannobio

Cannobio, a pretty place, is on the Italian side, about 5km/3mi from the border. A popular market is held here every Sunday between 8am and 1pm. At the end of the lakeside promenade, near the boat pier, stands the pilgrimage church S. Pietà. It was built in 1571 in the style of Bramante to designs by Pellegrino Tibaldi. The votive image inside (c1400), painted on parchment and once held to work miracles, depicts the dead Christ with St John and the Virgin. The altarpiece of 1536 represents Christ carrying the cross. Next to the Baroque parish church of S. Vittore stands the castle-like Palazzo della Ragione (1291). Here lanes lead down to the shore, where the promenade is lined by houses with colourful façades and galleries open to the lake. To see some fine scenery, take a trip away from the lake, for example to **Orrido di Sant' Anna** about 2km/1mi away, where the Cannobino has carved a spectacular gorge into the rocks. **Val Cannobina**, nestling between Gridone (2188m/7179ft) and Monte Zeda (2156m/7074ft), is also very beautiful.

Drive a further 7km/4.5mi south of Cannobio to Cannero Riviera, which has a lovely setting on the western bank of the lake amongst vineyards, olive groves and orchards. From the lakeside road two islands, the **Castelli di Cannero**, can be seen. The islands were once the stronghold of infamous robber barons, until in 1414 they were executed and their castle razed. In 1519 Lodovico Borromeo built a castle named La Vitaliana here, but only its ruins remain.

Cannero Riviera

Verbania (16km/10mi south of Cannero Riviera), the largest town on Lago Maggiore, consists of two districts: Intra, the industrial and commercial centre and port for the car ferry to Laveno, and Pallanza, a holiday resort of fine residences on the slopes of the 693m/2274ft Monte Rosso.

Verbania

The two parts of Verbania are separated by the peninsula Punta della Castagnola, most of which is occupied by the extensive **park** of Villa Taranto. In 1931 Neil MacEacharn, a Scotsman, bought the 20ha/50-acre estate and painstakingly created a park that combines the principles of an English garden with those of the Italian garden tradition. Thousands of native and exotic plants flourish here on extremely diverse terrain that was specially landscaped for them; the park is famous for its beeches, magnolias, dahlias and camellias, as well as 500 different types of rhododendron. Opening times: late March– Oct daily 9am–6.30pm.

✶ ✶
◄ Villa Taranto

Piazza IV Novembre, the centre of Verbania and the starting point of its promenade, is the site of the **Palazzo Pretorio (town hall)** and close by the **mausoleum of General Cadorna**, commander-in-chief of the Italian army in the First World War. The conductor Arturo Toscanini liked to stay on the small island of **S. Giovanni**. The 18th-century Baroque **Palazzo Viani-Dugnani** north of the piazza houses the **Verbania Museo**. It displays archaeo-

The park of Villa Taranto

logical finds, some paintings of the 19th and 20th centuries and sculptures by Paolo Trubeckoj (1866–1938). Opening times: early April–late Oct Tue–Sun 10am– noon, 3.30pm–6.30pm. At the northern end of Viale Azari, 1km/0.5mi outside the town centre, is one of the finest Renaissance churches of the area. **Madonna di Campagna**, built in the style of Bramante, probably between 1519 and 1527, has an octagonal dome with a columned gallery. Its campanile survives from an earlier Romanesque church. Inside note the frescoes dating from the 15th to 17th centuries, choir stalls of 1582 and a 13th-century votive painting of the Madonna delle Grazie.

Hinterland ►

Here too there are attractive excursions in the hinterland of the lake. For a superb view of the Borromean Gulf climb **Monte Rosso** (693m/2274ft), which takes about two hours. The panorama from **Monte Zeda** (2156m/7074ft), the highest mountain near the lake, is even more comprehensive. It is also well worthwhile making the detour to **Val Grande**, part of a nature reserve, passing **Ponte Romano** on the way. This bridge over the S. Bernardino is believed to date back to Roman times.

Lago di Orta

A further side trip leads to the westernmost of the north Italian lakes, Lago Maggiore's »little brother«: Lago di Orta, which is 13km/ 8mi long and on average 2km/1mi wide. It lies between low wooded

A place of mystery: Isolo S. Giulio in Lago di Orta

hills, with Monte Mottarone (1491m/4892ft) as a backdrop to the north-east. The main settlement here is **Orta S. Giulio**. From the car park take steep narrow alleys down to the lake and piazza, which is lined with Baroque buildings of the 17th and 18th centuries. At the centre is the Palazzo della Comunità, a Renaissance building of 1582 with a little tower. From the ground floor with its broad arcades an external stairway leads to the upper storey, where the Great Council met.

In the lake the small Isola S. Giulio is shrouded in an aura of mystery. Around 390 St Julius of Aegina founded a church here. Today the **basilica of S. Giulio** occupies the site. The interior is a mixture of different styles, including late Gothic frescoes (14th–16th centuries), and Baroque stucco decorations and marble intarsia work. The most precious of the church furnishings is the Romanesque pulpit made of black serpentine, carved with scenes that have still not been deciphered. The figure supported by a staff probably represents Guglielmo da Volpiano, a prominent Benedictine abbot, monastery founder and author who was born on the island in 962. The relics of St Julius are kept in the crypt in a sumptuous shrine.

✷
◄ Isola S. Giulio

There is a wonderful view of the lake and island from the 400m/ 1312ft Sacro Monte, which is dedicated to St Francis of Assisi. A path with 20 chapels leads up to the Franciscan monastery, which was built in 1583. The chapels, dating from the period 1591–1788, are adorned with frescoes and terracotta figures depicting the passion of Christ and scenes from the life of St Francis.

✷
◄ Sacro Monte

The spa and holiday resort Baveno lies at the foot of Monte Camoscio. For centuries its pink granite has been used for building. In the 19th century high society and artists came here: Queen Victoria, for example, as well as Lord Byron and Richard Wagner. The **church of SS. Gervasio e Protasio** originated in the Romanesque period, and its octagonal baptistery was designed in Renaissance style.

Baveno

The four Borromean Islands, the »pearls of Lago Maggiore«, can be reached by boat from all surrounding lakeshore settlements. Many kings and queens have visited them, and many poets and novelists, including Stendhal, Dickens, Dumas, Turgenev, Flaubert and Anatole France, have commemorated the islands in their works. It is therefore not surprising that they are overcrowded in summer. Isola Bella and Isola Madre still belong to the **Borromeo family**. Lago Maggiore, which had been the subject of disputes with Switzerland for 200 years, was granted to their ancestors, an ancient line of counts from Milan, by the Visconti dukes of Milan in 1439. From 1630 the islands were transformed into a man-made landscape that is unique in Europe.

✷ ✷
Isole Borromee

The focus of attention is the much-lauded Isola Bella, which Alexandre Dumas described as »an incomparably magical place«. As early as the Baroque period, this »beautiful island« was considered a won-

✷ ✷
◄ Isola Bella

The splendid Baroque gardens on Isola Bella

der of the world. When Count Carlo Borromeo and the architect Angelo Crivelli began to remodel the island in about 1630, it was no more than a flat slate rock. After the completion of the work in 1670 by his son Vitaliano Borromeo, the island – named after Carlo's wife Isabella d'Adda – had become **an outstanding masterpiece of the art of the Italian garden**. Then as now this superb Baroque garden takes up almost the entire island. In ten terraces of diminishing size it rises from the bank of the lake and is opulently adorned with statues, grottoes, arcaded galleries and exotic plants. The magnificently furnished Palazzo Borromeo, which was built in 1632, is now a museum. Opening times: late March to mid-September daily 9am–5.30pm.

The **Isola dei Pescatori** is about 500m/500yd to the north-west. Until the early 20th century fishermen and their families lived here. Today tourism is the dominant feature of the island.

◄ Isola Madre

The »mother island«, Isola Madre, is the largest of the Isole Borromee. In 1502 **Lancilotto Borromeo** began to construct a palazzo with a garden here. Its present appearance dates from the 18th and 19th centuries, when Vitaliano Borromeo remodelled it in the style of an English garden. Its special charm is the wonderful botanical garden, where large peacocks roam among ancient trees, magnificent rhododendrons, and subtropical and exotic plants. The Palazzo Borromeo, a fine 16th-century residence, houses collections of dolls and ceramics (opening times: March–Oct 9am–12.30pm, 1.30pm–6pm). Next to it stands the little funeral chapel of the Borromeo family (1858). The fourth island, Isola S. Giovanni, is privately owned and not open to the public.

Stresa

Stresa lies at the entrance to the Borromean Gulf beneath the 1491m/4892ft Monte Mottarone. In the 19th century it was one of the highest-class spas in Italy. The palatial hotels that keep the memory of those times alive, though now somewhat faded, accommodated illustrious members of the aristocracy from all over Europe as well as such guests as Stendhal, Dickens, Hemingway and Richard Wagner.

The centre of the town is the lake-side promenade, where there are lovely views of the Borromean Islands and the lake and where the parish church and most of the large hotels are to be found. The sights include the **Villa Ducale** (1770) and the 19th-century **Villa Pallavicino**, the latter at the southern end of the town surrounded by a beautiful botanical garden which includes a small zoo. Opening times: mid-March to mid-Oct daily 9am–6pm.

Baedeker TIP

Musical highlights

Stresa has a tradition of concerts with star performers. The Settimane Musicali di Stresa, an internationally renowned festival of classical music, is held in August and September. www.stresafestival.eu

★★ Monte Mottarone

The summit of the 1491m/4892ft Monte Mottarone is one of the most impressive viewing points of the whole region. It can be reached by car (toll road), cable car or on foot (about four hours). Halfway up at 700m/2300ft is Gignese, home to the **Museo dell' Ombrello**, an unusual museum of umbrellas (opening times: early April– late Sept Tue–Sun 10am–noon, 3pm–6pm). A little higher up in Alpino (768m/2520ft) over 2000 alpine plants are cultivated in the **Giardino Alpino**.

Arona

The tour around the lake continues via Belgirate and Lesa, from where a superb view across the lake takes in the summit of Campo dei Fiori near Varese, to Meina with its magnificent Villa Farragiana. Shortly before reaching Arona look up to see the **Colosso di S. Carlone**, supposedly the largest statue in Europe, on its hilltop site. It commemorates Saint Carlo Borromeo, the most famous member of this Milanese family, who was born in 1538 in Arona. At the age of just 22 he was Cardinal Archbishop of Milan and a committed opponent of the Reformation. It was he who prevented an agreement between the conflicting religious parties at the Council of Trent (1545–63) and thus triggered the Counter-Reformation. He was canonized by Pope Paul V as early as 1610. An internal spiral staircase leads to the head of the 23m/75ft-high statue, which was erected in 1697. The diocesan seminary next to it was built by Francesco Maria Richini between 1620 and 1643.

Arona itself is a small commercial and industrial town with a long lakeshore promenade. In the **Museo Civico** on Piazza De Filippi the oldest exhibits, dating from 1200 BC, testify to a long history of settlement. The church of **S. Maria Nascente** in the lower town dates from the 15th and 17th centuries. It is worth visiting the church to see Gaudenzio Ferrari's folding altar depicting the *Adoration of the Christ Child* (1511) and the *Assumption of the Virgin* (c1617) by Morazzone.

Sesto Calende

Sesto Calende, at the southern end of Lago Maggiore, is an industrial town whose long history is documented in the **Museo Civico**

🕐 (opening times: Mon–Thu 8.30am–12.30pm, 2.30pm–4.30pm, Sat 3pm–7pm, Sun 3pm–5pm).

The **church of S. Donato** on the road to Angera dates from the 12th century but was much altered in the Baroque period. The narthex, some capitals and the crypt remain from the Romanesque building; the frescoes in north apse are late Gothic, those in the choir from the 17th century.

Parco Regionale Lombardo della Valle del Ticino

The Ticino Park was Europe's first »river park«. It encompasses the river bed and a broad strip along the banks of the Ticino between the south end of Lago Maggiore and its confluence with the Po, an area totalling 90,000ha/350 sq mi. Internet: www.parcoticino.it

✳ ✳ **Eastern Bank**

Angera
✳
Rocca ▶

The little town of Angera on a peninsula on the eastern shore of Lago Maggiore is no more than 2km/1mi from Arona, which lies opposite. The crenellated Rocca di Angera, which looms above the town, is a reminder of its former strategic importance. The castle rock was a stronghold securing the rule of the Lombards and later of powerful noble families. It owes its present form to the Visconti, and passed to the Borromeo family in the 15th century. It is now home to the **Museo della Bambola**, a doll museum (opening times: mid-March–mid-Oct daily 9am–5.30pm). Murals survive in some of the rooms. The victory of Archbishop Ottone Visconti over the Torriani is the subject of the cycle of frescoes in the Sala della Giustizia (1314). 15th-century frescoes from the Palazzo Borromeo in Milan decorate the Sala delle Cerimonie. From here there is a fine view of the Sacro Monte near Varese, the southern tip of the lake and the small island of Partegora. Exhibits in the archaeological museum show that this area was settled as early as 1200 BC. Traces of the cult of Mithras, a Persian god of light who was widely worshipped in imperial Roman times, were found in the **Antro di Mitra** (Cave of Mithras) halfway up the Rocca.

✳
S. Caterina del Sasso

Pass Ispra and continue to Reno (10km/6mi north). Here it is worth visiting the pilgrimage church of S. Caterina del Sasso, which was built into the rock on the steep banks of the lake and is accessible only on foot or by water. The hermit Alberto Besozzo lived here in the 13th century. Near his cave a chapel dedicated to St Catherine was built, and in the 14th and 15th centuries a church and a Dominican monastery were added.

Laveno

The industrial town of Laveno lies in the shadow of the Sasso del Ferro (1062m/3484ft). A cable car runs to the summit of this »iron rock«, where there is a splendid view. The **Museo di Terraglia** in Cerro, a district of Laveno, displays a collection of ceramics and earthenware and informs visitors about the tradition of pottery in Laveno (opening times: Tue–Sun 2.30pm–6pm, Fri–Sun also 10am–noon).

Fans of contemporary art should take the trip to **Arcumeggia**, a village 13km/8mi to the east, where Italian artists have painted the façades of the houses. Nearby in Sangiano the theatre director and author **Dario Fo** was born in 1926 (▶Famous People).

Luino, the economic centre of the Lombard side of Lago Maggiore, lies on a large bay at the mouth of the river Tresa. In the pretty old quarter on the slopes above the lake note the houses of prosperous burghers, some of them with sizeable inner courtyards. Although

S. Caterina del Sasso clings to the rocks above the lakeshore

the town is thought to be the birthplace of the **Renaissance painter Bernardino Luini** (1480/82–1532), only one fresco there is attributed to him: the *Adoration of the Magi* in the church S. Pietro in Campagna. This church near the cemetery is Romanesque in origin but was restored in the 17th century.

Destinations in the hinterland between Luino and ▶Locarno include Agra (655m/2150ft), a resort above the entrance to the delightful Val Veddasca, and Monte Lema (1620m/5315ft). This summit with its panoramic view, which can be reached by cable car from Miglieglia, rises above the Malcantone, as the densely populated country on the Swiss border between Tresa in the south and Ticino in the north is called.

Agra

✳
◀ Monte Lema

Maccagno is a small resort at the end of Val Veddasca close to the Swiss border. A serpentine road connects it to Indemini, a mountain village that has preserved its historic look, with closely built stone-roofed houses, wells, stepped alleys and passages. Immigration since the 1990s has breathed new life into the village.

✳
Indemini

From Indemini it is a further 17km/11mi to Vira on a road over a pass. The curving route passes Monte Tamaro (1962m/6437ft), where a cable car goes up to one of the finest mountain-top views in Ticino.

✳
Monte Tamaro

The spectacular church of S. Maria degli Angeli (1996) on Monte Tamaro is the work of **Mario Botta**, a well-known Ticino architect. A walkway resembling a viaduct leads along the mountain top to the circular chapel, which is entered through its roof.

✳
◀ S. Maria degli Angeli

Vira Vira is the main town of Gambarogno, an area between Caviano on the Swiss part of the lake and the mouth of the river Ticino that takes its name from Monte Gambarogno (1739m/5705ft). Nature lovers appreciate this attractive countryside near the lake for its craggy mountains, magnificent views, lovely hiking trails and sequestered villages. Vira itself has a long history; the **church of S. Pietro** by the lake was founded in the Middle Ages and restored in the 17th century, and has a fine Renaissance font dating from 1589.

Bolle di Magadino The broad plain around the delta of the river Ticino at the north end of the lake, a nature reserve, is known as the **Bolle di Magadino**. Over 300 species of birds live in the marshes. In **Magadino**, an important centre of trade in the Middle Ages, two painted panels attributed to Bernardino Luini and frescoes by the German painter Richard Seewald (1889–1976) can be admired in the parish church of 1847, which is dedicated to S. Carlo.

✴ ✴ Locarno

E 3/4

Switzerland: Canton of Ticino	**Population:** 14,000
Altitude: 205m/675ft	

The ancient city of Locarno is situated at the north end of ▶Lago Maggiore. Sheltered from winds by the foothills of the Alps, camellias azaleas, mimosas and magnolias bloom here, and oleander, palm, fig, olive and almond trees flourish. The city has a worldwide reputation as a winter sports resort, and in the summer months is an excellent base for hiking and boat trips.

History The **name Locarno** derives from the Celtic Leukarni, who lived around the mouth of the river then called the Leukera (»white«), and now known as the Maggia. Numerous finds from excavations show that the settlement, which owed its importance to its site on the route to the alpine passes, grew quickly and was a centre of **glass-making**. In the Middle Ages the town, which became rich from trade, especially **the silk trade**, was ruled by families of Lombard nobles. Its decline began in 1512, when a devastating landslide in the mountains made the traditional trading routes across the Alps impassable, and continued during the turmoil of the Reformation, when all Protestant families were expelled from the city in 1555, and the highly profitable silk trade disappeared with them. After the foundation of the canton of Ticino (Tessin), Locarno alternated with Lugano and Bellinzona as capital of the canton (1803–78). Its fortunes did not revive until the beginning of tourism in the 19th century. The city became widely known in 1925, when a peace con-

VISITING LOCARNO

INFORMATION

Lago Zorzi 1
CH-6600 Locarno
Ente Turistico Lago Maggiore
Tel. 0 91 7 91 00 91
Fax 0 91 7 85 19 41
www.maggiore.ch

WHERE TO EAT

► Moderate

① Bar/Restaurant Balena
Porto Regionale
Tel. 09 17 51 90 32
Restaurant on a ship serving fish specialities, but also a pleasant place to enjoy an aperitif

② Locanda del Vino
Viale Verbano 27
Tel. 09 17 44 69 40
A young crowd comes here to drink wine, and the food is good too.

► Inexpensive

③ Cantina Canetti
Piazza Grande 13
Tel. 09 17 51 07 97
Closed Tue evening, Sun
A cosy, low-lit rendezvous for the locals, who come here for light meals and a good range of wines by the glass or carafe

WHERE TO STAY

► Luxury

① Grand Hotel
Via Sempione 17
Tel. 0 91 7 43 02 82
Fax 0 91 7 43 30 13
www.grand-hotel-locarno.ch
The 19th-century Grand Hotel is still the finest in Locarno, despite its advanced years; the chandelier of Murano glass in the hall is the world's largest; the rooms are extremely spacious, and several boast furniture by early 20th-century designers.

► Mid-range

② Millenium
Via Dogana Nuova 2
Tel. 0 91 7 59 67 67
Fax 0 91 59 67 68
www.millenium-hotel.ch
This small hotel in the old customs house right on the lakeshore has a jazz theme: the rooms have names like Duke Ellington and Charlie Parker.

ference between Great Britain, France and Germany resulted in the **Locarno Pact** and the admission of Germany to the League of Nations.

Since the Middle Ages Locarno has changed its appearance radically. This is due firstly to the Maggia, which flows into Lago Maggiore here and has carried such enormous quantities of sediment in the course of the centuries that the shoreline has been pushed far out into the lake. The Piazza Grande, and the Castello Visconteo, the historic centre, originally stood directly on the lake. Today modern buildings and heavily built-up mountain slopes characterize the scene.

Maggia

Locarno Map

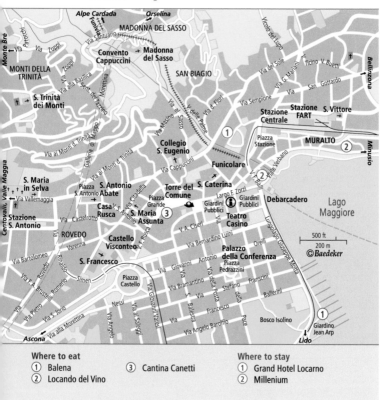

Where to eat
① Balena
③ Cantina Canetti
② Locando del Vino

Where to stay
① Grand Hotel Locarno
② Millenium

What to See in and around Locarno

Piazza Grande

✷ The hub of the town is the long Piazza Grande, one of the **loveliest squares in Switzerland**. Its north side is lined with elegant arcaded buildings in the Lombard style. They house banks, shops, cafes and restaurants, and mainly owe their present appearance to the 19th century. The oldest building is the 14th-century **Torre del Comune**. The piazza is a busy place, the site of a long-established market on Thursday mornings. For a long time there have been plans to close the square to traffic.

Old quarter

Behind the piazza several picturesque lanes lead up to the old quarter, where the principal sights of Locarno and many imposing houses of rich merchants dating from the 16th and 17th centuries are to be seen. **Via S. Antonio** is one of the prettiest lanes.

Castello Visconteo forms the western corner of the city centre. Today's castle with its round tower is no more than a fragment of what was a much more substantial building. After defeating the local noble families in 1432, the **Visconti** from Milan built the castle, and the later feudal lords who ruled the city extended it. In 1532 the Swiss Confederation razed most of it. Only the Palas – the residential quarters – and the 13th-century round tower remained, serving as the seat of the Swiss bailiff until 1798. Following a thorough restoration they are now home to the Museo Civico e Archeologico, the municipal and archaeological museum. The beautiful galleried courtyard, the Renaissance loggia, the fresco in the staircase and the nicely carved ceiling beams are noteworthy features of the interior. The exhibits include numerous finds ranging from the Bronze Age to the Middle Ages, a fine collection of Roman glass, sculptures from the church of S. Vittore in Muralto, furniture, wooden sculpture and crafts, and an interesting section on the Locarno Pact. Opening times: April–Oct Tue–Sun 10am–5pm.

★ **Castello Visconteo**

★ ◄ Museo Civico e Archeologico

☉

In the 16th century the so-called **Casorella**, one of Locarno's most splendid patrician houses, was built onto the castle. It is now devoted to an exhibition of work by the painter Filippo Franzoni (1857–1911).

The church of **S. Francesco**, above the Visconti castle and some distance to the west, was probably founded by St Anthony of Padua in 1229, one year after the canonization of St Francis. In its present form the church dates from the period 1528–72. Parts of the previous building and the demolished Castello Visconteo were incorporated in the Renaissance façade, which in its simplicity is typical for an order of mendicant friars. A door to the right of the apse gives access to the former monastery, where the most notable sight is the **refectory** with its trompe l'oeil frescoes.

> ! **Baedeker TIP**
>
> **Film festival**
>
> Locarno's international reputation is also based on its film festival, which has been held each August since 1946 and is the second oldest in Europe after that in Venice. Makers of movies and – since 1983 – TV films from all over the world compete for the coveted Golden Leopard, the heraldic animal of the city. Open-air screenings on the Piazza Grande are the highlight of the festival. Information: festival office, tel. 09 17 51 02 32, www.pardo.ch.

The main Catholic church of Locarno, visible from afar with its five-storey campanile, is on the north-western border of the old quarter. It was constructed between 1668 and 1674, but the furnishings and decoration largely date from the 19th century.

S. Antonio Abate

The 17th-century Casa Rusca on the south side of Piazza S. Antonio is **one of the finest palazzi in Locarno**. It houses the municipal art gallery, the basis of which is the collection of Jean (Hans) and Marguerite Arp, who lived in Locarno for many years. Many works by

★ **Casa Rusca/ Pinacoteca Comunale**

the Surrealist Arp and other artists who were his friends, such as Max Ernst, Georges Braque, Picasso and Chagall, can be admired. Changing exhibitions of the works of 20th-century artists are also held here regularly. Opening times: Tue–Sun 10am–noon, 2pm–5pm.

S. Maria in Selva

A little to the west of S. Antonio Abate, in Via Vallemaggia, lies S. Maria in Selva, now a little cemetery chapel but in fact the remains of a monastery church (15th–16th century) that was demolished in

1884. It is richly decorated with late Gothic frescoes dating from the 14th–15th centuries. It is also worth looking at the cemetery, where some of the many monuments are highly elaborate; sculptures adorn the **grave of Jean Arp** (1886–1966).

Return to Piazza Grande past the fine houses of wealthy burghers, for example **Casa Simona** (16th century, altered in the 18th century) in Via S. Antonio 3 and **Casa del Negromante**, probably one of the oldest noble residences of the city (14th century; Contrada Borghese no. 14). In Via Citadella note the **church of S. Maria Assunta**, consecrated in 1636. A large statue of St Christopher dominates the façade. The building adjoining the church is the **Casa dei Canonici**. It was built between 1590 and

Sumptuous Baroque stucco work in the church of S. Maria Assunta

1605 with an arcaded courtyard as the palazzo of the founder of the church. A park, the **Giardini Pubblici** (1825), extends from the south side of Piazza Grande down to the lake piers. Here a theatre, casino and the tourist office are accommodated in the **spa building** of 1909–10. Via della Pace leads south to the **Palazzo della Conferenza**, venue for the peace conference of 1925.

Lakeside promenade

On Lago Maggiore an attractive promenade, Lungolago Giuseppe Motta, runs around the bay. The boat pier (debarcadero) is here, and sculptures by Arp can be seen in the **Giardini Jean Arp** at its southern end.

S. Vittore

Locarno's oldest church is in the Muralto quarter, east of the station. Lombard architects built S. Vittore between 1090 and 1110. The massive campanile was added in the 16th century and raised to its present height in 1932. A marble relief of St Victor on horseback (*c*1460) adorns the south wall; the three heads of bearded saints on a standard represent the Holy Trinity. The interior was covered in frescoes between 12th and 17th centuries; the wonderful cycle of Romanesque paintings on the south wall of the nave dates from the 12th century, the frescoes on the choir walls from the 15th century; the *Pentecost* in the apse is by Hans Schmidt of Augsburg (1583). Beneath the choir is **one of the most beautiful Romanesque crypts in Switzerland**. Note the imaginatively carved figures and ornamental motifs on the capitals; the late Gothic frescoes in the first bay of the vault were painted around 1500.

✶ ✶
◀ Crypt

Halfway up the mountain above Locarno, at a height of 355m/ 1165ft, the landmark of the city, the pilgrimage church of S. Maria Assunta, generally known as Madonna del Sasso (Madonna of the Rock), has a commanding position in the district of Orselina. To get there the options are to take the rack-and-pinion railway (funicolare, from Stazione Via Ramogna), to drive or to walk, either on the Via Crucis (Way of the Cross) or via the Sentiero della Valle. According to tradition the church stands on the spot where a Franciscan friar named Bartolomeo d'Ivrea had a vision of the Virgin Mary in 1480.

✶ ✶
Madonna del Sasso

The pilgrimage church Madonna del Sasso watches majestically above the town

and 17th centuries, but much altered at later dates. The west façade with its five-arched portico dates from the 19th century. The whole interior is covered with stucco and adorned with frescoes. The wealth of fittings includes countless votive tablets donated in gratitude for the many miracles attributed to the Madonna of the Rock. The most valuable treasure in the church is the **panel painting of the *Flight into Egypt*** (c1520) in the south aisle by Bartolomeo Suardi, known as Bramantino; the ***Entombment of Christ*** in a side chapel was painted by Antonio Ciseri in 1870. A number of interesting chapels in the monastery include the **Von Roll Chapel** with a 15th-century wooden sculpture representing the *Mourning of Christ* or the *Holy Tomb*; the **Pietà Chapel** and its altar date back to the time of Fra Bartolomeo (under the second arch of the Casa del Padre); in two further chapels **terracotta figures** depict scenes from the New Testament, including the *Last Supper* and *Pentecost*.

Church museum ▶ In the adjacent church museum, Museo Casa del Padre, more votive images, sculptures, paintings, liturgical items and robes are on ⏱ display. Opening times: Easter to mid-Oct Mon, Fri, Sun 10am–noon, 2pm–5pm.

Via Crucis ▶ Few chapels remain from the original Way of the Cross (Via Crucis). The terracotta figures in two of them were made by Francesco Silva in about 1620. The Oratorio dell'Annunziata at the bottom of the processional way, which was consecrated in 1502, contains the tombstone of Bartolomeo d'Ivrea.

✳ **View ▶** There are superb views over Locarno and Lago Maggiore from the terrace of the church.

✳ **Cardada** From the pilgrimage church Madonna del Sasso a cable car (all year except Nov 8am–8pm, journey time ten minutes) runs up to Cardada (Alpe Cardada; 1350m/4430ft). The celebrated architect **Mario Botta** designed it in 1999. From Cardada it is possible to continue by chair lift (six minutes) or on foot (one hour) to Cimetta (1676m/5499ft), which lies in a winter sports area with several ski lifts. For a truly fantastic view, climb a further hour from Cimetta to the summit of Cima della Trosa (1863m/6112ft); from here there is a descent via Alpe Bietri to the mountain village Mergoscia.

✳ **Cimetta ▶**
✳ ✳ **Cima della Trosa ▶**

Lodi

Provincial capital   **Altitude:** 87m/285ft
Population: 42,500

This little town on the river Adda is the capital of the province of the same name, which lies between the Adda in the east, the Lambro in the west and the Po in the south.

● VISITING LODI

INFORMATION

A. P. T., I. A. T.
Piazza Broletto 4
I-26900 Lodi
Tel. 03 71 42 13 91
Fax 03 71 42 13 13
www.commune.lodi.it

WHERE TO EAT

► Inexpensive

I due Agnelli
Via Castelfidardo 12
Tel. 03 71 42 67 77
Closed Sun evening, Mon
Traditional trattoria that serves a good
risotto, ossobuco and fish specialties;
small but well-chosen wine list

WHERE TO STAY

► Mid-range

Anelli
Viale Vignati 7
Tel. 03 71 42 13 54
Fax 03 71 42 21 56,
www.albergoanelli.com, 29 rooms
Dependable hotel on the
southern edge of the
historic old town.
Air-conditioned
rooms and garage.

The origins of Lodi are to be found in the neighbouring Lodi
Vecchio, where the Romans founded the settlement Laus Pompeia.
Lodi Vecchio was an important town until the 12th century, when
the power-hungry Milanese destroyed it in order to eliminate
competition. After this, Emperor Frederick Barbarossa established
the new town, Laus Nova, on a small area of elevated ground in
1158.

Founded by the Romans

What to See in Lodi

The focus of municipal and cultural life in Lodi is the generously
proportioned Piazza della Vittoria, which gained its present appearance surrounded by arcades in the 15th and 17th centuries. Festivities, concerts and election rallies take place here, and the numerous
cafes and bars are rendezvous for locals and tourists alike.

★ **Piazza della Vittoria**

The cathedral of S. Bassiano, which was founded in 1160, stands on
the piazza. A statue of the patron saint, Bassianus, can be seen right
at the top of the façade. Construction of the church nave took almost
100 years, and in 1284 the last details were added to the façade. The
porch supported by lions – the figures came from the old church in
Lodi Vecchio – was built then. To the left and right of the entrance
note the figures of Adam (with no head) and Eve, which along with
the lions are the oldest decorative elements of the façade. The rose
window and the double arches on either side of the door were added

★ **Cathedral**

in the 16th century. The church, originally Romanesque, was much altered in the following centuries. The relics of the patron saint rest in the crypt.

The **town hall** of Lodi with its loggia and portico on the main façade to the left of the cathedral was built in the 18th century. The portico leads to the little Piazza del Broletto and the remains of the old Broletto (medieval town hall) dating from 1284.

Broletto

Behind the cathedral is Piazza del Mercato, site of the Palazzo Vescovile, which was built in 1730 by Giovanni Antonio Veneroni. The piazza hosts a lively market four times weekly.

Piazza del Mercato

The church of S. Maria Incoronata, an architecturally interesting Renaissance work, lies to the west of the cathedral. It was begun in 1488 to designs by **Giovanni Domenico Battagio**. Inside the influence of Bramante is recognizable. The dome of 1513 covers an octagonal space with chapels and double arches. The murals inside the church mainly date from the 16th century.

★
S. Maria Incoronata

The former monastery of S. Filippo (Corso Umberto 63) is now home to the Museo Civico, which displays archaeological finds from Lodi Vecchio. Opening times: Sat 8am–12.30pm, Sun 3.30pm–6.30pm, June–Sept Sun 9.30am–12.30pm. Closed for renovation.

Museo Civico

☉

Follow Via Strepponi and Via S. Francesco to reach the Gothic church of S. Francesco on Piazza Ospedale. It dates from the 13th century, but was never completed. The interior is decorated with 14th and 15th-century frescoes.

S. Francesco

The Ospedale Maggiore, also on the piazza of that name, was established in 1459 by the bishop of Lodi. The 15th-century chiostro (cloister) with its terracotta adornments is worth visiting.
The Museo Paolo Gorini in one wing of the cloister (key from the porter's lodge at the main entrance to the Ospedale) presents the research of the scientist **Paolo Gorini** (1813–81), principally preserved parts of the human body, for which he tried out alternative methods of preservation. The ceiling above this strange collection of exhibits is gaily painted with grotesque motifs.

Ospedale Maggiore

◄ Museo Paolo Gorini

Around Lodi

6km/4mi to the west of Lodi is Lodi Vecchio. It is difficult to believe that this scene of rural tranquillity was once the site of the second most important city in Lombardy. The **church of S. Bassiano** outside today's settlement has survived from old Lodi. It is said to derive

★
Lodi Vecchio

← *The church of S. Maria Incoronata has an impressive dome*

Sant'Angelo Lodigiano, a medieval castle

from a church founded by St Bassianus in the 4th or 5th century. Between 1320 and 1323 – long after the city was destroyed – it underwent thorough alterations in the Gothic style. Only the apse remains of the earlier church. The dominant feature of the bright interior are the extensive frescoes, some of them Gothic.

At the centre of **Sant'Angelo Lodigiano** (10km/6mi south of Lodi Vecchio) a fortress of the 13th and 14th centuries contains the Museo nel Castello, including an art collection, a museum of bread and a museum tracing the development of agriculture from the Neolithic period to the present day. Opening times: March–late July, early Aug–late Oct 8.30am–12.30pm, 2pm–6pm.

The plain known as **Lodigiano** extends around Lodi from the east bank of the Adda to the Lambro. Rows of poplars and canals set the scene. The main waterway is the Canale Muzza, which is almost 60km/40mi long and was built in 1220 as the centrepiece of the irrigation system for the fields of the Lodigiano plain.

✳ **Abbadia Cerreto**

The attraction in the village of Abbadia Cerreto, 10km/6mi southeast of Lodi, is the 12th-century church of S. Pietro. It survives from a Benedictine monastery of the 11th century which was taken over in 1135 by Cistercians from Chiaravalle. The notable part of the monastery church is its east end with an elegant octagonal crossing tower.

✳✳ Lugano

F 4/5

| **Switzerland:** Ticino/Tessin canton | **Population:** 56,000 |
| **Altitude:** 272m/892ft | |

Lugano, the true capital of Ticino (Tessin), derives its charm from its wonderful setting on ▶Lago di Lugano. However, Lugano is also the third most important financial centre in Switzerland.

Lugano nestles on the northern bank of ►Lago di Lugano between the two conspicuous peaks of Monte Brè and Monte S. Salvatore. In its vegetation and way of life, Lugano is pervaded by a Mediterranean-style atmosphere. All year round there is a colourful mix of peoples and languages. Exclusive boutiques and jewellers add a note of fashionable elegance. In just a few decades the town grew at a rapid pace to become a **prosperous economic centre** (textile and high-tech industries), the cultural capital of southern Switzerland and an extremely popular holiday resort. However, a high price has been paid for this: although Lugano still has a charming little old quarter and extensive parks, it is high-rise buildings, hotels and apartment blocks that are its dominant features. The 925m/3035ft Monte Brè is covered with buildings almost to its summit, and the town centre now merges seamlessly with the suburbs Paradiso in the south, and Cassarate and Castagnola in the east. Lugano is an unattractive example of modern overdevelopment in Switzerland, but this doesn't seem to have diminished its appeal.

Unofficial capital of Ticino

Thanks to its location on the old trading route between northern Europe and Italy, the area around Lugano was settled in pre-Roman times. In the Middle Ages it was ruled by the bishops of Como and thus repeatedly became involved in the bitter conflicts between Como and Milan. In 1512 the Swiss conquered the town. Starting in Napoleon Bonaparte's time, from 1803 to 1868 Lugano alternated with Bellinzona and Locarno as the capital of Ticino. The **opening of the Gotthard railway** in 1882 led to the rapid economic development of the region. Tourism, in particular, began on a large scale and became one of the main sources of income in the area.

History

What to See in and around Lugano

Three connecting squares, Piazza della Riforma, Piazza Rezzonico and Piazza Manzoni, along with the pedestrian zone, are the heart of the old quarter of Lugano. Piazza della Riforma, lined by fine 19th-century town houses, is the main square. Street cafes, restaurants and shops do their business under its arcades. A food market is held here on Tuesdays and Fridays, and in the summer months an art and antiques market on Saturdays. On the side towards the lake stands the impressive **Palazzo Civico**, built as government offices in 1844–45; a statue representing *Spartacus* (1850) has been placed in the northern archway. The little Piazza Riziero Rezzonico adjoins Piazza della Riforma to the south-west, and to the north-east the gardens of Piazza Alessandro Manzoni with the Palazzo Riva, now seat of the Banca della Svizzera Italiana, one of three fine 18th-century Baroque town houses that share the same name; the others stand on Piazza Cioccaro and at Via Pretorio 7. On the lakeshore not far from the three squares is the main pier (**debarcadero**) for ships to other places on the lake and round trips.

✴ Old quarter ✴ ◄ Piazza della Riforma

▶ VISITING LUGANO

INFORMATION

Lugano Turismo Infopoint
Palazzo Civico, Riva Albertolli
Tel. 0 91 6 05 26 43, fax 0 91 6 13 05 36
www.lugano-tourism.ch

WHERE TO EAT

▶ Expensive

① *Orologio*
Via Nizzola 2
Tel. 09 19 23 23 38
www.ristorante-orologio.com
Closed Sun, holidays
Elegant restaurant opposite the bus station; both the menu and the wine list offer a fine selection.

▶ Inexpensive

② *Grotto Morchino*
Via Carona 1, Pazzallo
Tel. 09 19 94 60 44
www.morchino.ch
Closed Sat midday, Mon
This wonderful grotto is in a wood above Lugano Paradis; guests are served grilled food under enormous trees.

WHERE TO STAY

▶ Luxury

① *Ticino*
Piazza Cioccaro 1
Tel. 09 19 22 77 72, fax 09 19 23 62 78
www.romantikhotels.com/Lugano
This cosy hotel occupies a 14th-century palazzo; the rooms are small but equipped with modern bathrooms.

▶ Mid-range

② *Lido Seegarten*
Viale Castagnola 24
Tel. 09 19 72 63 63, fax 09 19 73 62 62
www.hotellido-lugano.com
This hotel lies right on the lake at the northern end of the bay, towards Brè, and has a swimming pool; ask for a room with a view of the lake.

▶ Budget

③ *Montarina*
Via Montarina 1
Tel. 09 19 66 72 72, fax 09 19 66 00 17
www.montarina.ch
Just above the station; a budget hotel and hostel, but it has a pool.

Shopping streets ▶ The old quarter and its narrow alleys, some lined with arcades, encloses Piazza Riforma and rises from there to the west. The main shopping streets are Via Nassa and Via Pessina. The latter, which leads north, has retained its old appearance. Here there are tempting food shops and delicatessens. To the south Via Nassa, lined by chic shops, leads to Piazza Bernardino Luini.

★★
S. Maria
degli Angioli

S. Maria degli Angioli on Piazza Bernardino Luini was built from 1499 to 1515 as the church of a Franciscan monastery. Plain from the outside, it is one of the **artistic highlights of Ticino**. Inside a three-arched screen separates the nave from the monks' choir. Its façade depicting the passion and crucifixion of Christ (1529) is the principal work of **Bernardino Luini**, a pupil of Leonardo and one of

Lugano Map

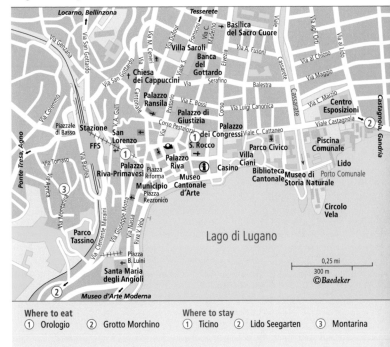

Where to eat
① Orologio   ② Grotto Morchino

Where to stay
① Ticino   ② Lido Seegarten   ③ Montarina

the most important Renaissance painters of Lombardy. The fresco of the Last Supper on the south wall of the nave and the graceful Madonna with the young Jesus and John in a side chapel are also by Luini. Note also the frescoes depicting the Flight into Egypt and the Adoration of the Magi (1520) by Domenico de Pet.

Nearby, the little pilgrimage church S. Maria di Loreto of 1524 is an oasis of peace among modern residential and hotel buildings. The church, which at first sight looks like a palazzo, once belonged to a monastery of the Carlist order. The charming porch and tower date from 1633. Inside, the church is notable for its sumptuous stucco decorations and 17th-century frescoes. **S. Maria di Loreto**

San Lorenzo, the main church in Lugano, stands in a wonderful and commanding position above the old quarter. In its present form it dates from the 13th century and has been altered a number of times. The fine Lombard Renaissance façade was built between 1500 and 1517. The principal architect is thought to have been Gian Gaspare ★ **S. Lorenzo**

Pedoni from Carona. In the 18th century, when the church was renovated, the side chapels were added. Only some fragments of Gothic cycles of frescoes remain.

✳ **Buildings by Mario Botta**

In 1985 **Mario Botta**, a star architect from Ticino (born 1943), designed **Palazzo Ransila**, a commercial building on Corso Pestalozzi, with a beehive structure whilst keeping its old façade. In 1987 he built the fortress-like headquarters, clad in natural stone, of the **Banca del Gottardo** (Viale Stefano Franscini), which houses a gallery dedicated to contemporary painting and photography (opening times: Tue 2pm–5pm, Wed–Sat 11am–5pm). In 1990 Botta built his own **atelier** (Via Ciani 16) and several villas.

! **Baedeker TIP**

For lovers of jazz
Each year in late June and early July the internationally renowned Festival Jazz Lugano draws big names from the jazz scene and large audiences. www.estivaljazz.ch

✳ **Museo Cantonale d'Arte**

The Museo Cantonale d'Arte (Via Canova 10), the cantonal art gallery north-east of Piazza della Riforma, occupies a group of three palazzi (16th–18th centuries). It exhibits paintings by Swiss and other European artists of the 19th and 20th centuries such as Hodler, Klee and Bill, and French Impressionists (Renoir, Degas and others). Temporary exhibitions are also held. Opening times: Tue 2pm–5pm, Wed–Sun 10am–5pm.

✳ **Parco Civico**

East of the old quarter along the banks of the lake is a beautiful park filled with old trees, subtropical plants and sculptures. The Villa Ciani, constructed here in Neoclassical style in 1840 for the brothers Giacomo and Filippo Ciani, houses the **Museo Civico di Belle Arti**, an excellent collection of works by foreign and Swiss Impressionist and modern artists (opening times: Tue–Sun 10am–noon, 2pm–6pm). The **Museo Cantonale di Storia Naturale** (Cantonal Museum of Natural History) on the east side of the Parco Civico displays zoological, botanical, palaeontological, geological and mineralogical collections. Opening times: Tue–Sat 9am–noon, 2pm–5pm.

✳ **Giardino Belvedere**

The long lake promenade from Lugano to Paradiso is flanked by the Giardino Belvedere, where sculptures by well-known international artists stand between subtropical plants. The promenade is also the site of **Villa Malpensata** (Riva Caccia 5), a 19th-century building by Gianfranco Rossi. It is home to the **Museo d'Arte Moderna**, where temporary exhibitions on modern art and architecture are held. Opening times: Tue–Sun 10am–6pm.

Castagnola ✳ **Villa Favorita** ▶

In Castagnola, an upmarket little town on the shore of the lake to the east of Lugano, Villa Favorita lies in the middle of a lovely park. It originated in a residence built in 1687 for the von Beroldingen family, which passed to the Riva family in 1732 and to Baron von Thyssen in 1932. Until 1991 the Collezione **Thyssen-Bornemisza**, one of the world's most important private collections of paintings, occupied the wings that were added at that time. Most of the works are now exhibited in the Palacio de Villahermosa in Madrid, and since 1993 Villa Favorita has held a smaller collection by great artists of the 19th and 20th centuries acquired by Thyssen's daughter Francesca von Habsburg. Opening times: April–Oct Fri–Sun 10am–5pm.

Not far to the east of Villa Favorita (Via Cortivo 24), Villa Heleneum is situated in a lovely park. It was built around 1930 in Neoclassical style as a copy of the Trianon Palace at Versailles and now houses the Museo delle culture extraeuropee, where exhibits from Oceania, Indonesia and Africa can be viewed. Opening times: April–Oct Tue–Sun 10am–6pm.

◄ Villa Heleneum/ Museo delle culture extraeuropee

Picturesque Gandria, once a fishing village, clings to the steep and rocky slopes of Monte Brè above Lago di Lugano, about 5km/3mi east of Lugano. It can be reached by boat or via the northern lakeshore road (head towards Lago di Como), but the most attractive way to get there is to walk from Castagnola (about 3km/2mi). With

★ ★
Gandria

Villa Favorita was once home to a famous art collection

its narrow flights of steps, arched and crooked passageways and terraces for vines, the little village possesses great charm.

✳
Swiss Customs Museum

Cross by boat to the opposite bank to visit the Museo Doganale Svizzero, the Swiss Customs Museum. The exhibition in this former customs house of 1904 presents the working life of customs officers, including weapons and some highly unusual and interesting vessels and containers used by smugglers. Opening times: end of April to mid-Oct 1.30pm–5.30pm.

✳✳
Monte Brè

The cable car (Via Pico) from Cassarate takes 20 minutes to the 925m/3035ft summit of Monte Brè (runs every 30 minutes, 8am–6pm). This mountain, a popular destination as a lookout point, forms the eastern border of the bay of Lugano. It can also be climbed on narrow paths and steps in about three hours, or reached by car on a serpentine mountain road. At the top is a restaurant, from whose terrace the magnificent **panoramic view** reaches as far as the Alps of Valais and the Bernese Oberland. The Swiss architect and painter Wilhelm Schmid (1892–1971) lived in the mountain village of **Brè**; Museo Schmid commemorates him. Opening times: mid-April to mid-Oct Wed–Sun 2pm–5pm.

✳✳
Monte S. Salvatore

Monte S. Salvatore, Lugano's second mountain, is 915m/3002ft high. The lower station of the funicular railway to the top is in Paradiso, on the south side of the town (Viale delle Scuole; mid-March to early Nov, every 30 min). Museo S. Salvatore is devoted to a collection of minerals (opening times: Wed–Sun 10am–noon, 1pm–3pm). From the summit there is a fantastic all-round view of Lugano and Lago di Lugano, the Alps of Valais and the Bernese Oberland, and the north Italian plain. A gourmet restaurant and a self-service cafe await visitors to the summit.

✳✳ Mantua · Mantova

R 10

Provincial capital
Population: 49,000

Altitude: 20m/66ft

Mantua is attractive for its lakeside location alone. In addition it possesses well-preserved historic buildings and squares. The numerous arcades, all with different capitals, are a beautiful testimony to the Renaissance era.

City of Manto

Historic Mantua is a prosperous city. The province of Mantua derives its income from the chemical industry and oil reserves, but above all from profitable agriculture, as most of the famous Parma ham is produced here. The foundation of Mantua is attributed to

● VISITING MANTUA

INFORMATION

A. P. T./I. A. T.
Piazza Mantegna 6
I-46100 Mantova
Tel. 03 76 43 24 32, fax 03 76 36 32 92
www.turismo.mantova.it

WHERE TO EAT

▶ **Moderate**

① *Taverna S. Barbara*
Piazza S. Barbara 19
Tel. 03 76 32 94 96
Closed Mon, Tue evening
Typical Mantuan food; guests are
seated in an inner courtyard of the
Palazzo Ducale or in the smart and
cosy tavern.

② *L'Ochina bianca*
Via Finzi 2
Tel. 03 76 32 37 00
Closed Mon, sun evening, Aug
www.ochinabianca.it
Modern, pleasantly furnished osteria
that offers a huge choice of dishes and
has an extensive wine list.

③ *Ristorante Pavesi*
Piazza delle Erbe 13

Tel. 03 76 32 36 27
Closed Thu
It is impossible to miss this likeable
family-run restaurant in the midst
of bustling Piazza delle Erbe; Mantuan
cuisine, various pasta and meat dishes
and salads; try the delicious streusel
cake sbrisolona with coffee here.

WHERE TO STAY

▶ **Mid-range**

① *Rechigi*
Via Calvi 30
Tel. 03 76 32 07 81
Fax 03 76 22 02 91
www.rechigi.com, 32 rooms
Well-furnished and equipped hotel
with good service in a central location

▶ **Inexpensive**

② *Bianchi Stazione*
Piazza Don Leoni 24
Tel. 03 76 32 64 65
Fax 03 76 32 15 04
www.albergobianchi.com, 51 rooms
Well-run and friendly hotel opposite
the station; many rooms face the
quiet inner court; parking spaces
available.

Manto, the daughter of the seer Tiresias from Thebes. She is said to
have discovered this lovely spot, which was later named after her,
and lived there.

The site of Mantua, elevated terrain in the middle of a large marshy
area, was already settled in Etruscan times. It was resettled under Octavian in 41 BC as a Roman colonia for veterans. The city was an island for a long time; only in the 12th century was the river Mincio
embanked, and Mantua then expanded on a peninsula. As an important seat of rulers of a marcher county, the city flowered culturally
from the 10th century until the death of the last marchioness, Matilde di Canossa, in 1115. After this Mantua developed as a free comune, until the Bonacolsi family took control in 1273. From 1328

History

Mantua Map

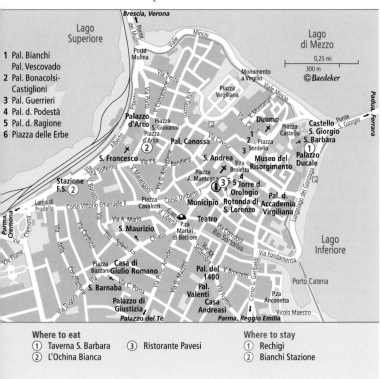

1 Pal. Bianchi
  Pal. Vescovado
2 Pal. Bonacolsi-
  Castiglioni
3 Pal. Guerrieri
4 Pal. d. Podestà
5 Pal. d. Ragione
6 Piazza delle Erbe

Where to eat
① Taverna S. Barbara
② L'Ochina Bianca
③ Ristorante Pavesi

Where to stay
① Rechigi
② Bianchi Stazione

the **Gonzaga** were the rulers. In 1707 power passed to the Austrian Habsburgs. The numerous cultural jewels which can be visited in Mantua today are mainly the heritage of the 300 years of Gonzaga rule. The Gonzaga dynasty increased their power and wealth purposefully through marriages and skilful ecclesiastical policy: several Gonzaga were cardinals.

Leading architects such as Leon Battista Alberti and later Giulio Romano, a pupil of Raphael, were brought to Mantua. The painters Antonio Pisanello, Andrea Mantegna and Peter Paul Rubens and the composer Claudio Monteverdi (▶ Famous People) worked for the Gonzaga court, which enjoyed its golden age during the Renaissance under **Francesco II** (1466–1519), **Isabella d'Este** (▶ Famous People) and her son Federico II (1500–40). However, a war over the succession (1627–31) devastated the city. In 1708, after the death of the last Gonzaga, Ferdinando Carlo, the Austrian Habsburgs took power in

Mantua and held it until 1866 – except during the reign of Napoleon I, who had the Tyrolean freedom fighter **Andreas Hofer** shot here in 1810.

What to See in Mantua

Markets are still held on Piazza delle Erbe. The name of the square is a reminder that vegetables and herbs have been sold here since the Middle Ages.

★
Piazza delle Erbe

The Rotonda di S. Lorenzo occupies the south-west corner of the square. Marchioness Matilde di Canossa had it constructed in the late 11th century. The church was secularized in 1579 and surrounded by other buildings for centuries, but reopened as a church in 1926. It lies almost 2m/6ft below the level of the square today. Features of the circular, two-storey domed rotunda, which was built of brick with a semi-circular apse, are two Roman columns, cushion capitals and the remains of frescoes. A depiction of the martyrdom of St Lawrence can be seen on the right in the apse. Opening times: summer Tue–Fri 10am–1pm, 3pm–7pm.

★
◄ Rotonda di
S. Lorenzo

☉

The Palazzo della Ragione on the north-east side of the piazza, once the city hall, was built in the 13th century with early Gothic influences. As with other palazzi in Mantua, the code di rondine, the »swallow-tail« crenellations, are a noticeable feature. The arcade gallery was added during the Renaissance. Frescoes from the first period of construction survive on the upper floor.

★
◄ Palazzo
della Ragione

The Torre dell'Orologio was built next to the Palazzo della Ragione in 1473 by Luca Fancelli, the court architect of the Gonzaga. The mathematician, mechanic and astrologer Bartolomeo Manfredi made the magnificent astronomical clock. It served not only to give the exact time, but also to provide astrological information relating to the day and month as well as to influences on agriculture. The Madonna on a crescent moon (late 16th century) symbolizes the victory of Christianity over unbelievers.

★
◄ Torre dell'
Orologio

On the opposite side of the square stands the church of S. Andrea, with a façade giving onto the little Piazza A. Mantegna. The church was built from 1472 to designs by Leon Battista Alberti to replace a Benedictine monastery. The early 15th-century campanile in late Gothic style remains from the monastery. Alberti's church is regarded as **a pioneering Renaissance work in Lombardy**. The spatial scheme carried out here had a long-lasting influence on architectural history. The façade, a portico with tall rounded arches, pilasters and a pediment, combines the design of an ancient temple with that of a triumphal arch. **Inside the church** the motif of the façade is repeated twice on each side of the nave, with the tall round arches now housing side chapels.

★ ★
◄ S. Andrea

The innovative aspect of Alberti's plan was the unified space, which is centred on the crossing. The triumphal arch is continued inside in the shape of a coffered barrel vault. The frescoes were painted

The evening sky over Mantua

around 1550 to designs by Giulio Romano. The dome, the work of Filippo Juvarra, was not added until the years 1733–56. The first chapel in the left aisle holds the tomb of **Andrea Mantegna**, who died in Mantua in 1506. The bust of the painter, which is thought to be a self-portrait, is famous. A relic of the **blood of Christ** is kept in the crypt of S. Andrea. According to legend, earth soaked with Christ's blood was brought to Mantua by St Longinus. The relic, which was in the possession of the Gonzaga family, is shown to the faithful just once a year, during the Good Friday procession.

Palazzo dell' Accademia Virgiliana
East of Piazza delle Erbe at Via Accademia 47 stands the Palazzo dell' Accademia Virgiliana, which was built in 1767 and remodelled in Neoclassical style a short time later. The Austrian Habsburg ruler Maria Theresia was an active patron of this Mantuan academy for literature and art. Inside, the 400-seater **Teatro Bibiena** survives unchanged from the first period of construction, which took place from 1767 to 1769 under the direction of Antonio Galli Bibiena. Bibiena brought the young Wolfgang Amadeus Mozart to Mantua especially for a concert to inaugurate the late Baroque theatre. Opening times: Tue–Sun 9am–noon, 3pm–6pm.

! **Baedeker TIP**

Boat trips

Mantua looks especially beautiful from the water. In summer boats run to the Lotus Flower Isles, and there are longer trips to the river Po. Information: tel. 03 76 32 28 75, www.motonaviandes.it.

The continuation of Piazza delle Erbe to the north-east is the little Piazza Broletto, site of the Palazzo del Podestà, an originally Romanesque structure that was altered in the 15th century in Renaissance style and now accommodates the conservatory of Mantua. The **Torre Civica** on the corner is a survivor from the Middle Ages. A seated 13th-century figure on the north side next to the passage leading to Piazza delle Erbe is said to represent Virgil.

At the corner of Via Cavour stands one of the old family towers that testify to the conflicts between Ghibellines and Guelphs. Rival families built fortified towers in which to take refuge. The Torre della Gabbia (»cage tower«), which dates from around 1300, takes its name from a method of execution common in those times: condemned persons were put on view in a cage attached to the tower, in which they died slowly of hunger and thirst.

The long Piazza Sordello is the oldest square in Mantua. For centuries it was the seat of Gonzaga rule and thus the cultural and political centre of the city.
The cathedral, at the northern corner of the piazza, was begun in about 1131. Today the campanile (1140) is the only remaining part of the Romanesque cathedral, which was originally built in the form of a basilica and remodelled in the Gothic style under Francesco I Gonzaga; in the 18th century the façade was again altered, now in the Baroque style. Only the right-hand outer wall is Gothic. The **in-**

Piazza Broletto: a pleasant place to end the day

terior was rebuilt in the 16th century to created double aisles. The classical Chapel of the Sacrament (1784) is in the north transept. The design of the Incoronata Chapel (*c*1482) in front of it is ascribed to Leon Battista Alberti.

✷ ✷ Palazzo Ducale

Opening hours:
Tue–Sun
8.30am–7pm
www.mantova
ducale.it ▶

On the east side of Piazza Sordello lies the jewel of the city of Mantua, **the largest palace ensemble in Italy**: the Palazzo Ducale. From outside it is hard to imagine the immense size of the residence of the Gonzaga dynasty. After passing through a little gate, visitors to the palazzo have entered a complex of buildings that resembles a city within the city. The palace consists of eight large buildings with a total of 500 rooms.

Palazzo Ducale *Plan*

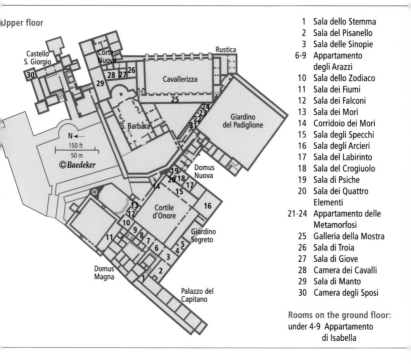

Upper floor

1　Sala dello Stemma
2　Sala del Pisanello
3　Sala delle Sinopie
6-9　Appartamento degli Arazzi
10　Sala dello Zodiaco
11　Sala dei Fiumi
12　Sala dei Falconi
13　Sala dei Mori
14　Corridoio dei Mori
15　Sala degli Specchi
16　Sala degli Arcieri
17　Sala del Labirinto
18　Sala del Crogiuolo
19　Sala di Psiche
20　Sala dei Quattro Elementi
21-24　Appartamento delle Metamorfosi
25　Galleria della Mostra
26　Sala di Troia
27　Sala di Giove
28　Camera dei Cavalli
29　Sala di Manto
30　Camera degli Sposi

Rooms on the ground floor:
under 4-9　Appartamento di Isabella

The individual components that make up the Palazzo Ducale origi-nated between the 13th and 17th centuries. The earliest palaces were the Domus Magna (1299) and the Palazzo del Capitano (1308). From 1395, as a defence against attacks by the neighbouring Viscon-ti, the fortress Castello S. Giorgio, a fine example of late Gothic mili-tary architecture, was built. The Domus Nuova dates from 1480–84, the Corte Nuova and Rustica from about 1539. In 1565 the Cavaller-izza and palace church of S. Barbara brought to an end the main work on the palace complex.

The entrance to the Palazzo Ducale is on Piazza Sordello. Only a small part of the grounds, changing according to the time of year, is opened to visitors. The numbers used in the following description of the principal rooms relate to the ground plan.

Tour

A painting by Domenico Morone in the Sala dello Stemma (»Hall of Weapons«) depicts the expulsion of the Bonacolsi by the Gonzaga in 1328 and includes a veduta of Piazza Sordello on which the cathedral can be seen with its Gothic façade.

◄ Sala dello Stemma

PALAZZO DUCALE

✳ ✳ Mantua's showpiece, the largest palace in Italy, lies on the east side of Piazza Sordello: the Palazzo Ducale. From outside it is difficult to imagine the enormous size of the residence of the Gonzaga dynasty. Visitors step through a little gate to enter a complex of buildings which is almost like a city within the city and has a total area of 34,000 sq m/40,000 sq yd. The palace consists of eight main buildings with more than 500 rooms, in addition to 15 gardens and courtyards.

🕐 Opening times:
Tue–Sun 9am–9pm

① Sala dello Stemma

In the »Armoury Hall« a painting by Domenico Morone depicts the expulsion of the Bonacolsi by the Gonzaga in 1328. A veduta of Piazza Sordello was used as a basis for 20th-century restoration of the Palazzo Ducale.

② Sala del Pisanello

The remains of murals are part of a cycle of frescoes by Antonio Pisanello (⊲1440) on the theme of life at the court of King Arthur. Through their possession of a relic of Christ's blood, the Gonzaga identified with the world of Arthurian chivalry and the legend of the Holy Grail.

③ Appartment degli Arazzi

The 16th-century Brussels tapestries (»arazzo« means »tapestry«) in this succession of four rooms were woven on the basis of designs by Raphael for Pope Leo X. Cardinal Ercole Gonzaga acquired them for the palace church.

④ Sala dello Zodiaco

The room takes its name from the ceiling painting by Lorenzo Costa il Giovane, which dates from around 1579 and portrays Diana amongst the signs of the zodiac. Napoleon is said to have slept here.

⑤ Sala dei Fiumi

The »Chamber of Rivers« was used as a banqueting hall. The walls are adorned with 18th-century allegorical representations of the six rivers of the province of Mantua, which was larger then than today. From this room there is a view of a hanging garden, laid out on the first floor in the 16th century by Pompeo Pedemonte for guests of court.

⑥ Sala degli Specchi

There are no longer any mirrors in the Sala degli Specchi, the »Hall of Mirrors«. The Mannerist ceiling paintings in this room are the work of 16th-century Mantuan artists, and the wall decoration dates from 1779. The trompe-l' oeil effect of the pairs of horses at both ends of the hall is extremely well executed. The horses seem to follow visitors as they walk through. The figure of a woman holding a circlet (5th picture on the left) appears to be reaching out to beholders wherever they are standing.

⑦ Sala degli Arcieri

The »Hall of Archers« houses valuable 17th-century paintings, including a Rubens family portrait of the Gonzaga adoring the Holy Trinity.

⑧ Cavallerizza

Here the famous horses of the Gonzaga stud could be admired.

⑨ Galleria della Mostra

The Galleria della Mostra was home to the important Gonzaga art collection. Some of the paintings were destroyed by fire, and the others have finished up in European museums. Roman sculpture is now on display here.

⑩ Camera degli Sposi

One of the main sights, painted between 1465 and 1474 by Andrea Mantegna, is in the Castello S. Giorgio. The walls depict members of the Gonzaga family, and above the entrance putti hold a dedicatory inscription. The artist immortalized himself in the form of a small self-portrait on one of the pilasters.

⑪ Appartamento di Isabella

After the death of her husband in 1519, Isabella d' Este moved into the Corte Vecchia. Wooden intarsia work depicting musical instruments and city views, as well as a Roman bust of Faustina, have survived in the Studio, which she used as a study and has a coffered ceiling, and in the Grotta. The outstanding marble doorway is by Cristoforo Romano. Note also the motto of Isabella d' Este, »Nec spe, nec metu« (»Neither from hope nor fear«), and the musical scales with the symbol for a rest – a means of expressing silence.

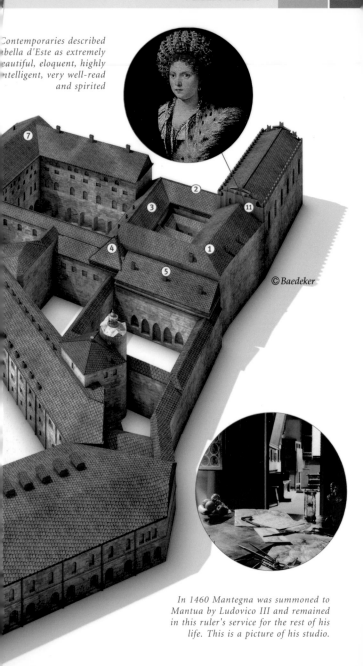

Contemporaries described bella d'Este as extremely beautiful, eloquent, highly intelligent, very well-read and spirited

© Baedeker

In 1460 Mantegna was summoned to Mantua by Ludovico III and remained in this ruler's service for the rest of his life. This is a picture of his studio.

The golden age of the Gonzaga court was during the Renaissance under Francesco II and his wife Isabella d'Este

Ludovico II in conversation with his son Francesco Gonzaga in the Camera degli Sposi

Sala del Pisanello ►	Remains of murals in the Sala del Pisanello are part of a cycle of frescoes (c1440) by **Antonio Pisanello** on the subject of life at the court of King Arthur. Through their possession of the relic of Christ's blood, the Gonzaga identified with the world of Arthurian chivalry and the legend of the Holy Grail.
Appartamento degli Arazzi ►	The 16th-century Brussels tapestries (»arazzo« means »tapestry«) in this succession of four rooms were woven on the basis of designs by Raphael for Pope Leo X. Cardinal Ercole Gonzaga acquired them for the palace church.
Sala dello Zodiaco ►	The room takes its name from the ceiling painting by Lorenzo Costa il Giovane, which dates from around 1579 and portrays Diana amongst the signs of the zodiac. Napoleon is said to have slept here.
Sala dei Fiumi ►	The »Chamber of Rivers« next to the Sala dello Zodiaco was used as a banqueting hall. The walls are adorned with 18th-century allegorical representations of the six rivers of the province of Mantua by Giorgio Anselmi. From this room there is a view of a hanging garden, laid out on the first floor in the 16th century by the architect Pompeo Pedemonte for guests of court.
Sala dei Falconi ►	To the right of the Sala dello Zodiaco visitors enter the Sala dei Falconi, where falcons have been painted on the ceiling, and pass via the Sala dei Mori (13), where ebony figures are intended as representations of negroes, into the adjoining Corridoio dei Mori (14).
✱ Sala degli Specchi ►	There are no longer any mirrors in the Sala degli Specchi, the »Hall of Mirrors«. The Mannerist ceiling paintings in this room, in which festivities were held, are the work of 16th-century Mantuan artists, and the fine wall decoration dates from 1779. Note the extremely effective trompe l'oeil effect of the pairs of horses at both ends of the hall, which seem to follow visitors as they walk through.
✱ Sala degli Arcieri ►	The »Hall of Archers« houses valuable 17th-century paintings. **Peter Paul Rubens**, who was court artist here from 1600 to 1608, painted the portrayal of the Gonzaga adoring the Holy Trinity. The work was cut into pieces, and only a small section of it can be viewed today.
Sala del Labirinto ►	The painted ceiling in this room depicts a **labyrinth** as a symbol of the uncertainty of life. The inscription reads »forse che si, forse che no« (»maybe yes, maybe no«).
Appartamento delle Metamorfosi ►	The precious library of the Gonzaga once occupied these four rooms. The 17th-century depictions of **Ovid's *Metamorphoses*** by Antonio Maria Viani are incomplete. The busts, copies of Greek originals, date from the 1st and 2nd centuries AD.
Cavallerizza, Galleria della Mostra ►	In the Cavallerizza the famous horses of the Gonzaga stud could once be admired. The Galleria della Mostra, which runs along the Cavallerizza, was home to the important Gonzaga art collection. Some of the paintings were destroyed by fire, and the others have finished up in European museums. A number of busts of Roman emperors and sculptures are now on display here.

The murals in the Sala di Manto depict scenes from the history of the city, including a representation of the legendary founder of Mantua, Manto (in a green dress).

One of the main sights, painted between 1465 and 1474 by **Andrea Mantegna**, is in the Castello S. Giorgio: the Camera degli Sposi or »Wedding Chamber«. It is shown as a pavilion with members of the Gonzaga family on the walls: Ludovico with his consort Barbara of Brandenburg, their children and courtiers. Above the entrance putti hold a dedicatory inscription. The artist immortalized himself in the form of a small self-portrait on one of the pilasters. Women and putti look down into the room over a balustrade, while others direct the viewer's gaze to the ceiling painting, which opens up a view of the heavens.

After the death of her husband in 1519, Isabella d'Este moved out of her former apartments in the Castello S. Giorgio and into the Corte Vecchia. Wooden intarsia work depicting musical instruments and city views has survived in her study, the Studio, which has a coffered ceiling, and in the Grotta. The outstanding marble doorway is by Cristoforo Romano. Note also the motto of Isabella d'Este – »nec spe, nec metu« (»neither from hope nor fear«) – and the scales with the musical notation for a rest, a means of expressing silence.

In the Camera degli Sposi the viewer's eyes are directed to the heavens

★
◄ Appartamento di Isabella

Other Sights in Mantua

Palazzo Canossa on the piazza of the same name was built in 1560 in the Mannerist style by Giovanni Battista Bertani for the marquises of Canossa and lengthened considerably in 1660. Its most magnificent feature is the stairway with Baroque sculptures.

Palazzo Canossa

At Piazza Carlo d'Arco it is worth paying a visit to the Palazzo d'Arco, an 18th-century aristocratic residence with a small 19th-century garden. The last member of the Arco family who lived there laid down in her will that the rooms should be opened to the public after her death just as they were when she occupied them. This provides an excellent impression of the style of living of Mantuan nobles, and includes furnishings and art from the 15th to 18th centuries; the old

★
Palazzo d'Arco

kitchen is most impressive. The family owned an extensive collection of paintings and a valuable library. Opening times: March–Oct Tue–Sun 10am–12.30, 2pm–5pm; Nov–Feb Sat, Sun 10am–noon..

S. Francesco

From here it is not far to the church of S. Francesco, south of the palazzo. It originated in the 14th century as a Franciscan monastery church and is now the **most important medieval church in Mantua**. However, the existing building is largely a reconstruction following severe damage in the Second World War. The Cappella Gonzaga remains of the original church: the Gonzaga used S. Francesco as their burial church for a long period. Some surviving 14th-century frescoes depict scenes from the life of St Louis of Toulouse.

✶ ✶ Palazzo del Tè

Opening hours:
Mon–Fri 9am–6pm
www.centro
palazzote.it ►

Palazzo del Tè to the south of the city centre is regarded as the principal work of the architect **Giulio Romano**. From 1525 until 1535 the art-loving first **Duke of Mantua, Federico II**, built a summer palace outside the city on the island of Tè, which lay where the Mincio had been dammed to form lakes. The result was not the usual princely villa, but an extensive garden palace with ponds, gardens and stables, which later was to be a model for such palaces as Versailles, Nymphenburg and Schönbrunn. Federico II spent time here not only with his wife Margarita Paleologa, but also with **Isabella Boschetti**, with whom he had a passionate relationship for years. In the Palazzo del Tè celebrations were held and guests received: Emperor Charles V stayed here, for example. The four wings of the main building, which has only 1½ storeys, surround a square inner courtyard. The frescoes that decorate the rooms were designed by the architect, Romano, but most were painted by his pupils.

Each room is dedicated to a particular theme, and the whole ensemble was planned according to the teachings of philosophers, philologists, astrologers and scholars. The architecture, painting, sculpture and stucco work adopt elements of ancient Roman art, but then – and this is the remarkable aspect of Giulio Romano's work – exaggerate and distort them. The structure of the buildings seems at first sight to be simple, clear and transparent, but the execution is in fact astonishing and complex. Numerous breaches of the rules of ancient architecture, for example symmetry, were deliberately employed in the endeavour to introduce an element of gaiety to court architecture.

Tour

The first rooms on the tour were furnished for Isabella Boschetti. The following wing was used for receptions and large festivities and dances, and the third part of the building was fitted out for Charles V.

Sala dei Cavalli ►

The Sala dei Cavalli, a reception room, is dedicated to the horses of the Gonzaga stud. Six horses are represented with an ideal landscape as the background. Here Rinaldo Mantovano executed Giulio Romano's designs. The heraldic symbols of Federico catch the eye: Mount Olympus, a symbol of power, and the fire salamander – a reference to the flame of his passion for Isabella Boschetti.

In the Sala di Psiche, the dining room, the marriage of Amor and Psyche is represented; here the gods assemble for a banquet. According to the neo-Platonic interpretation the room is an invitation to Federico to progress from carnal love to spiritual love.

◄ Sala di Psiche

The Sala dei Giganti is the **most important room in the palace**. It depicts the **destruction of the Titans**, who hatched a plot against the gods. On the ceiling Jupiter, surrounded by the alarmed gods, sits on a cloud and hurls thunderbolts into the hall of the power-hungry giants in punishment. On the walls the horrified Titans are crushed by masses of falling rock. The decoration of this chamber, like that

◄ Sala dei Giganti

Palazzo del Tè was designed by Raphael's pupil Giulio Romano

of the neighbouring rooms, was done in honour of Charles V. The room, which has outstanding acoustics, was illuminated in the evenings from the fireplace, which made the scenes on the wall and ceiling appear even more frightening.

Gardens ► An airy loggia opens up the palace to the gardens, with depictions of plants to emphasize the transition. The architectural effects of the water were planned: the arches are mirrored in the calm surface of the water to form circles. In order to light up the garden at night, candles were placed in the mouths of the mythical beasts. To the north-east the gardens terminate in an arch-shaped exedra, which was added in the 17th century in the period of Austrian rule.

Appartamento della Grotta ► In a secluded corner of the garden Federico ordered the construction of a small house for his exclusive personal use. Its decoration of mosaics, mythological subjects and floral ornamentation was modelled on that of a Pompeian villa. The octagonal Grotta is designed in the manner of Roman baths.

What to See around Mantua

S. Benedetto Po South-east of Mantua, beyond the Po, lies S. Benedetto Po, site of the basilica of the same name. S. Benedetto Po was once an important monastery. The Benedictine monks, and later Cistercians, made cultivable the land which was often flooded by the Po. The monastery originated in a foundation by Tedaldo di Canossa in 1007. Visitors can see 32 life-size terracotta figures of doctors of the church, apostles and saints, the Renaissance arcà of Cesare Arzago (1528) and the sarcophagus of Marchioness Matilda di Canossa (died 1115), who mediated in the Investiture Controversy between Pope Gregory VII and Emperor Henry IV. 500 years after her death, her mortal remains were translated to St Peter's Basilica in Rome.

S. Maria delle Grazie In Curtatone, a few miles west of Mantua, it is worth visiting the pilgrimage church of S. Maria delle Grazie, which was built in the 15th century by **Bartolino da Novara** to fulfil an oath taken by Francesco Gonzaga I in 1399. Construction continued until the 16th century. The most notable features of the interior are concerned with the theme of deliverance from perils in many different forms. For example, just inside the main entrance an embalmed crocodile of unknown origin is suspended from the roof, and on one wall is a depiction of a man who has been weighed down with a stone before being thrown into a well. Votive offerings adorn the pilasters and columns. Paintings, photographs and embroidery or crochet work record private mishaps such as a snake-bite, traffic accident or illness. Each of them bears the initials P. G. R., meaning »Per Grazia Ricevuta« (»received by grace«). Every year on 15 August (the feast of the Assumption of the Virgin) Curtatone is the venue for an international **competition of Madonnari**, pavement artists who specialize in religious themes.

★ Milan · Milano

Capital of the Lombardy region
Altitude: 122m/400ft

Provincial capital
Population: 1,310,000

Milan has earned all the superlatives: the leading Italian city for industry, finance, trade and trade fairs, the fashion capital of Italy, a city of media, music and theatre. However, with Milan it is not a case of love at first sight. Those who know the city compare it with an oyster, which shows strangers its dull outer shell and hides the pearl within.

Milano, the capital of Lombardy, is the undisputed centre of northern Italy and the second-largest city in Italy after Rome. It is an important traffic hub with two airports, several railway stations and a dense network of motorways and other main roads. Milan is known far beyond the borders of Italy as **the capital of Italian fashion and design**, and also as a major centre for music and theatre. The name of the city means a lot to football fans, as two Milanese clubs, AC Milan and Inter (FC Internazionale Milano), have played in Serie A for many years and are among the world's most famous clubs.

Centre of northern Italy

After fighting the Etruscans, a Celtic tribe called the Insubres founded a settlement in 396 BC. In 222 BC it came under the hegemony of the Romans, and under the name **Mediolanum** was the centre of transport and trade in the province of Gallia Cisalpina. Under Emperor Diocletian it was the capital city for a time, and after Emperor Constantine's Edict of Toleration of 313 Mediolanum also became a religious centre and the base of Bishop Ambrose, one of the fathers of the church (►Famous People). After suffering devastation repeatedly in the period after the fall of the Western Roman Empire, in 569 Milan fell under Lombard rule, and from 774 under that of the Franks.

History

From the 11th century Milan strove for autonomy as a comune, a movement which was only temporarily held up when Emperor Frederick Barbarossa destroyed the rebellious city in 1162, while sparing the churches. The ultimate victors in conflicts with the Holy Roman Empire and internal struggles in the city were the **Visconti** family. In 1277 they took control of Milan and in 1395 gained the title of dukes.

The Ambrosian Republic between 1447 and 1450 was only a short interlude before **Francesco Sforza** inherited the position of the Visconti. As an economic centre with 200,000 inhabitants, the city also attracted covetous neighbours, starting with the kings of France, who occupied Milan several times up to 1525. After the death of the last Sforza in 1535, the Duchy of Milan reverted to the Holy Roman

▶ VISITING MILAN

INFORMATION

I. A. T.
Via Marconi 1 (next to the cathedral)
I-20100 Milano
Tel. 02 72 52 43 01/2
Fax 02 72 52 43 50
www.milanoinfotourist.it

I. A. T.
Galleria di Testa (at the railway station)
Tel. 02 72 52 43 60

TRANSPORT

The metro lines M1, M2 and M3 are a fast means of transport. Tram no. 30 and buses 96 and 97 serve the inner city. In 2007 a toll was introduced for drivers entering the city centre by car.

SHOPPING

Via Montenapoleone, Via della Spiga and Via Andrea are the famous »golden triangle« where the great fashion designers showcase their work. For boutiques with reasonable prices and specialist shops, go to the Brera quarter. Greatly reduced designer fashion is available from the stock houses, e.g. Libero (Via Dante 14 and Via Solferino 11) and Il Salvagente (Via Fratelli Bronzetti 16). Designer goods are sold on Corso Garibaldi and Corso Matteotti.

WHERE TO EAT
▶ **Moderate**
① *Capolinea*
Via Lodovico il Moro 119

Milan: the perfect place for high-end shopping

Tel. 02 89 12 20 24
Closed Mon
A rendezvous for Milan's night owls
and artists; excellent home-made
pasta dishes, tasty vegetables and the
famous escalope milanese. A jazz bar
is attached.

② *Trattoria Milanese*
Via S. Marta 11, tel. 02 86 45 19 91
Closed Tue
Traditional family restaurant serving
Milanese specialities such as risotto
milanese, costoletta milanese and
ossobuco; for dessert try the home-
made zabaione.

③ *Torre di Pisa*
Via Fiori Chiari 25
Tel. 02 87 48 77
Closed Sat midday
Small restaurant in the Brera quarter
with good home-made cooking, deli-
cious pasta and excellent meat dishes.

④ *Le Vigne*
Ripa di Porta Ticinese 61
Tel. 02 8 37 56 17
Closed Sun
A pleasant osteria in the Navigli
quarter for a light snack or a proper
meal; delicious desserts and good
wines. High prices.

▶ **Inexpensive**
⑤ *Bottiglieria da Pino*
Via Cerva 14
Tel. 02 76 00 05 32
Opens only for lunch, closed Sun
Reasonably priced restaurant near the
cathedral with tasty light dishes; the
desserts are also recommendable.

⑥ *La Cantina di Manuela*
Via Poerio 3, tel. 02 76 31 88 92
www.cantinadimanuela.it
Popular place near Piazza Risorgimento with excellent food, an out-

standing wine list and very reasonable
prices.

WHERE TO STAY
▶ **Luxury**
① *Diana Majestic*
Viale Piave 42
Tel. 02 2 05 81
www.sheratondianamajestic.com,
94 rooms
Comfortable Art Nouveau hotel near
Porta Venezia with a garden in which
to relax after strenuous sightseeing.

② *Grand Hotel et de Milan*
Via Manzoni 29
Tel. 02 72 31 41, fax 02 86 46 08 61
www.granhoteletdemilan.it, 95 rooms
Extremely central luxury hotel with
great charm – Giuseppe Verdi liked it.

▶ **Mid-range**
③ *King*
Corso Magenta 19
Tel. 02 87 44 32, Fax 02 89 01 07 98
www.hotelkingmilano.com, 48 rooms
Venerable, cosy hotel on Corso Magenta; pretty rooms with sound-
proofed windows; from the upper
floor there are great views across the
roofs of the city.

④ *Casa Svizzera*
Via S. Raffaele 3
Tel. 0 28 69 22 46
Fax 02 72 00 46 90, 45 rooms
Attractive, well-fitted hotel with a very
pleasant atmosphere on the cathedral
square.

⑤ *Antica Locanda Leonardo*
Corso Magenta 78
Tel. 02 48 01 41 97, fax 02 48 01 90 12
www.anticalocandaleonardo.com
12 rooms
Small hotel in a central location. The
rooms are tastefully furnished and air-
conditioned; small garden.

Empire and was given by Emperor Charles V to his son Philip II. Under the Spanish Habsburgs the city was a stronghold of the Counter-Reformation, with Carlo Borromeo (1538–84) and Frederico Borromeo (1595–1631) as its archbishops. After the War of the Spanish Succession Milan passed to Austria from 1714 to 1796, and – following the intermezzo of Napoleonic rule – from 1814 to 1859. The 19th-century movement for Italian unification, the **Risorgimento**, found vehement support in Milan. Initially Field Marshal Count Radetzky thwarted its efforts by bloodily suppressing the revolution of 1848.

Not until 1861, with the help of France and the neighbouring Kingdom of Sardinia-Piedmont, was Milan able to join the newly proclaimed Kingdom of Italy. This was followed by industrialization and rapid economic growth, accompanied by a rise in population and workers' revolts in the period before the First World War. In 1919 the first groups of Fascist Blackshirts were formed in the prelude to Mussolini's dictatorship. In 1943 Milan suffered severe damage in the Second World War.

The city's appearance

In comparison to many smaller towns in Lombardy, Milan has a modern appearance. In the centre around the cathedral there are still some narrow alleys, but also wide shopping streets. Between Castello Sforzesco and Piazza S. Babila a pedestrian zone has been created. Italy's most famous shopping streets are here: Via Monte Napoleone, Via della Spiga, Corso Venezia. The city centre is encircled by a belt of wide roads which follow the course of the former »bastioni«, the old fortifications of the Spanish Habsburgs. Outside this belt, highrise buildings have proliferated, and sprawling suburbs have sprung up on the edge of Milan.

City Centre

★★ Piazza del Duomo

The heart of Milan and its bustling centre is Piazza del Duomo. The piazza was laid out in its present form in 1865 as a cathedral square, although work on the cathedral had not yet been completed. On the north side of the square is the entrance to the famous **Galleria Vittorio Emanuele II**, on the south side the two symmetrical 20th-century **Arengario** buildings, home to the tourist information office. Opposite the north side of the cathedral is the well-known department store **La Rinascente**. The **equestrian statue** of 1896 represents Vittorio Emanuele II, King of Italy.

★★ Duomo

The best-known historic building in Milan is its »duomo«, the cathedral of S. Maria Nascente, which is dedicated to the birth of the Virgin. Covering an area of 11,700 sq m/ 125,000 sq ft, it is the **second-largest church in Italy** after St Peter's in Rome. It holds about 40,000 people and is adorned by 3000 statues. In 1386 the foundation stone for a completely new cathedral in the Gothic style was laid on the

Highlights *Milan*

Cathedral of S. Maria Nascente
The ascent to the roof of the cathedral is a highly recommended and thoroughly enjoyable break in your sightseeing programme.
▶ page 270

Galleria Vittorio Emanuele II
Not exactly cheap, but certainly chic: Milan's high-class promenade is ideal for a stroll, even when the weather is bad.
▶ page 272

Castello Sforzesco
Michelangelo's famous Pietà Rondanini and other wonderful sculptures are on show in the municipal collections in the Sforza fortress.
▶ page 278

Pinacoteca di Brera
Masterpieces of Italian painting from a period of 800 years – a delight for everyone, not just for art lovers.
▶ page 282

S. Maria delle Grazie
The world's most famous mural, Leonardo da Vinci's *Last Supper*, is a magnet for visitors.
▶ page 282

site of previous churches dating back to early Christian times. By 1419 work on its eastern end had been finished, enabling Pope Martin V to consecrate the choir. Although some parts remained to be completed, the final consecration was performed in 1572 by Archbishop Carlo Borromeo. The crossing tower was not finished until the years 1765–69.

In the early 19th century, on the occasion of the coronation of Napoleon as king of Italy, the west façade was largely completed in neo-Gothic style, but work on details and restoration continued until 1935. Smog and car exhaust gases, as well as vibrations from the heavy traffic that shakes the building, constitute a serious threat that necessitates permanent restoration work on a large scale.

The five-part façade is a mixture of Baroque and neo-Gothic elements. The most notable of the five entrances is the **main door** at the centre. In the early 17th century it gained its Baroque frame, but the bronze door with neo-Gothic and Art Nouveau influences was not installed until 1900. It depicts scenes from the life of the Virgin. The second door from the right shows scenes from the history of Milan.   ◀ Façade

The gigantic interior consists of a nave and double aisles, which are slightly lower. The transept has single aisles. The total length is 148m/486ft, the width at the transept 89m/292ft and the height of the nave 46m/151ft at the centre. In their present form most of the glass dates from the 19th century, but some of the original 15th-century windows have survived and can be seen in the north transept. The windows of the choir were inserted in 1402. In the oldest part, the east end, are **two Gothic doorways** from the first years of con-   ◀ Interior

Milan Map

Where to eat
① Capolinea
② Trattoria Milanese
③ Torre di Pisa
④ Le Vigne
⑤ Bottiglieria da Pino
⑥ La Cantina di Manuela

Pirelli Tower, Stazione Centrale F.S.

Monza, Lecco

0,25 mi

300 m

© Baedeker

S. Angelo

S. Bartolomeo

Piazza della Repubblica

Via Pafini
Via Nuova
Porta Nuova
Via Moscova
Largo Donegani
Montebello
Corso

Via Filippo
Via Fatebenefratelli
Via Annunciata

Pal. Borromeo

Archi di Porta Nuova

Palazzo Dugnani
Museo d. Cinema
Centro Svizzero

Giardini Pubblici

Via Tarchetti
Bastioni di Porta Venezia

S. Carlo al Lazz.

Viale Vittorio Veneto
Viale di Porta Orientale
I Palazzi

Piazza Sta. Franc. Romana

Buenos Aires
Gregorio
Tunisia
Lecco
Via V. G. B. Morgagni
Lazater

Piazza Oberdan

Porta Venezia

Piazza VII Novembre 1917

Via A. Stoppani
Don Sturzo

Piazza G. Ascoli

Viale Abruzzi

Piazza Cavour

Civica Galleria d'Arte Moderna
Giardini di Villa Reale

Piazzale Morandi

Palazzo d. Senate

Planetario
Civico Museo di Storia Nat.

Piazza Duse

Via Marina
Via della Spiga
Via S. Spirito
Via Gesù
Via Monte Napoleone
Via S. Andrea
Via Borgospesso
Via del Giardini
Via Manzoni
Via Senato
Via dei Cappuccini
Palestro

Nino
Bixio
Carlo
Via Cirro
Piacenza
Via G. Modena
Via Castel
Via Morrone
Uberti
Menotti
Goldoni

Via Bellotti
Plave

S. Pietro Celest.

Museo Poldi Pezzoli
Pal. Belgioioso
Mus. Manzoniano
S. Fedele
Municipio
Pal. Marino

Duomo

Pal. Serbelloni
Prefettura

Istituto dei Ciechi

S. Cuore di Gesù

Piazza del Tricolore
Corso Concordia

Piazza Risorgimento
Corso Indipendenza

Piazzale Dateo

Via Mozart
Via S. Damiano
Monforte
Corso Monforte

Porta Monforte

Via Carlo
Via Sottocorno
Via Goffredo Mameli
Via Fratelli
Via Sismondi

Macedonio

S. Babila
Piazza S. Babila

S. Carlo

Corso
Corso Matteotti
P.zza Meda

Via Borgogna
Via Pietro Mascagni
Via Bellini
Viale Majno
Viale Bianca Maria
Via Archimede
Premuda

Corso Vitt. Emanuele II
Via Durini
Via Cino
Via Larga

Largo Augusto
Via Battisti

Pal. Reale

Palazzo Arcivescovile
Piazza Fontana
Piazza Beccaria

S. Maria d. Passione

Conservatorio Verdi

S. Pietro in Gess.

Corrigioni

Piazza Giornato

Marcona
Via B. Cellini
Fiamma
Via B. Calvi

Orfanatrofie Femm.

S. Maria d. Suffragio
XXII

S. Gottardo
Uff. Comunale
S. Stefano Magg.
Piazza S. Stefano
S. Antonio Abate
Teatro Lirico

Corso di Porta Vittoria

Porta Vittoria

Corso

Via Anfossi
Via Sidoli
Bezzecca

Mon. al Marinaio d'Italia
Largo Marinai d'Italia

Stazione Porta Vittoria F.S.

Ospedale Maggiore/ Università

Via Sforza

Palazzo di Giustizia

Via Freguglia
Via V. Malpi
Via Besana
Rotonda

Via Fontana

Via della Commenda

San Barnaba
SS. Paolo e Barnaba
S. Maria d. Pace
Soc. Umanitaria
Piazza Umanitaria

Giardino Guastalla

Largo Richini
S. Nazaro Magg.
Piazza S. Nazaro

Policlinico

Via M. Fanti
Via Lamarmora
V. Curtatone
Caldara

Regina Margherita
Nero
Augusto
Via Spartaco

Bergamo
Botta
Viale Lazio

Fogazzaro
Via A. Maffei
Emilio
Via Cadore
Via M. Campionesi
Friuli

Via Perugino
Via Sim. d'Orsenigo

S. Calimero
Piazza Card. Ferrari

S. Maria al Paradiso

Corso di Porta Vigentina
Via Orti

S. Pietro d. Pellegrini

Via Lazzaro Papi
Viale Lombardia

Piscina Caimi

Pier Vasari
Via S. Lattuada

Piazzale Libia

Via Comelico
Via A. Maj
Viale Girone
Via Ferrini
Viale Umbria
Via Tito Livio

S. Pio

Porta Vigentina
Pavia

Via Crivelli
Beatrice
Via d'Este

Piazzale Med. d'Oro
Porta Romana

Piacenza, Parma

Where to stay

1. Diana Majestic
2. Grand Hotel et de Milan
3. King
4. Casa Svizzera
5. Antica Locanda Leonardo

struction: the door of Christ (1389, on the left by the north sacristy) and the door of the Virgin (1391, on the right by the south sacristy). Otherwise the furnishings of the cathedral mainly derive from the 16th century, when Archbishop Carlo Borromeo commissioned his favourite architect, **Pellegrino Tibaldi**, to remodel the interior. Tibaldi also designed the **Cripta di S. Carlo** under the choir. In the octagonal Cappella di S. Carlo the mortal remains of Archbishop Carlo Borromeo, who was canonized in 1610, are kept in a sarcophagus of rock crystal.

The **Tesoro del Duomo**, the cathedral treasury, is also beneath the choir. Its exhibits include a late Romanesque processional cross from Chiaravalle (with admission to crypt; opening times: 9am–noon, 3pm–6pm).

The **tombs of prominent people** can be found in the aisles: in the south aisle (from west to east) the sarcophagus of Archbishop Ariberto da Intimiano (died 1045), the red marble tomb of archbishops Ottone Visconti (died 1295) and Giovanni Visconti (died 1354), the marble monument to Marco Carelli (died 1394) and the tomb of Gian Andrea Vimercati (died 1548); the wall monument to Gian Giacomo Medici (died 1555) in the south transept was made in 1563 by Leone Leoni. In the north aisle note the baptismal font made by Pellegrino Tibaldi from a Roman porphyry bowl, and in the north transept the seven-branched, plant-like **Trivulzio candelabrum**, a 5m/16ft Romanesque masterpiece in bronze (1200–20).

Battistero Paleocristiano ► Inside the cathedral next to the main entrance steps lead down to the Battistero Paleocristiano. When the Metro was being constructed under the cathedral square, walls of the churches that preceded the cathedral were discovered. Remains of the early Christian basilica of S. Tecla, which stood here in the 4th century, can be seen, as well as remains of the baptistery, S. Giovanni alle Fonti, probably the place where St Augustine was baptized by Bishop Ambrose in 387. Opening times: March–Oct 9am–5pm.

★ ★
Terrazzi ► Don't miss going up to the terrazzi, the roof terrace of the cathedral. The steps and the lift are outside on the north side of the cathedral. Unusually, it is possible to walk along the building past innumerable slender, pointed finials, which are crowned by figures, as far as the crossing tower. The statue of the Madonnina looks down on the roof. In good weather the view from the terrazzi extends all the way to the plain of the Po and the Alps. Opening times: March–Oct daily 9am–5pm.

Palazzo Reale In its present form with a classical façade, the Palazzo Reale opposite the south side of the cathedral was designed in 1772. In 1138 the old city hall was built on this site, then altered in the 14th century by the Visconti and used as the **seat of government**, the Corte Ducale. The

*The cathedral is in the heart of Milan and provides a superb view →
of Galleria Vittorio Emanuele II and the city*

CATHEDRAL OF S. MARIA NASCENTE

✱ ✱ If Gian Galeazzo Visconti had had his way, Milan cathedral would have been built in a single phase. This ambitious prince doubled the working hours and introduced fines for slacking, but his efforts were in vain: the construction of the cathedral was not completed until the 20th century.

🕐 Opening times:
March–Oct daily 9am–5pm

① The second-largest church in Italy
With a length of 148m/486ft, a width of 89m/292ft and an interior height of up to 68m/223ft, the cathedral is Italy's second-largest church after St Peter's Basilica in Rome.

② Heavenly host in stone
About 3400 figures crown the pinnacles of the cathedral. Soaring above them all, the 4m/13ft Madonnina shines out far and wide.

③ First stages of construction
The choir, part of the transepts and the first two bays of the nave had been built by about 1415.

④ Precious stained glass
The oldest windows of the cathedral glow colourfully in the north sacristy.

⑤ Trivulzio candelabrum
The seven-armed bronze candelabrum in the north transept is said to date from the 13th century.

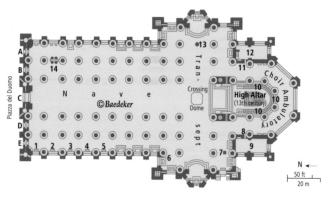

Themes of the bronze doors (19th and 20th centuries)
A Edict of Milan
B Life of St Ambrose
C Life of the Virgin
D History of Milan
E History of Milan Cathedral

Furnishings
1 Sarcophagus of Archbishop Ariberto da Intimiano (✝ 1045)
2 Sarcophagus of Archbishops Ottone Visconti (✝ 1295) Giovanni Visconti (✝ 1354)

3 List of archbishops of Milan
4 Sarcophagus of the merchant Marco Carelli (14th century)
5 Tomb of Gian Andrea Vimercati (✝ 1548)
6 Tomb of Gian Giacomo Medici (✝ 1555; by Leone Leoni, 1560–1563)
7 St Bartholomew (by Marco d'Agrate, 1562)
8 Door of the south sacristy (reliefs by Hans von Fernach and other Rhenish masters, 1393)

9 South sacristy (cathedral treasury)
10 Wood carvings of choir stalls (1572–1620)
11 Door of the north sacristy (by Giacomo da Campione and assistants, 14th century)
12 North sacristy (remains of the first phase of building)
13 Trivulzio bronze candelabrum (13th century)
14 Font (by Pellegrini, 16th century)

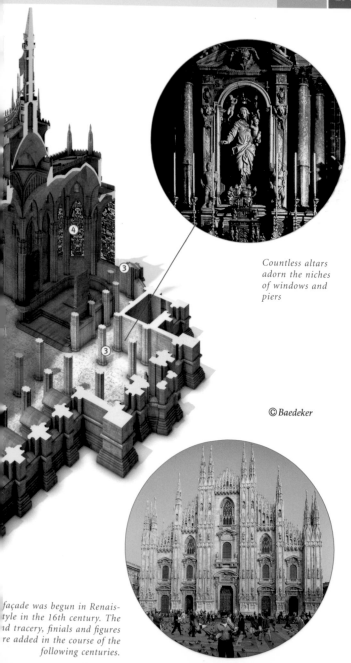

Countless altars
adorn the niches
of windows and
piers

© Baedeker

façade was begun in Renais-
tyle in the 16th century. The
ld tracery, finials and figures
re added in the course of the
following centuries.

The most precious treasure in the cathedral is a nail from Christ's cross. It is kept in a crucifix high up in the apse.

itors can climb to the roof of cathedral

Sforza made further alterations, but moved into the Castello Sforzesco in the 15th century. In 1943 the interior was destroyed in a bombing raid.

Civico Museo d'Arte Contemporanea ►
Museo del Duomo ⏱

The Palazzo Reale is home to the Civico Museo d'Arte Contemporanea with its large collection of 20th-century painting.

The cathedral museum, which is also part of the palazzo, recounts the history of Milan cathedral through documents, sketches and designs. It also displays architectural fragments and valuable works of art from the church. Closed for renovation..

Palazzo Arcivescovile

The bishop's palace to the south-east was first built in the 12th and 13th centuries. The entrance and inner courtyards were designed in the 16th century by **Pellegrino Tibaldi**, the classical east front in the 18th century by **Giuseppe Piermarini**.

★ ★
Galleria Vittorio Emanuele II

Galleria Vittorio Emanuele II on the north side of Piazza del Duomo is the most famous sight in the city apart from the cathedral and La Scala. A colourful mix of locals and visitors frequent the galleria: bank employees, salespeople and tourists flock to the cafes and restaurants, while fast food outlets attract the younger generation. The galleria, which opened in 1878, was designed by the Bolognese architect **Giuseppe Mengoni** and named after the first king of a united Italy. It was built on a cross-shaped ground plan in an elegant and ostentatious manner and roofed in glass. A magnificent 47m/155ft-high glass dome rises at the centre.

Mengoni came up with an outsized triumphal arch as the entrance; on its lower floor the founders of the companies Campari and Motta set up shop. The three other entrances are less spectacular. In 1943 the galleria was largely destroyed by bombs, but was rebuilt fairly quickly. To celebrate its centenary, a mosaic floor was laid below the dome in 1978.

★
Piazza Mercanti

Piazza Mercanti borders the cathedral square to the west. In the Middle Ages it was the focus of municipal life. Then Via Mercanti was laid out through the middle of the piazza.

Palazzo della Ragione ►

The long Palazzo della Ragione was the»new« city hall in the Middle Ages. It was built between 1228 and 1233 under the first mayor of Milan – a stone equestrian portrait of him can be seen in a round-arched niche on the outside of the south wall. The palazzo was constructed in a plain Romanesque style. Markets took place here when the traders set up their stalls under the arcades. The room above was used for assemblies, and until 1770 the palazzo was the seat of city government. The **Loggia degli Osii** (Piazza Mercanti 9) has a conspicuous black and white marble façade. Judgments and important communal announcements were once

Galleria Vitorio Emanuele II: not just a place for promenading →
and luxury shopping, but also an example of magnificent architecture

made from the little balcony. The building to the right of the loggia, the **Palazzo delle Scuole Palatine** (Piazza Mercanti 11), was built in 1644–45, incorporating a medieval city gate, as a counterpart to the Palazzo dei Giureconsulti opposite. The **Palazzo dei Giureconsulti**, which forms the north side of the piazza, has a Mannerist design and dates from 1560–68.

S. Maria presso S. Satiro

South of Piazza Mercanti on Via Torino is the church of S. Maria presso S. Satiro, which originated in the 9th century. In the second half of the 15th century it was altered to designs by Donato Bramante. The church is known for its **painted trompe l'oeil architecture**: as there was not enough space to extend the choir in the 15th century, Bramante painted a deceptively genuine-looking choir with a barrel-vaulted coffered ceiling. The Cappella della Pietà, built in the form of a Greek cross, with a Pietà (1482) by Agostino de Fondutis is also impressive.

Pinacoteca Ambrosiana

South-west of Piazza Mercanti lies Piazza Pio XI, where the Palazzo dell'Ambrosiana, opened on St Ambrose's day 1609, houses the Pinacoteca Ambrosiana. The collection includes outstanding paintings, including works by Botticelli, Ghirlandaio, Titian, Caravaggio and Tiepolo, as well as Raphael's enormous cartoon for his famous *School of Athens* in the Vatican and Leonardo da Vinci's *Portrait of a Musician*. Opening times: Tue–Sun 10am–5.30pm.

The **Biblioteca Ambrosiana**, one of Europe's first public libraries, is attached. Its holdings include 750,000 books and 35,000 manuscripts. Opening times: Mon–Fri 9am–5.30pm.

Ospedale Maggiore/ Università

The Ospedale Maggiore south of the cathedral was begun in 1456 in the early Renaissance style by Filarete. It is a rectangular brick complex around four courtyards, and remained unchanged up to the 18th century. Until 1942 it served as a hospital, but now accommodates faculties of the university.

Teatro alla Scala

North of the cathedral lies **Piazza della Scala**, site of a monument to Leonardo da Vinci made in 1872 by Pietro Magni and the opera house, which takes its name from the former church of S. Maria della Scala and is known far beyond the city: the world-famous Scala. The designs for this classical edifice were done by **Giuseppe Piermarini**, who was the leading architect in Milan at that time. On 3 August 1778 the theatre was inaugurated with a performance of an opera by Antonio Salieri. In 1943 La Scala was destroyed by bombs. Following reconstruction in the old style, it reopened in 1946 with seats for an audience of 2800. The present façade, which dates from 1830, is composed of classical columns, pilasters and windows. A pediment with a relief of Apollo on his sun chariot in the tympanum crowns the central doorway (►Baedeker Special p.276). **Tickets** for La Scala are available from: Biglietteria Centrale, Piazza del Duomo, Galleria del Sagrato, daily noon–6pm; reservations and information: tel. 02 72 00 37 44, www.teatroallascala.org.

One wing of La Scala houses an excellent theatre museum, displaying portraits and busts of great figures from the world of opera, costumes, models of stage sets and Franz Liszt's grand piano. One room is devoted to Giuseppe Verdi (▶Famous People), another to Gioacchino Rossini. Visitors can also learn about **the history of theatre in Europe**, theatre in the ancient world and Commedia dell' arte, as well

◀ Museo Teatrale alla Scala

To have performed at La Scala is to belong to the pantheon of opera greats

Most of the world's gr opera singers have performed in these splendid surroundings

A WORLD-FAMOUS THEATRE

A performance at La Scala is still a society event. In Milan almost everybody knows what the current production is – *Tosca* or *Lucia di Lammermoor* – and who is in the cast.

The premiere may be an event where the »great and good« of the city keep to themselves, but on the very next evening opera fans of all classes will be present, just as at a football match. Those who cannot afford an expensive seat buy a ticket to stand on one of the upper tiers. And more than a handful of fans attend performances several times in succession.

The **opening of the season** on 7 December, St Ambrose's Day, is the society event of the year. On this day La Scala is the meeting place of Milanese high society. All the notables and celebrities of the city get in on the act, and well-known faces can be seen, dressed up to the nines, emerging from luxury limousines into a crowd of journalists and photographers on the square in front of the theatre. Probably all the world's great musicians have passed through La Scala's doors. **Arturo Toscanini** made it a world-famous venue in the 1920s, and conducted the reopening concert in 1948. »The divine« **Maria Callas** enjoyed her greatest triumphs at La Scala. In 1953 Leonard Bernstein made his opera debut there. In 1960

the celebrated Dimitri Mitropoulos died at the rostrum, at the age of 64, during a rehearsal of Gustav Mahler's Third Symphony. **Claudio Abbado** became permanent conductor at the age of 35, and musical director of La Scala four years later. He was succeeded in 1986 by **Ricardo Muti**, and since 2005 **Stéphane Lissner** has had the leading role. But times have changed nevertheless. There have been complaints about the quality of the singers, and increasing financial difficulties. In 1991 the ministry of finance in Rome cut the subsidies. This meant a significant drop in income for La Scala, which received the highest subsidies. Closure of the theatre was only just prevented, and in 1995 La Scala was made into a joint stock company. The state holds 51% of the shares, and the remainder is in the hands of a foundation. As the fabric of the building was decaying, it had to be rebuilt. The theatre moved to a temporary location and reopened in 2004 in the Piazza Scala.. The architect **Mario Botta** has constructed a new building around the old auditorium.

as taking a look at the auditorium. A library of theatre studies containing 90,000 volumes is attached. Opening times: daily 10am–noon, 2pm–5pm.

Opposite La Scala stands the most important private palazzi of the city, Palazzo Marino. Its Mannerist design influenced several generations of Lombard architects. The commission was awarded in 1558 to **Galeazzo Alessi** from Perugia. The façade to Piazza della Scala was not added until the late 19th century, but corresponds to designs by Alessi. The four wings of the palazzo enclose two courtyards and now house the **city hall** of Milan.

Palazzo Marino/Municipio

The house in which the well-known Italian **poet Alessandro Manzoni** lived from 1814 to 1873 is now the Museo Manzoniano (Via Morone 1). His study, salon and the room in which he died can be visited, and pictures, manuscripts and documents are on view. Opening times: Tue–Fri 9–noon, 2pm–4pm.

Museo Manzoniano

Palazzo Pezzoli (Via A. Manzoni 12) accommodates the **art collection of Gian Giacomo Poldi Pezzoli**. It includes valuable paintings by such artists as Botticelli, Piero della Francesca and Canaletto, porcelain, fine pieces of furniture (16th–18th centuries), Murano glass, jewellery dating from several centuries and collections of clocks and compasses. Opening times: 10am–6pm.

✱ **Museo Poldi Pezzoli**

Northern City Centre

From Piazza Duomo cross Piazza Cordusio with its big bank and insurance buildings to reach Via Dante, a broad and busy shopping street which connects to Castello Sforzesco. The 14th-century Palazzo Carmagnola at the corner of Via Dante and Via Rovello houses the Piccolo Teatro, founded in 1947 by **Giorgio Strehler**, Nina Vinchi and Paolo Grassi as the first Italian teatro pubblico. It became world-famous under Strehler, who directed works by Goldoni, Shakespeare, Chekhov and Brecht and took up the tradition of Commedia dell' arte.

Piccolo Teatro

Although it is one of Europe's leading theatres, for a long time it seemed makeshift in terms of its size and technical equipment. In 1977 the star architect and designer Marco Zanuso was commissioned to built a new theatre. Political quarrels and corruption scandals held the work up, and the cost of the project escalated from year to year. After a 15-year construction period the new theatre was finally inaugurated in 1998. Strehler, who died in 1997, did not live to see it completed.

Beyond Largo Cairoli the route leads direct to the main gate of the magnificent Castello Sforzesco. After the old Visconti castle was devastated and plundered, **Duke Francesco** (reigned 1450–66) initiated

✱✱ **Castello Sforzesco**

work on the present building, a fortified residence for the Sforza family, in 1450. To protect the Palazzo Ducale, the existing square complex with its characteristic towers was built by renowned military architects. The central gate tower, Torre del Filarete, was constructed in 1452, destroyed by an explosion in 1521 and rebuilt only in the early 20th century.

The fortress builder Bartolomeo Gadio from Cremona was responsible for the two corner towers with diamond-patterned stonework. The citadel, the Rocchetta, towers on the west side. Duke Galeazzo Maria Sforza made the Corte Ducale, the dukes' residence, the seat of government, and had it magnificently furnished between 1466 and 1476, when he was murdered.

The work of well-known painters, including Vincenzo Foppa, Cristoforo Moretto and Benedetto Ferrini, adorned the interior. After Galeazzo's death, his widow, Bona di Savoia, had the 30m/100ft-high central tower, Torre di Bona di Savoia, erected as a safe place to live. The artistic golden age of the ducal residence was the time of **Ludovico il Moro** and **Beatrice d'Este**, who brought Leonardo da Vinci and Donato Bramante to Milan. Bramante built a portico in the court of the Rocchetta and a bridge to the Corte Ducale at the north-eastern corner. Leonardo da Vinci was commissioned to paint the walls of some of the palace rooms. Other projects fell victim to political events, as the French invaded and took over the fortress in 1499.

After the death of the last Sforza, Francesco II, the Duchy of Milan reverted in 1535 to Emperor Charles V, who handed it to his son Philip II. The Spanish viceroys made the fort into an impressive stronghold. The inner court, Piazza d'Armi, was used as a parade ground. In the late 19th century restoration of the fortress began. Bombs caused severe damage in 1943, and following post-war reconstruction several rooms in the former ducal palace and the Rocchetta were opened as a museum (**Musei Civici del Castello Sforzesco**).

⏱ Opening times: Tue–Sun 9am–5.30pm.

Ground floor ► The highlights on the ground floor of the Corte Ducale are the **equestrian statue of Bernabò Visconti** (14th century; room 2) by Bonino da Campione and the frieze of the Porta Romana (room 6; 1171) by Anselmo da Campione depicting the Ambrosian troops who defended the church of Milan against the Arians. The Sala delle Asse (room 8) was painted by **Leonardo da Vinci** to create the illusion of an open bower of oaks. Frescoes by Lombardy painters have survived in the **Cappella Ducale** (room 12). In the Sala degli Scarlioni (room 15) the famous Pietà Rondanini, Michelangelo's last work, which he was forced to leave unfinished in 1564, can be admired. This Pietà, timeless in its simplicity but harrowing at the same time, was in the possession of the Rondanini family until 1953, when it was bought by the city of Milan.

✷
Pietà Rondanini ►

Renowned architects and artists, including Leonardo da Vinci, →
took part in the construction of Castello Sforzesco

Castello Sforzesco Plan

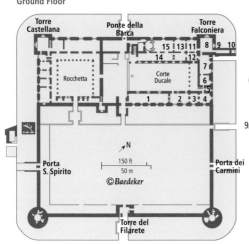

Ground Floor

1 Sala della Cancelleria
  Sculpture, frescoes, mosaics (4th–11th centuries)
2 Romanesque and Gothic sculpture
3 Frescoes (15th century)
4 Frescoes (14th–15th centuries)
5 Religious art (14th–15th centuries)
6/7 Exhibits on city history
8 Sala delle Asse
  Wood carvings by Leonardo da Vinci
9/10 Saletta negra
  Renaissance sculpture
11 Sala dei Ducali
  Sculpture (15th century)
12 Capella Ducale
13 Sala delle Colombine
  Sculpture (15th–16th century)
14 Sala delle Armi
  Weapons
15 Sala degli Scarlioni
  Sculpture (16th century)

First floor ► On the first floor valuable furnishings from the 15th to 17th centuries are exhibited and a separate little room, the **Camera di Griselda**, is used to display frescoes from Roccabianca castle with scenes taking Boccaccio's *Decamerone* as their literary source. After this visitors enter the **pinacoteca**, where Italian paintings, mainly from the 15th to the 18th century, including works by Bellini, Mantegna, Tintoretto, Canaletto and Tiepolo, are on show.

Rocchetta ► The first and second floors of the Rocchetta house one of the largest and most important collections of musical instruments in Europe, as well as arts and crafts in glass, ceramics and porcelain dating from various centuries and scientific instruments of the 14th to 18th centuries. The Trivulzio tapestries in the ballroom on the first floor, made to designs by Bramantino (1503–09), are masterpieces of craftsmanship. The lower floor accommodates prehistoric and Egyptian collections illuminating various aspects of life in ancient Egypt.

★
Trivulzio tapestries ►

Biblioteca Trivulziana ► The Biblioteca Trivulziana, also housed in the Rocchetta, is regarded as the most renowned private library in Europe. It was amassed over centuries by generations of the Milanese Trivulzio family. Among its holdings are 170,000 manuscripts going back as far as the 8th century, miniatures and numerous printed works (16th–18th century).

Parco Sempione Ponte della Barca leads to Parco Sempione, which adjoins to the north-west. Opening times: daily 7am–7pm. The **aquarium** in the eastern corner of the park was one of the best in Europe before the Second World War. Its Art Nouveau building of 1906 was bombed in

1943 and did not open again for 20 years. Marine fauna and freshwater fish can be seen in its tanks and pools. Opening times: Tue–Sun 9am–5pm.

S. Simpliciano on the piazza of the same name to the east of the aquarium is **one of the city's oldest churches**. It originated in early Christian times and was rebuilt in the late 12th century as a Romanesque hall church. The doorway decorated with sculptures is of interest. Above the left entrance the figures of three martyrs who are buried in the church, Martirio, Sisinio and Alessandro, can be seen. Inside, a fresco of the *Coronation of the Virgin* (1508) adorns the apse. Each year on 29 May white doves are set free on the square in front of the church. This custom derives from a legend: it is said that during a battle in which Barbarossa was fighting against the Lombard comuni, the martyrs Martirio, Sisinio and Alessandro rose from their graves, creating confusion on the battlefield and bringing about the victory of the Lombards. Opening times: 7am–noon, 3pm–7pm, Sun 7.30am–11.30am, 4pm–7pm.

S. Simpliciano

! *Baedeker* TIP

Tram tour

A round trip on a historic tram (1920) is recommended not only for fans of nostalgic transport. It takes in the main sights such as the cathedral, Santa Maria delle Grazie and La Scala. Information about the tour is provided via headsets, and passengers can hop on and off. Departures: 9am, 11am, 1pm, Piazza Castello; information: Tram Turistico, tel. 02 86 71 31.

The Brera quarter east of Parco Sempione is **one of the liveliest and trendiest districts of the city** with narrow streets, many little shops and boutiques, galleries, bars and restaurants.

Brera quarter

The Palazzo di Brera with its art gallery Pinacoteca di Brera (Via Brera 28), once a seat of the Jesuit order, was completed in 1686. After the prohibition of the order in 1773 the complex of buildings was extended in 1784 to accommodate an academy of art and the pinacoteca. The inclusion of the Gothic church of S. Maria di Brera, which formerly lay on waste land (»brera«), is still visible in rooms III and IV of the art gallery, which were once the nave of the church. To this day the Palazzo di Brera houses the academy of art and an observatory. Enter the gallery of paintings on the first floor through the arcaded courtyard, where there is a statue of Napoleon (1809) by Antonio Canova.

✳ Palazzo di Brera

The Pinacoteca di Brera is **one of the leading art galleries in Italy**. It possesses an outstanding collection of paintings by almost all important Italian artists since the 13th century. In 1776 Maria Theresia installed a collection in the Palazzo di Brera for the purpose of studies in the newly founded academy of art. It has been open to the public since 1809. The works are hung in a total of 38 rooms, not all of

✳ ✳ ◄ Pinacoteca di Brera

which are always accessible. The collection, part of which derives from the Jesuit order, consists mainly of high-calibre Italian, Flemish and Dutch painting of the Renaissance, Mannerist and Baroque periods.

Highlights include a cycle by Vittore Carpaccio, *The Lamentation over the Dead Christ* by Mantegna, a *Pietà* by Giovanni Bellini, *St Peter Enthroned* by Cima da Conegliano, portraits by Titian, *The Miracle of St Mark* by Tintoretto, the famous large panel depicting *Madonna with Saints and Frederigo da Montefeltre* by Piero della Francesca, in a separate room, and Raphael's world-famous *Betrothal of the Virgin Mary*. Equally famous are Caravaggio's *Last Supper in Emmaus*, portraits by **van Dyck** and **Rembrandt** and vedute of Venice by Bellotto, Canaletto and Guardi. Recently, major 20th-century works, including paintings by Boccioni, Morandi and Balla and sculptures by Marini and Rosso, have been added to the collection.

Opening times: Tue–Sun 8.30am–7.15pm.

Museo del Risorgimento

The Museo del Risorgimento (Via Borgonuovo 23) east of the Palazzo di Brera uses a variety of documents and visual materials to recount the history of the unification of Italy from Napoleon's first campaign in 1796 to the foundation of the Kingdom of Italy in 1870. Opening times: Tue–Sun 9am–1pm, 2pm–5.30pm.

Giardini Pubblici

The Giardini Pubblici, a pretty park in the English style to the east of the Brera quarter, is home to the **Planetarium** and the **Civico Museo di Storia Naturale**, a museum of natural history that contains geological, mineralogical and zoological departments as well as dinosaur skeletons (opening times: Mon–Fri 9.30am–1pm, 2pm–4.30pm, Sat, Sun, holidays 9.30am–1pm, 2pm–5.30pm).

Civica Galleria d' Arte Moderna

The Neoclassical Villa Reale (1790) on the south side of the Giardini Pubblici houses the Civica Galleria d' Arte Moderna, where paintings of the 19th and 20th century (Balla, Boccioni, Segantini, Corot, Cézanne, Millet, Gauguin, Manet, Picasso, Modigliani) and a collection of sculptures by Marino Marini can be admired. Entrance: Via Palestro 16; opening times: Tue–Sun 9.30am–1pm, 2pm–5.30pm.

Next door the **Padiglione d' Arte Contemporanea** (P.A.C.) is devoted to temporary exhibitions by contemporary artists.

Western City Centre

S. Maria delle Grazie

The church of the reformed Dominican congregation S. Maria delle Grazie on Corso Magenta has great significance for the history of art. Its eastern part, designed by **Donato Bramante**, had a strong influence on Lombard Renaissance architecture around 1500. In the attached monastic complex Leonardo da Vinci's world-famous mural of the *Last Supper* can be seen. The church was built between 1463 and 1469 under Guiniforte Solari. In 1490 the chancel and apse were

Pinacoteca di Brera *Plan*

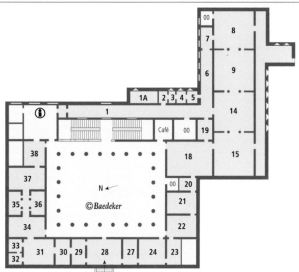

Main entrance (ground floor)

1 20th-century painting and sculpture (Boccioni, Carrà, De Pisis, Marino Marini, Modigliani, Morandi, Medardo Rosso)

1A Mocchirolo Chapel, 14th century

2,3,4 Italian painting, 13th-16th centuries (Giovanni da Milano, Andrea di Bartolo, Gentile da Fabriano, Stefano da Verona)

5,6 Venetian painting, 15th and 16th centuries (Bellini, Carpaccio, Cima, Liberale, Mantegna)

7 Venetian portraits, 16th century (Lotto, Tizian, Paris Bordon, Moroni)

8 Venetian painting, 15th century (Giovanni and Gentile Bellini, Cima da Conegliano, Vivarini, Montagna)

9 Venetian painting, 16th century (Tizian, Veronese, Tintoretto, Jacopo Bassano)

14 Venetian painting, 16th century (Bonifacio Veronese, Savoldo, Moroni)

15 Lombard painting and frescoes, 15th-16th centuries (Foppa, Bramantino, Marco d'Oggiono, Gaudenzio Ferrari)

18 Lombard painting, 16th century (A. Melone, Lomazzo, i Campi)

19 Religious paintings and Lombard portraits, 15th-16th centuries (Bergognone, Cesare da Sesto, Luini, Solario)

20 Painting from neighbouring regions Ferrara and Emilia Romana,15th century (Del Cossa, Tura, Costa)

21 Polyptychs from Le Marche, 15th century (Niccolò, Alunno, Girolamo di Giovanni, Carlo and Vittore Crivelli)

22,23 Painting from neighbouring regions Ferrara and Emilia Romana,15th and 16th centuries (De Roberti, Garofalo, Ortolano, Dossi, Corregio)

24 Piero della Francesca, Raphael, Bramante

27 Painting from central Italy, 15th and 16th centuries (Genga, Bronzino, Signorelli)

28 Painting from central Italy, 17th century (Carracci, Reni, Guercino, Barocci)

29 Caravaggio and painters influenced by him

30 Lombard painting, 17th century (Procaccini, Cerano, Morazzone, Cairo)

31 Dutch and Italian painting, 17th century (Rubens, Van Dyck, Jordaens, Pietro da Cortona, Strozzi)

32,33 Dutch painting, 16th and 17th centuries (Jan de Beer, Rembrandt, Bruegel the Elder, Santvoort)

34 Religious painting, 18th century (Tiepolo, Subleyras, Batoni)

35 Venetian painting, 18th century (Piazzetta, Canaletto, Guardi, Bellotto)

36 Italian genre painting and portraits, 18th century (Crespi, Ceruti, Fra Galgario)

37,38 Italian painting, 18th century (Appiani, Hayez, Fattori, Pellizza da Volpedo)

demolished, as Ludovico il Moro wanted it to hold the tombs of the Sforza family. He commissioned Bramante to do the work.

Even from outside, S. Maria delle Grazie is captivating: the façade has five bays and a Renaissance doorway. To the east rises the massive domed crossing tower with a gallery on all sides. The use of differently coloured materials creates a strong decorative effect.

✶ ✶
Interior ▶

The spacious interior shows that the change from Gothic to Renaissance style in Lombardy took place during the relatively short construction period. The Gothic elements in the nave – pointed arches and a cross vault – contrast with the eastern section, which was built in early Renaissance style on a central ground plan. Adjoining the crossing are lateral apses and to the east the choir, which also terminates in an apse.

Bramante's colour scheme and proportions lend a striking and coherent design to the imposing dome of the crossing. In the whole eastern part of the interior, the circle is the dominant shape in individual elements of composition, decoration and the clerestory windows. At the end of the left-hand aisle is the entrance to the votive chapel with its panel painting of Maria delle Grazie (c1462).

The lovely **cloister** with its well and small trees was also built to designs by Bramante. From here, too, there is an excellent view of the crossing tower.

Cenacolo
Vinciano ▶

✶ ✶
Last Supper ▶

In the refectory, to which a separate door to the left of the church gives access, one of the most famous murals in the world can be seen: **Leonardo da Vinci's *Last Supper*** (▶ Baedeker Special p.42). Commissioned by Ludovico il Moro, the artist worked from 1495 until 1498 on the *Cenacolo*, which takes up the north wall of the refectory. It represents the Last Supper at the moment when Christ tells his disciples that one of them will betray him. The work is famous above all for its impressive composition and its almost psychological portrayal of the actors. The disciples, who are in uproar, are depicted in groups of three. Peter bends towards John, a hand on his shoulder, and in doing so has unintentionally pushed Judas (4th from left) forwards, with the result that Judas' face is the only one in shadow.

Restoration work and the removal of later overpainting has made the original lighting of the scene clear: light appears to enter through the windows on the west side of the refectory. For the monks who ate there, the opening up of the space to the rear as a continuation of their own dining room must have had a powerful effect (▶ Baedeker Special p.42). Visits by appointment only, book well before travelling since tickets are sold out weeks in advance: tel. 02 89 42 11 46. www.milano24ore.de

✶
Museo Nazionale
della Scienza e
della Tecnica
Leonardo da
Vinci

The Museo Nazionale della Scienza e della Tecnica Leonardo da Vinci (Via S. Vittore 21) to the south of the church displays architectural and technical models that were built to designs by Leonardo (1452–1519). However, most of the museum is dedicated to techni-

Crowds come to see Leonardo da Vinci's »Last Supper«

cal progress from Leonardo's time to the 20th century. Opening times: Wed–Fri 9.30am–5pm, Sat, Sun 9.30am–6.30pm.

Milan's oldest church can be found on Piazza S. Ambrogio, somewhat to the east of the museum. The **most significant church in Lombard Romanesque style** was built here in the 12th century on the site of an early Christian cemetery. Its patron saint was Archbishop Ambrose (►Famous People), who built the church before 386. His relics have been venerated in the crypt since his burial there in 397. The church was attached to a Benedictine monastery in the 8th century, extended in the 9th century and altered again in the late 11th century. Following religious and political turbulence and damage to the fabric, rebuilding ensued in the course of the 12th century and was completed in 1196.

Chapels and interior decorations in the Gothic style were added around 1400. In the late 15th century Donato Bramante designed two cloisters and the arcade passage on the north wall of the church, the Portico della Canonica. Visitors pass through the spacious atrium, a place for the faithful to assemble and wash, to the west façade, which is flanked by two bell towers, the pre-Romanesque Campanile dei Monaci (9th century, on the right) and the Romanesque Campanile dei Canonici with blind arcades (12th century, left). The main entrance is richly adorned with Lombard decoration – the characteristic interweaving and various animal sculptures; the doors, which depict the story of David and Saul, were completed in the 18th century.

★★
S. Ambrogio

Interior ► The nave of S. Ambrogio is the oldest part of the whole complex. The vaulting consists of cross vaults in the nave and aisles, a dome above the crossing and a lower barrel vault over the choir. Note the beautiful **decorated capitals** and the **ciborium**, the altar canopy below the crossing dome, which is borne by Roman porphyry columns (early 12th century). Below it is the 9th-century **Altare d'Oro**, famous for the paliotto, Carolingian decoration of the altar with Christ enthroned, and scenes of the Nativity and Passion in gilded silver relief.

The **marble pulpit** of 1212 is a further treasure of the church. It was made by combining parts of different ages. Below it is the early Christian sarcophagus of Flavius Stilicho, who was regent during the minority of the West Roman emperor Honorius after the death of Emperor Theodosius in 395. Below the choir the remains of saints Ambrose, Gervase and Protasius rest in the crypt.

The last chapel in the right-hand aisle leads to the **funeral chapel S. Vittore in Ciel d'Oro** (4th–5th century), which is known for its very ancient mosaics dating back to about 470. One of the very earliest portraits of St Ambrose can be seen here. The left-hand aisle gives access to Bramante's Portico della Canonica. Opening times: Mon–Sat 7am–noon, 2.30pm–7pm, Sun 7am–1pm, 3pm–8pm.

A haven of peace in the city bustle: the courtyard of S. Ambrogio

From the Portico della Canonica enter the Museo di S. Ambrogio, which explains the history of the church and displays religious artefacts and works of art. Opening times: Mon, Wed, Thu, Fri 9.30am–noon, 2.30pm–5pm; Sat, Sun 3pm–5pm.

◄ Museo di
S. Ambrogio
🕓

The Museo della Criminologia e Armi Antiche opposite the entrance to S. Ambrogio is devoted to the centuries-long history of torture. The cage hanging in front of the museum is a reminder of a method of execution in the Middle Ages: the condemned were put on show in a cage until they starved to death. Opening times: daily 10am–1pm, 3pm–7.30pm.

**Museo della
Criminologia e
Armi Antiche**
🕓

At Corso Magenta 15 the former Benedictine nunnery Monastero Maggiore houses a small archaeological museum, in which finds from excavations of Etruscan, Roman and Greek culture are exhibited. Opening times: Tue–Sun 9.30am–5.30pm.

**Museo
Archeologico**

🕓

Southern City Centre

S. Lorenzo Maggiore, which goes back to the mid 4th century, is **one of the oldest Christian buildings with a central plan**. The church was destroyed by fire in the 11th century and rebuilt in Romanesque style up to 1104. The conspicuous feature of the square in front of the church, where a bronze statue of Emperor Constantine stands, is a row of 16 **colossal columns** from the imperial Roman period, probably deriving from baths. They were moved here in the 4th century with the intention of integrating them into the entrance to the church. The portico and Neoclassical west façade date from the 19th century. The dome was restored in the Renaissance style by the architect Martino Bassi after collapsing in the 16th century. In order to gain an impression of the original building, walk around the church and take a closer look at its eastern side. The church with its central ground plan has an impressive **spatial composition**. An ambulatory with two-storey exedras (extensions similar to an apse) enlarges the interior, which centres on the circular space below the dome. The southern exedra opens to the baptistery, which consists of an anteroom and the Cappella di S. Aquilino; the mosaics and murals date from the late 4th century. Behind the high altar it is possible to take a look inside the Cappella di S. Ippolito (early 6th century), where Roman columns have been built into the corners. Finally, on the north side, note the Cappella di S. Sisto (around 500). Opening times: daily 7.30am–6.30pm.

★ ★
**S. Lorenzo
Maggiore**

🕓

S. Eustorgio, further south, originated in an early Christian church of the 4th century, where the ninth bishop of Milan, the Greek Eustorgios, was buried in 349. In the 11th century remains of this building were integrated into a new church. Further renovation took place from 1218, when it became a monastery church for the Dominicans.

★
S. Eustorgio

The Romanesque church S. Lorenzo Maggiore seen through Roman columns

They erected the bell tower, at almost 80m/260ft the **tallest campanile in Milan**, around 1300. In the 15th century several chapels were added, including the well-known Cappella Portinari built onto the end of the choir. The **interior** of S. Eustorgio consists of a nave and side aisles, all with cross-vaults. The chapels in the right aisle accommodate several Visconti tombs, of which the two-storey late Gothic **wall tomb in the Visconti Chapel** (about 1360, 4th chapel) is the most impressive. The sarcophagus in the **Cappella dei Magi** in the south transept is said to have held the bones of the Three Magi, which were brought here from Byzantium, before they were taken to Cologne in 1164 after the capture of Milan by Emperor Frederick Barbarossa.

✳ Cappella Portinari ►

The chapel in the axis of the choir was built between 1462 and 1468 as a funeral chapel for the banker Pigello Portinari. The architect was Michelozzo, who designed it in Renaissance style with a dome on a central plan. It is adorned with frescoes by Vincenzo Foppa. At its centre a huge marble tomb catches the eye: it contains the mortal remains of St Peter Martyr, the inquisitor of Milan, who died in 1252 and was canonized a year later. In 1339 Giovanni Balduccio made this tomb, which is regarded as the outstanding example of Lombard Gothic sculpture of the 14th century. Opening times: daily 7.45–noon, 3pm–6.30pm.

✳ Navigli quarter

The Navigli quarter, not far south-west of S. Eustorgio beyond the Porta Ticinese, is known for its many little restaurants, bars with music and lively nightlife. Two canals, the Naviglio Grande and Naviglio Pavese, the last remaining parts of a canal network that was once extensive, meet in the Darsena, the former harbour. Construction of the Naviglio Pavese, which enters the Ticino at Pavia and thus leads to the Po, gave Milan a link to the Mediterranean. The Naviglio Grande, a canal branching off from the Ticino which was extended as far as the centre of Milan in the 14th century, also played an important role. Construction of this waterway began around 1200. In 1257 it was lengthened to the edge of Milan, and in 1395 reached the city centre close to the cathedral. The canal was then used to transport building materials for the cathedral direct to the construction site. This part of the canal was later filled in.

Outside the City Centre

✳ Stazione Centrale

To the north-east of the city centre the main railway station, built by Ulisse Stacchini between 1912 and 1931, is one of Europe's largest terminus buildings. An imposing roof of glass and iron spans the platforms. A mixture of Art Nouveau and monstrous Neoclassicism characterizes the composition of the façade and the interior design. Opposite the station the 32-storey **Pirelli skyscraper**, built from 1955 to 1958 to designs by Gio Ponti and others, rises to a height of 127m/417ft on its boat-shaped ground plan.

It is well worth taking a walk in the Cimitero Monumentale, where prosperous citizens of Milan have been laid to rest. The cemetery, which was founded in the 19th century, has a wealth of buildings that give it the character of a necropolis: small temples, octagons, round churches – all of Lombard architecture seems to be represented here. The tombs of the Campari, Toscanini and Motta families are especially worth seeing. The grave of **Alessandro Manzoni** is in the cemetery chapel. Opening times: Tue–Sun 8am–6pm.

✷ **Cimitero Monumentale**

🕑

5km/3mi south-east of the city centre, at the junction of Via Sant' Arialdo and Via S. Bernardo, lies the abbey of Chiaravalle Milanese, which **Bernard of Clairvaux** established in 1126. It is a typical example of the French Gothic style that the Cistercians brought to northern Italy. The architecture of Cistercian monasteries is characterized by great simplicity and absence of decoration, as can be seen on the façade of the **abbey church of S. Maria**. The only exception is the finely crafted crossing tower of the church. The rectangular choir is a further characteristic of Cistercian architecture. Only parts of the cloister and chapter house have survived in their original condition. Opening times: Mon–Sat 9am–11am, 3pm–6pm, Sun from 11am.

✷ **Chiaravalle Milanese**

! Baedeker TIP

Antiques

Lovers of fine antiques should note the name Bollate, a district of Milan in which an enormous antiques market takes place on Sundays. It runs along Naviglio Grande from Viale Gorizia to the bridge in Via Valenza. There is a local rail connection to Bollate.

Monza

H 7

Province: Milano
Population: 122,000

Altitude: 162m/530ft

Many residents of Monza work in the nearby city of Milan. The former importance of Monza, which was the seat of dukes in the time of the Lombards, is scarcely apparent today in this somewhat faceless industrial town – except in the cathedral precinct.

After the period of Roman settlement, the city flourished in the Lombard period under the name Modoetia, when Queen Theodelinda chose it as her dowager place of residence. In the Middle Ages

History

▶ VISITING MONZA

INFORMATION

I.A.T.
Palazzo Comunale, Piazza Carducci
I-20052 Monza
Tel. 0 39 32 32 22

WHERE TO EAT

▶ **Moderate**
Prater
Piazza S. Paolo
Tel. 0 39 32 33 35
Closed Mon

A pleasant place to eat, both inside and outside on a terrace screened from the street by bamboo plants.

WHERE TO STAY

▶ **Budget**
Antica Trattoria dell' Uva
Piazza Carrobiolo 2
Tel. 0 39 32 38 25, fax 0 39 32 38 47
www.anticatrattoriadelluva.it, 10 rooms
Small, basic, long-established hotel in

Monza looked to the emperors for support against its powerful neighbour Milan. However, in 1324, weakened by internal conflicts, it fell to the Visconti and subsequently for the most part shared the fate of the Duchy of Milan.

What to See in Monza

✶
Duomo
S. Giovanni
Battista

The main sight in Monza is undoubtedly the cathedral, which goes back to a first church built in about 595. The founder of this first church was a **Lombard queen, Theodelinda**, who played a decisive part in converting the Lombards, followers of the heretic Arius, to Nicene Christianity. Construction of the existing cathedral began in 1260. It was initially a Romanesque structure on a central plan, which was extended in the following century by the addition of the nave and side apses. By 1396 the work had largely been completed. The five-part façade of the cathedral is decorated in green and white marble, but the overall impression is dominated by the Lombard ornamentation, which is particularly delicate on the upper part. As so often in Lombardy, the columns of the porch are borne by lions. The depictions on the tympanum include, in the upper part, Theodelinda giving the Lombard crown to John the Baptist. Below it is the baptism of Christ. The campanile, a 16th-century work by Pellegrino Tibaldi, is strangely out of tune with the façade.

Inside the church, Gothic elements can be seen in the transept and the apses; the nave has a barrel vault. Otherwise, the interior furnishings mainly date from the Baroque period. The principal attraction is the Cappella di Teodelinda to the left of the choir. It houses the early Christian sarcophagus of Theodelinda (died 628) and the greatest treasure of the church, kept in an imposing altar retable: the so-called **Iron Crown of the Lombards**, made from an iron nail from

The Lombard queen Theodelinda founded the cathedral

the crucifixion and decorated with precious stones. It is in fact a Carolingian work dating from the 9th century (closed Mon).

In the adjacent cathedral museum, Museo Serpero, some outstanding church treasure can be seen. The oldest items date from the early Christian period. The simply worked votive crown of Theodelinda and a depiction of a »hen with chickens« (6th–7th century) are especially charming. The church treasure also includes a significant cover of a book of gospels, which Pope Gregory the Great presented to Theodelinda on the occasion of the baptism of her son. Opening times: Tue–Sun 9am–1pm, 2pm–6pm, on public holidays from 11am.

★
◄ Museo Serpero

🕐

On Piazza Roma next to the cathedral the Arengario (13th century), the old town hall with its open loggia on the ground floor, is a reminder of the time when Monza was an independent comune. The tower of the town hall, the Torre del Comune, is of the same age.

★
Arengario

The classical Villa Reale north of the town centre was built for Ferdinand of Austria between 1777 and 1780. Giuseppe Piermarini designed the villa and its sumptuous interior, which can only be visited when temporary exhibitions are held there. Attached to the villa are the »royal gardens«, which merge into a park landscaped in the English style. The extensive park, which was commissioned by Napoleon's stepson Eugène de Beauharnais and laid out in the 19th century, is an oasis in the area north of Milan, which is densely built up and suffers from heavy traffic. In 1900 the king of Savoy, Umberto I, was shot here by the anarchist Gaetano Bresci. The famous Monza racing track was built in the park in 1922. It is the venue of the an-

Villa Reale

★
◄ Giardini Reali, Park

◄ Autodromo

Celebrations for winner Michael Schumacher at the 2001 Italian Grand Prix in the Autodromo

nual Italian grand prix in the Formula One championship. However, the autodromo finds little affection amongst those who would like to enjoy this small remaining patch of nature without the whine of engines. For fans of motor racing, on the other hand, there are many opportunities during the season to watch a race at the circuit or to take a look at the site. Opening times: 8am–6pm.

Around Monza

Brianza Brianza, once an area with beautiful hilly scenery, extends north of Monza as far as the southern part of the Lago di Como region. Large villas were built here even in Roman times, and later Milanese nobles built homes in Brianza. Today, the small villages have almost merged with each other. Something of the former beauty of the area has survived near **Carate Brianza**, 12km/7mi north of Monza. In the district of Costa an aristocratic villa from the late 18th century with an Italian garden occupies a lovely site above the Lambro. It is worth taking a detour to the district of Agliate to see the Basilica dei SS. Pietro e

Amaretto

If you are looking for a gift for friends or family back home, consider buying a bottle of Amaretto, a liqueur with a taste of almonds that is made in Saronno. As a sweet accompaniment to it, try amaretti almond candy, which also comes from Saronno.

Paolo. This plain Romanesque columned basilica (11th century) consists of a nave and two aisles, and a baptistery decorated with a round-arch frieze.

In the small industrial town of Saronno, some 15km/9mi west of Monza, the **church of Madonna dei Miracoli** is worth a visit. It was built in 1498 following a miracle performed by the Virgin Mary in 1447. The church was extended in the 16th century and given its Baroque façade in 1612. Inside there are 16th-century frescoes by Lombard painters, including outstanding works by Gaudenzio Ferrari (*Concert of the Angels*) in the dome and by Bernardino Luini in the chapel of the Madonna in the choir. Opening times: 7am–noon, 3pm–6pm.

Saronno

◄ ✷ Pavia

G/H 9

Provincial capital
Population: 72,000

Altitude: 77m/253ft

With its almost completely preserved centre, many Romanesque churches and old family towers, the ancient university town of Pavia has retained its medieval atmosphere. Petrarch and Leonardo da Vinci once researched here. Today Pavia University is home to many students from Italy and abroad.

The growth of the city began in Roman times, then under the name Ticinum. In the reign of Theodoric, Pavia was **a residence of the Ostrogoth rulers** (489–526). The most important period in its history began in 572, when Pavia became **capital of the Lombard kingdom**. It flourished for about 200 years, until **Charlemagne** was crowned king of the Franks and Lombards in Pavia in 774. The political influence of Pavia ended in 1360 when the Visconti took power and united the city with Milan. In 1525 history was made in Pavia once again, when the imperial armies of Charles V defeated King François I of France at the **Battle of Pavia**.

Capital of the Lombard kingdom

▶ VISITING PAVIA

INFORMATION
A. P. T./I. A. T.
Via Filzi 2, I-27100 Pavia
Tel. 0 38 59 70 01, fax 0 38 59 70 10
www.turismo.provincia.pv.it

WHERE TO EAT
▶ Moderate
① *Antica Osteria dei Previ*
Via Milazzo 65
Tel. 0 38 22 62 03
Old-established osteria near Ponte Coperto; good cooking and high-class wine list.

② *Osteria del Naviglio*
Via Alzaia 39 B
Tel. 03 82 46 03 92
www.osterianaviglio.it
This restaurant has an unbelievably good range of wines and excellent classic cuisine.

③ *Trattoria Ressi*
Via Ressi 8
Adeodato
Tel. 0 38 22 01 84
Closed Sun
This trattoria in a historic building in the centre of Pavia is not easy to find, but extremely charming; Lombard cooking – a limited range of dishes, but all freshly prepared, and a good wine list.

WHERE TO STAY
▶ Mid-range
① *Hotel Moderno*
Viale Vittorio Emanuele 41
Tel. 03 82 33 34 01
Fax 0 38 22 52 25
www.hotelmoderno.it, 52 rooms
Hotel close to the station, well equipped and well cared for; parking spaces available.

② *Aurora*
Viale V. Emanuele II, 25
Tel. 03 82 23 66 4
Fax 03 82 21 24 8
www.hotel-aurora.eu
This hotel close to the station offers modern rooms.

▶ Budget
③ *Excelsior*
Piazza Stazione
Tel. 0 38 22 85 96
Fax 0 38 22 60 30
www.excelsiorpavia.com
Charming breakfast hotel with garage, near the station; family atmosphere.

✳ *City plan*

The centre of this student town is extremely pretty. The main shopping streets are the east-west Corso Cavour/Corso Mazzini and Strada Nuova, which runs north-south down to the river. The Ticino divides the historic centre from newer quarters to the south.

What to See in Pavia

✳ *Piazza della Vittoria*

Piazza della Vittoria with its popular cafes is the bustling centre of town. The Broletto, next to which the rear side of the cathedral appears, is testimony to the long history of the piazza, from which narrow alleys branch off into the labyrinth of the surrounding

Pavia Map

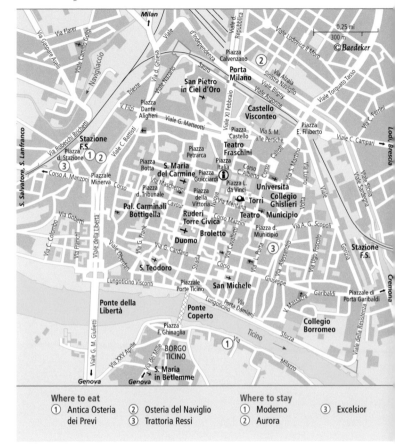

Where to eat
① Antica Osteria dei Previ
② Osteria del Naviglio
③ Trattoria Ressi

Where to stay
① Moderno
② Aurora
③ Excelsior

quarters. The Broletto of Pavia, which dates back to the 11th century, is the **oldest city hall in Lombardy**. It was altered a number of times over the centuries. Its relatively coherent façade with small, irregularly disposed windows is mainly 13th-century work, and the Renaissance loggia was added in 1539.

◄ Broletto

Apart from the enormous dome, which towers over the Broletto, the cathedral makes a rather unspectacular contribution to the church architecture of Pavia. It is a mixture of styles from different periods, and is somewhat dilapidated. It was built from 1488 to designs by **Donato Bramante**, **Giovanni Antonio Amadeo** and **Cristoforo Rocchi**. The work dragged on for centuries. The base of the dome was finally completed in 1750, but the roof of the dome and the façade

◄ Duomo

Piazza della Vittoria: Pavia's showpiece square

were not added until the 19th century and the transept in 1936. The tall dome is the dominant impression inside the cathedral: with a diameter of 30m/98ft and a height of 90m/295ft it is one of the **largest domes in Italy**, exceeded only by those of St Peter's Basilica in Rome and the cathedrals in Florence and Brescia.

★ ★

S. Michele

S. Michele, on the street of the same name, the **most significant church in Pavia**, developed from a previous church founded by the Lombards in the 7th century and is dedicated to their most important saint, the archangel Michael. It was the coronation church of the Lombard kings. Here Charlemagne, conqueror of Lombardy, is said to have placed the Lombard crown on his head in 774. The present church was built in the Romanesque style between 1117 and 1150 after an earthquake. Following the tradition of Charlemagne, German kings were crowned here as kings of Lombardy, which legitimized their rule in northern Italy. Emperor Frederick Barbarossa, for example, was crowned here in 1155.

The **façade** of S. Michele is composed of three parts and terminates in gallery of round-headed arches that rises parallel to the gable. At its centre the archangel Michael repels evil in the form of a dragon. The finely crafted decoration of the reliefs – animals, plants, warriors and mythical creatures – is outstandingly beautiful. The building material used for the façade was Arenaria sandstone from Oltrepò Pavese. This extremely sensitive stone crumbles in polluted air, and despite repeated attempts at restoration the reliefs and figural decoration are in an advanced state of disintegration.

Inside the church note the **Romanesque capitals** with ornamental, mythological and biblical themes in relief. The crypt is the best place for studying the details. The fresco paintings have various dates between the 13th and 17th centuries. The late Gothic crucifixion scene (15th century) in the arch of the choir is attributed to Urbanino da Surso. In the choir some remnants of the original 12th-century floor mosaic have survived. Black marble paving slabs in the nave mark the position of the throne during the coronation ceremony.

★
Università degli Studi

Pavia's **famous university** (Strada Nuova) was founded in 1361 by the Visconti ruler Galeazzo II. Its complex of buildings is grouped around several arcaded courts. Some of the venerable lecture halls have fine paintings on the walls and ceilings. Many alterations have changed the appearance of the university buildings. The most recent, initiated by Maria Theresia of Austria, remodelled the exterior in classical style and gave it the dark yellow colour that it still has today. The scientist Alessandro Volta from Como (►Famous People) made his pioneering discoveries at this university in the period around 1800.

The most famous student at Pavia was probably the dramatist **Carlo Goldoni**. He was expelled from the university at the age of 18 for mocking the women of Pavia in a satirical play. The citizens had a rule that a girl who consorted with a student would not be permitted to marry a man from Pavia.

★
Family towers

On Piazza Leonardo da Vinci south of the university stand remains from long-gone times: three family towers, mostly dating from the 12th century, the last of some 150 such towers that were built as places of refuge or fortifications during the time of the conflicts between the Guelphs and Ghibellines. Two further family towers can be seen on Via Luigi Porta.

Piazza Leonardo da Vinci is also the site of the archaeological excavations of the **crypt of S. Eusebio** (7th–11th century).

Only three of the once-numerous family towers are still standing

One of Pavia's main sights is **Castello Visconteo** in the north of the city centre. It was begun in 1360 for Galeazzo Visconti II, the new ruler of Pavia, who wished to have a second residence in addition to that in Milan. The brick-built castello was originally a square ensemble of four wings with four corner towers. During the Battle of Pavia in 1525 the north wing of Castello Visconteo with its two flanking towers was destroyed, and not reconstructed later. It is worth taking a look at the large inner courtyard, which is adorned with arcades and openwork tracery.

The castello houses the **Museo Civico** with its finds from excavations of Roman sites and architectural fragments from the Romanesque churches of Pavia. Here art lovers can get up close to study the outstanding decoration of church capitals. In the **Pinacoteca Malaspina** on the upper floor, paintings by Lombard and Venetian painters of the 14th to 17th centuries are exhibited. Opening times of the museums: Tue– Sun 10am–6pm, Jan, Juli, Aug, Dez 9am–1pm.

✳
S. Pietro in Ciel d'Oro

A basilica built at the time of the Lombard kingdom was replaced between 1120 and 1200 by S. Pietro in Ciel d'Oro (west of the castello). This church with its golden heaven – the painting on the ceiling was once gilded – is the **second great Romanesque church in Pavia** together with S. Michele. The tomb of St Augustine, the large Arca di S. Agostino in the choir (1362) by Giovanni di Balduccio, is one of the most important 14th-century works of sculpture in Lombardy. It has been the last resting place of Augustine, one of the fathers of the church, since the translation of his bones from Hippo Regius in the 8th century. The urn containing the remains of the Roman philosopher, author and statesman **Boethius** (480–524) can be seen in the 19th-century neo-Romanesque crypt. He was accused of high treason when he came to the defence of a friend who was on trial. During his imprisonment he wrote a philosophical treatise, *The Consolation of Philosophy*, which was highly popular in the Middle Ages. Opening times: 7am–noon, 3pm–6pm.

✳
Arca di S. Agostino ▶

⏱

S. Maria del Carmine

To the west of the university on Piazza stands the late Gothic Carmelite church of S. Maria del Carmine. Construction began in 1370 to designs by **Bernardo da Venezia** and was completed just under a century later with a brick west façade in late Gothic style including a rose window. There are interesting remains of 15th-century frescoes inside, in both the north and south transept.

S. Teodoro between the cathedral and the banks of the Ticino, a brick-built Romanesque church, was founded during the age of the Lombard kingdom and rebuilt in the 12th century. Inside the church note the frescoes, including a well-known Renaissance view of Pavia showing the city with its castello, Romanesque cathedral and many family towers in 1522.

S. Teodoro

Follow Strada Nuova to reach the bank of the river Ticino and the famous Ponte Coperto that crosses it. The bridge, the entire length of which is roofed, was constructed in 1352 on Roman foundations. Today's bridge is a reconstruction, as the original was destroyed by bombing in 1944.

Ponte Coperto

The Collegio Borromeo in the south-east district of the city centre was founded for the benefit of poor students in 1559 by Cardinal Carlo Borromeo, archbishop of Milan. This university college is a Mannerist work by **Pellegrino Tibaldi**, one of the leading architects of the period in Lombardy.

Collegio Borromeo

To the west of the centre, close to the Ticino, is the church of S. Lanfranco, a simple brick construction that was consecrated in 1236. It holds the **marble arca** of Bishop Lanfranco (died 1198), a masterpiece of Lombard sculpture made in about 1498 by **Giovanni Antonio Amadeo**. The remains of frescoes on the south wall date from the late 13th century. Their theme is the murder of Thomas Becket in Canterbury. Amadeo was responsible for what remains of the cloisters, which have rich terracotta decorations.

S. Lanfranco

Oltrepò Pavese

The area south of Pavia, called Oltrepò Pavese, is perhaps the most charming countryside in Lombardy. An open plain near the Po, to the south it becomes a region of rolling hills with orchards and vineyards, while wooded slopes and mountains rising to 1700m/5500ft characterize the scenery in the northern Apennines. Oltrepò Pavese is **one of the main wine-growing areas in Lombardy**, producing more than half of the total output of Lombard wine and two thirds of its DOC wines. It is known for spumante, which takes the appellation »Classese« when it is made using the classic method.

The garden of Lombardy

The capital of Oltrepò Pavese is Voghera. Here the **cathedral of S. Lorenzo Martire** on Piazza del Duomo was built between 1605 and 1611. It has the plan of a Greek cross, above which a massive dome rises. The other notable building in the town is the **Teatro Sociale** with its interesting classical façade of 1845.

Voghera

Salice Terme ✳ Salice Terme is a well-known and beautiful spa with a quiet, restorative atmosphere. The water of the thermal springs contains sulphur and iodine salt, and provides relief for rheumatic complaints and diseases of the bronchial system. Salice Terme is a good base for exploring Oltrepò Pavese.

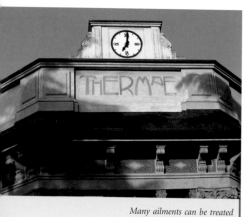

Many ailments can be treated in the spa at Salice Terme

In the mountains east of Ponte Nizza (10km/6mi south-east of Salice Terme) lies **Abbazia S. Alberto di Butrio**, a monastery that originated as a hermitage in the 11th century. Monastic buildings and three churches were added in the 15th century. Late Gothic frescoes can be seen in the chapel of S. Antonio.

Sabbioneta

Q 10/11

Province: Mantova	**Altitude:** 18m/60ft
Population: 4300	

Sabbioneta is situated in one of the loneliest parts of the Po plain. The little town, which makes a sleepy impression today, is important in art-historical terms due to a very short but interesting period in the 16th century, when Vespasiano Gonzaga set up his residence here and planned to create an »ideal city«.

Ideal city **Vespasiano Gonzaga** was 14 years old when he inherited the castle of Sabbioneta and a few villages from his grandfather in 1525. In the following years he pursued a military career, and made Sabbioneta his residence in 1554. Here he built a new city, his own creation to rival the works of his cousins in Mantua, aiming to put into practice the ideas of the Renaissance. The theories of Vitruvius, an author of the 1st century BC, were his model for urban planning. The ground plan was an irregular octagon surrounded by deep moats, which was divided into 30 blocks of buildings. Sabbioneta gained the name **»Piccola Atene«** (Little Athens), a comparison to which the statue of Pallas Athene on Piazza d'Armi refers. In the lifetime of Vespasiano Gonzaga, culture blossomed briefly in Sabbioneta, but after the death of its creator in 1591 the doors of the imposing buildings were closed

▶ VISITING SABBIONETA

INFORMATION

I. A. T.
Piazza d' Armi 1
I-46018 Sabbioneta
Tel. 03 75 22 10 44
Fax 03 75 22 21 19

WHERE TO EAT

▶ **Moderate**
Parco Cappuccini
Via Santuario 30
Tel. 0 37 55 20 05
Closed Mon, Wed evening
In a pretty little palazzo near the
historic town centre with a park full

of old trees, the restaurant serves
typical Mantuan meat dishes.

WHERE TO STAY

▶ **Mid-range**
Don Camillo
Via Cisa 60
Brescello
Tel. 05 22 96 00 67, fax 05 22 68 71 90
43 rooms
The hotel is located 15km from
Sabbioneta and was opened in 2008.
The "Don Camillo and Pepone"
movies were filmed in Brescello.

as quickly as they had once been opened, and the residence rapidly
became a »junk room of history«.

What to See in Sabbioneta

The Palazzo Ducale (1568) on the piazza of the same name makes a
very plain external impression. The trompe l'oeil exterior paintings
have disappeared, and much of the once magnificent furnishings
have been lost. Nevertheless, the heavy gilded coffered ceilings and
stucco decoration (1574–91) remain impressive.

★
Palazzo Ducale

In the Sala delle Aquile (Hall of Eagles) four life-size equestrian statues represent the founder and members of his family. In the Sala degli Antenati, the Hall of Ancestors, note reliefs depicting the Gonzaga
and a ceiling painting on which Phaeton with his sun chariot can be
seen. Some of the paintings are by Bernardino Campi of Cremona.

The church of S. Maria Assunta on Piazza Ducale was built in
1580–82. **Ferdinando Galli Bibiena** painted the vault of the Chapel of
the Sacrament as a pierced dome that allows a view of the sky – an
architectural innovation.

S. Maria Assunta

The church S. Maria Incoronata is an important art-historical monument. It was built as a domed octagon in late Renaissance style,
based on models which had been executed a century earlier. The
church houses the Mannerist tomb of Vespasiano Gonzaga and an
outstanding **bronze statue of Vespasiano**, done in 1588 by Leone
Leoni.

S. Maria Incoronata

Teatro all' Antica

※ The Teatro all' Antica was built by **Vincenzo Scamozzi** between 1588 and 1590. The Olympian gods stand above the audience on an arch borne by Corinthian columns. Trompe l'oeil paintings adorn the wall. Few plays were performed in this little theatre, as Vespasiano Gonzaga died shortly after its completion and the building was neglected. It later served as a cinema, and is now occasionally used as a theatre.

! **Baedeker TIP**

Antiques

Sabbioneta is a destination for lovers of fine antiques. In addition to several shops, the "market of little antiques" is held on the first Sun of every month except Jan and Aug. Information: tel. 03 75 22 10 08.

Vespasiano Gonzaga ordered the construction of the **Palazzo del Giardino** on Piazza d' Armi as his private garden palace. Of the once richly fitted interiors, the large Sala degli Specchi, adorned with landscapes, is the finest. Pretty paintings in the grotesque manner remain in the Gabinetto delle Grazie. The most eye-catching building in Sabbioneta, also on Piazza d' Armi, is the **Galleria degli Antichi** (1584) with its decorative trompe l'oeil painting. The collection of antiquities was taken to Mantua long ago.

The Olympian gods look down on the auditorium

The greatest treasure in the Museo d'Arte Sacra is the **Golden Fleece**, which was found in the tomb of Vespasiano Gonzaga. From 1577 he was a member of the chivalric Order of the Golden Fleece, and wore the golden ram's fleece on a chain around his neck.

Museo d'Arte Sacra

The exhibition in the synagogue informs visitors about the large Jewish community that once lived in Sabbioneta. In Vespasiano's time Jews operated a mint and a printworks in Sabbioneta.

Sinagoga

Sondrio

M 3/4

Provincial capital
Population: 22,200

Altitude: 307m/1007ft

The lively provincial capital Sondrio lies approximately at the centre of ► Valtellina. Here the valley, surrounded by mountains that reach 2000m/6500ft, is very broad.

Sondrio is surrounded by wonderful vineyards – this is one of **the principal wine regions of Lombardy** (► Valtellina). The town is known for products made from pietra ollare, a type of steatite or soapstone. Sondrio is a popular resort for hikers, hunters and anglers and was the birthplace of the construction engineer and architect **Pier Luigi Nervi** (1891–1979). His works include the Pirelli Tower in Milan, the Olympic Stadium in Rome and the Tour de la Bourse in Montreal.

An attractive place to live

Sondrio Map

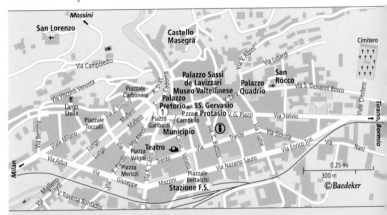

Where to stay
① Hotel della Posta

▶ VISITING SONDRO

INFORMATION

Ufficio Informazioni
Via Trieste 12
I-23100 Sondrio
Tel. 03 42 51 25 00
Fax 03 42 21 96 52
www.valtellina.it

WHERE TO EAT / WHERE TO STAY

▶ **Mid-range**

① **Grand Hotel della Posta**
Piazza Garibaldi 19
Tel. 03 42 51 04 04
Fax 03 42 51 02 10
40 rooms
A lovely hotel in a 19th century palazzo with a pleasant atmosphere; quiet but central location on Piazza Garibaldi; the rooms facing the piazza at the front are the best; good restaurant with international and Lombard cuisine; parking spaces next to the hotel.

What to See in Sondrio

Piazza Garibaldi

The broad Piazza Garibaldi with its statue of the eponymous libera-tor of Italy is the focal point of the town. The square was laid out under Austrian rule, when Sondrio flourished thanks to its location on the route from Austria over the Stelvio Pass to Lago di Como. Most of the buildings date from the 19th century.

Castello Masegra

The town is dominated by Castello Masegra, a 14th-century castle that was altered in the 15th century. It is worthwhile undertaking the climb for the fine view of the town and its surroundings.

Piazza Campello

Corso Italia leads to Piazza Campello, where the **church of SS. Gerva-sio e Protasio** catches the eye. This Baroque pilaster church and its detached campanile were built in the mid-18th century, while the façade was completed in 1838 to designs by Guiseppe Sertoli. On the same square the 16th-century **Renaissance-style Palazzo Pretorio** is home to the town hall; it is worth taking a look at the fine courtyard.

The historic town centre with all its little shops, cafes and restaurants, as well as a few pretty palazzi, lies beyond Piazza Campello.

Old quarter

The 17th-century **Palazzo Sassi de Lavizzari** in Via Maurizio Quadrivio houses the Museo Valtellinese di Storia e Arte with its archaeological, art and ethnological departments. The museum also possesses a collection of furniture from Valtellina and the area around Chiavenna dating from the 15th to the 19th century, as well as frescoes and paintings, mainly of the 17th and 18th centuries. Opening times vary.

Museo Valtellinese

3km/2mi west of the town, the 15th-century chapel Madonna della Sassella stands atop a rock. It is worth making the trip to see the interior frescoes dating from 1511 and the attractive site of the chapel.

Santuario della Madonna della Sassella

★ ★ Valcamonica

N–Q 3–6

Province: Brescia

Valcamonica, the valley through which the Oglio flows, stretches 80km/50mi from the northern shore of Lago d'Iseo to the Passo del Tonale in the north-east of Lombardy.

Ponte di Legno has excellent facilities for **winter sports**. From the mid-1950s headlines were made by the discovery and investigation of **prehistoric rock carvings** at various places in the valley (▶Baedeker Special p.310). This rock art has shown that Valcamonica was settled in the Neolithic period at the latest by the Camunni, a people of hunters and herdsmen about whom little is known and after whom the valley is named. Valcamonica has always been an important route of passage from the Alps and the regions north of them to the plain of the river Po. From 16 BC the Romans ruled the valley from its main settlement, Cividate Camuno. In the 8th century the Franks made Breno their centre of influence, and later Valcamonica passed into the hands of the Milanese Visconti.

Significant prehistoric finds

★ What to See in Valcamonica

Boario Terme in the southern part of Valcamonica owes its reputation as a spa to springs that contain sulphur and lime. The venerable

Boario Terme

⏵ VISITING VALCAMONICA

INFORMATION

I.A.T.
Corso Milano 41
I-25056 Ponte di Legno
Tel. 03 64 9 11 22, fax 03 64 9 19 49
www.pontedilegnoturismo.it

WHERE TO EAT AND STAY

▶ **Mid-range**
Mirella
Via Roma 21
Ponte di Legno
Tel. 03 64 90 05 00, fax 03 64 90 05 30

www.hotelmirella.it, 64 rooms
This hotel has a quiet location and
well-kept rooms, most of them with a
balcony.

▶ **Budget**
Pegrà
Via Nazionale SS 42 (near Esso petrol
station)
Ponte di Legno
Tel. 03 64 90 31 19, fax 03 64 90 36 45
www.hotelpegna.com
Good hotel with garage.

Grand Hotel, the spa facilities and the spa park date from around
1900, and classic spa events with a programme of music etc. provide
entertainment for guests visiting to take a health cure.

Cividate Camuno ⏲ The **Museo Archeologico della Valcamonica** exhibits archaeological
finds from the Roman period, when Cividate Camuno was the main
town of Valcamonica. Opening times: Tue–Sun, holidays 9am–2pm.

Breno ⏲ Breno, the old capital of the valley, occupies a site at the foot of a
high rock, on which remains of an 11th-century **castle** remain. The
14th-century **church of S. Antonio** is decorated with frescoes from
the 15th and 16th centuries depicting the legend of Daniel. The **Museo Camuno** (Via Garibaldi 4), next to the town hall, is rewarding
for its numerous relics of the Camunni (opening times: Tue–Fri
10am–noon, 2pm–5pm; Sat, Sun until 5.30pm).

★ ★
**Parco Nazionale
delle Incisioni
Rupestri** ⏲ In Capo di Ponte the main attraction of Valcamonica is reached:
above the town lies the Parco Nazionale delle Incisioni Rupestri,
where visitors can discover the famous **prehistoric rock carvings** on
five different routes. Approximately 30,000 figures have been carved
into around 100 rocks, all of which are numbered. A map showing
the sites is available in the Centro Camuno. Opening times: Tue–Sun
8.30am–4.30pm.

★
S. Salvatore The 11th-century Romanesque basilica of S. Salvatore lies out in the
countryside to the north of the park (ring the bell at the gate). It was
built by Cluniac monks. In its plain interior the **wonderful capitals**
with ornamentation, figures of animals and a representation of Jonah
appear to great advantage. A few remains of frescoes can be dis-

Breno, the main town of Valcamonica, with the remains of an old castle

cerned, and the outer wall incorporates some stones with rock carvings from the surrounding area. A prehistoric altar can be seen on the little path to the basilica.

On the opposite side of the valley from Capo di Ponte lies the district of Cemmo, where the little **Museo d'Arte e Vita Preistorica** provides insights into life in prehistoric times in Valcamonica and into the history and technique of the rock carvings (opening times: daily 8.30am–12.30pm, 1.30pm–5.30pm, Sun, holidays 8.30am–12.30pm, 2pm–6pm.

Cemmo

The rock carvings in Cemmo, which are regarded as the finest in Valcamonica, can be seen on two rocks, the **Massi di Cemmo**, which are opposite the museum beyond the football pitch. Their depictions of hunted animals are thought to have been made in the 3rd millennium BC.

> ## ! *Baedeker* TIP
>
> ### Life in prehistoric times
> A footpath in Cemmo leads up to the Archeodromo, a kind of teaching museum on the life, crafts and art of the population in the New Stone Age. A reconstruction of a Neolithic village shows how it may have been inhabited by an extended family about 6000 years ago. Opening times: daily 8.30am–12.30pm, 1.30pm–5.30pm.

Ponte di Legno (altitude 1260m/4130ft) at the upper end of Valcamonica is a **well-known ski resort** situated between the Ortles and Adamello ranges. Here a total of 80km/50mi of pistes are available to skiers; those at higher altitude are even suitable for summer skiing.

Ponte di Legno

What is the meaning of these mysterious rock carvings?

SYMBOLS IN THE STONES

Pizzo Badile, the mountain directly to the east of Naquane in Valcamonica, casts a shadow on the sky in early spring and autumn. This strange natural phenomenon may be the reason why there are so many rock carvings in this area.

Drawings incised in rock have been found in many places in the Alps, but those which are of higher quality and are more varied in terms of form and content appear to have been executed by especially gifted and trained artists. In some places, as in Valcamonica but also on Monte Baldo on Lago di Garda and in Valtellina, there are concentrations of figurative carvings with a symbolic meaning or whole compositions. About 300,000 of these more ambitious drawings have so far been discovered. The countless smaller, graphically less skilful symbols differ from these »professional« carvings. It can be regarded as certain that the rock carvings are an expression of religious feelings.

But who made them? The rock carvings in Valcamonica are said to derive from the **Camuni**, who settled here from the Neolithic period until Roman times and gave the valley its name. They left to posterity foot shapes, hands, human figures, female and male sexual symbols, dancing, riding and fighting humans, men with weapons, axes, arrows, lances, shovels and shield-like objects, domestic and wild animals, hunting scenes and depictions of crop cultivation, and last but not least a symbol of the sun, which **has become the emblem of Lombardy** as the Celtic or Camunic rose. Roman inscriptions and Christian crosses have also been discovered – evidence that this sanctuary of the Camuni was in use into Roman times. The story of research into the »incisioni rupestri« is relatively recent, as the first systematic investigations date from about 1820. In 1955 the Parco Nazionale delle Incisione Rupestri was established. When in 1979 it took its place alongside the Forum Romanum and Leonardo da Vinci's *Last Supper* as a Unesco World Heritage site, the prehistoric sanctuary had at last gained recognition in the 20th century.

✱ Valtellina

Province: Sondrio

Valtellina in the north-east of Lombardy is a valley with a length of about 100km/60mi, stretching from Bormio in the north-east to the northern end of Lago di Como. It divides the Bernina range to the north from the lower Bergamasche Alps to the south. The Adda flows through the valley and into Lago di Como.

Valtellina is the longest valley that crosses through the Alps not from north to south but from east to west. For this reason it was and remains one of the **principal arteries of traffic within the Alps** – an advantage that has turned into a disadvantage in recent decades, as the through-traffic has reached alarming levels. Today Valtellina's main source of income is **tourism**. In summer visitors come to hike, in winter to ski. Bormio is the most important Alpine resort in Lombardy; other major ski resorts are Livigno, the Valfurva valley and Aprica.

East-west Alpine axis

The route to Italy from the north has always passed through Valtellina. In consequence of this trade, the towns of Valtellina had special rights. From the 11th to the 13th century Milan and Como fought over Valtellina, which finally came under Milanese rule. In 1512 it fell to Grigioni (also Grisons or Graubünden), then independent and now a Swiss canton. The spread of Protestantism among the people of Grigioni led to continuing political and religious conflict. The differences between Catholics and the government of Grigioni culminated in the so-called **Valtellina Troubles** (1620–39), a war in which Spain and France intervened. In 1814–15, along with Lombardy, Valtellina passed to Austria and finally in 1859–61 to Italy.

History

The landscape of Valtellina is among the most fascinating in Lombardy. While the Adda has carved out its course through the broad valley, to the north the summits of the Bernina range reach heights of up to 4050m/13,300ft and to the south the Bergamasche Alps rise to almost 3000m/9850ft. At higher levels the terrain is increasingly barren and rugged. Lower down the scenery takes its character from little orchards and vineyards, and in places the valley is gentle and pretty. There is an impressive variety of flora and fauna in the areas that remain unspoiled.

✱ Landscape

Next to the regions of Oltrepò Pavese south of Pavia and Franciacorta in the province of Brescia, Valtellina is the most important wine region of Lombardy. On the terraced slopes of the valley grapes are grown on tiny plots of land which hardly permit the use of machinery. Valtellina is one of the few places outside Piedmont where the

Wine growing

▶ VISITING VALTELLINA

INFORMATION

Ufficio Turistico
Via Roma 131/B
I-23032 Bormio
Tel. 03 42 90 33 00
Fax 03 42 90 46 96
www.aptvaltellina.it

WHERE TO EAT

▶ Moderate

Vecchia Combo
Piazza Crocefisso 4
Bormio
Tel. 0 34 2 90 15 68
Closed Sun
Tiny restaurant serving excellent regional dishes from Valtellina such as delicious bresaola, good home-made pizzoccheri and a filling polenta taragna.

WHERE TO STAY

▶ Mid-range

Posta
Via Roma 66, Bormio
Tel. 03 42 90 47 53
Fax 03 42 90 44 84
www.hotelposta.bormio.it, 30 rooms
Well-run hotel in the centre; good-quality furnishings.

▶ Budget

Astoria
Via Roma 73, Bormio
Tel. 03 42 91 09 00, fax 03 42 90 52 53
www.astoria.bormio.it, 44 rooms
Quiet hotel in the historic town centre; the rooms are basic but well kept; there is a sunny terrace, a garage and parking spaces; specialities from Valtellina are served in the restaurant.

Nebbiolo grape flourishes. The other well-known varieties of grape here are Sassella, Inferno, Grumello and Valgella, which all yield full-bodied, strong red wines.

What to See in Valtellina

On this tour through Valtellina from west to east it is worth making stops in several places that are presented below. North of state route no. 38, in particular, there are many side roads from which the beautiful scenery can best be appreciated.

Morbegno

Morbegno, on the approach to the Passo di S. Marco in western Valtellina, already had a certain importance in the Middle Ages, as it lay on the trade route to Venice. Several elegant palazzi can be seen in the historic town centre. **Palazzo Malacrida**, hidden away in Via Malacrida, has a lovely columned porch with 18th-century frescoes by Cesare Ligari. The most rewarding of the churches is the 16th-century **S. Giovanni Battista** (Piazza S. Giovanni Battista) with its 18th-century Baroque frescoes by Pietro Ligari.

Valle del Bitto

South of Morbegno lies Valle del Bitto, which includes the valleys Gerola and Albaredo. Directly south of Morbegno is an interesting little place named Sacco, where the walls of some houses are adorned with frescoes. In Contrada Pirondini there is a popular painting on Casa Vaninetti depicting the legendary »Uomo Selvatico«.

Baedeker TIP

Try a bit of bitto!
Bitto, a hard cheese, is a speciality of the Gerols valley, where it has been made for centuries.

Valmasino, north-east of Morbegno, is popular amongst mountain hikers and climbers. To the north is Pizzo Cengalo (3367m/11,047ft), to the north-east Monte Disgrazia (3678m/12,068ft). One of Europe's toughest trekking routes connects the peaks around Valmasino. Hikers can recover from their exertions with a bath in the thermal springs at Bagni del Masino at the upper end of the valley, at a height of 1172m/3845ft. The region is also known for its variety of minerals: over 150 different types of stone have been identified here. **Valmasino**

►Sondrio **Sondrio**

Valmalenco, the valley north of Sondrio, is well developed for tourism. In summer it is a good hiking area, in winter well frequented by skiers. A good place to stop when travelling from Sondrio towards Lanzada is **Chiesa in Valmalenco**, a popular summer and winter resort at an altitude of 960m/3150ft. A little to the north at 1274m/4180ft lies **Primolo** with its chapel of the Madonna delle Grazie. Further east, **Caspoggio** (1098m/3603ft) is a well-known skiing resort where international championships are held. **Lanzada** (983m/3225ft) is the agricultural centre of the region. **Valmalenco**

From Sondrio a panoramic route with superb scenery leads east on minor roads through the little villages of Montagna in Valtellina, Poggiridenti and Ponte in Valtellina to Teglio. The road passes orchards and the vineyard-covered slopes of Grumello and Inferno, providing wonderful views of the Adda valley and the Alpine summits round about. Right at the start of the tour, the ruined **Castello Grumello** near Montagna in Valtellina is the sole castle on the »castle road«. The well-preserved historic centre of **Ponte in Valtellina** is an attractive place to stroll around. **★**
Strada Panoramica dei Castelli

The small town of Teglio (856m/2809ft) attracts plenty of visitors in summer and winter. The 16th-century Palazzo Besta is **one of the highlights of Valtellina**. In its plain surroundings Palazzo Besta makes a cheerful and inviting impression with a bright and long façade. Behind it is an arcaded courtyard, the walls of which are completely covered in frescoes of Virgil's *Aeneid*. The fantastical figures on the water spouts are also remarkable. A tour of the palazzo reveals rooms richly decorated with frescoes – the hall of honour, for example with scenes from the epic poem *Orlando Furioso* – beauti- **★**
Teglio
★
◄ **Palazzo Besta**

A fine fresco on the Renaissance arcades of the Palazzo Besta in Teglio

fully crafted wooden ceilings and heavy wooden furniture. Note particularly the stüa (parlour), a room typical of this region, here panelled with arollo pine; the adjoining heatable rooms for the lord of the house and his lady and the old kitchen are also impressive. In the room housing antiquities the famous Neolithic steles that were found near Teglio can be seen. Stele II from Caven depicts animals and a solar symbol, stele III from Caven spiral motifs and suns. Opening times: April–Sept Tue–Sun 8am–2pm, Oct–March Tue–Sat 8am–1pm 2pm–5pm.

South-east of Teglio state road no. 39 climbs in hairpin bends to **Aprica** (1172m/3845ft). In the Middle Ages this town was an important staging post between the Bernina Pass and the plains to the south. Aprica is now a flourishing winter sports resort and in summer a base for hikes and trips in the Alpine mountain world.

Tirano

✴

Basilica Madonna di Tirano ▶

Tirano lies on the banks of the Adda. From here it is only a few miles north-west to Switzerland, which pushes into Lombardy here like a wedge. Tirano's well-known cultural monument is the pilgrimage church Madonna di Tirano at the western edge of the town. It was built in 1505 at a place where a vision of the Virgin Mary had been seen, and was one of the foremost religious sites in Valtellina from the 16th to the 19th century. The square in front of the church was also an important market place. An unusually tall campanile towers over the High Renaissance church with its clear, simple and harmonious proportions. The interior is extravagantly decorated with **Mannerist and Baroque frescoes**.

The **Museo Etnografico Tiranese** in the 16th-century Palazzo S. Michele on the church square offers insights into the traditions and culture of Valtellina. Opening times: June–Sept Tue–Sun 10am–noon, 3.30pm–6.30pm; Oct–May Sat 10am–noon, 3pm–6pm.

Grosio

At Grosio the valley narrows and the road climbs through increasingly barren mountain scenery towards the Passo dello Stelvio. In Grosio two churches are worth a visit: the 14th-century S. Giorgio and the 17th-century S. Giuseppe on the edge of town. Palazzo Visconti Venosta houses the Museo Civico. Only ruins remain of Castello Nuovo, which the Visconti built in 1350.

A wonderful view of the broad valley of the Adda from →
the Strada Panoramico dei Castelli – here near Ponte in Valtellina

The octagonal baptistery San Giovanni ad Fontes in Lomello

on the road from Pavia to Gaul. The Lombards, too, built a castle here. It is worth inspecting the ensemble comprising the 11th-century **church of S. Maria Maggiore** and the octagonal 8th-century **baptistery S. Giovanni ad Fontes**. The **brick-built S. Maria Maggiore**, which was integrated into the Lombard castle in the 11th century as a fortified church, was much changed in the Baroque period but late restored to its original appearance. The castello on the little piazza is now used as the town hall. The **church of S. Michele** south-east of the centre is a lovely Romanesque structure of about 1200 with an 18th-century façade.

The Parco Nazionale dello Stelvio, which is managed jointly by Switzerland, Lombardy and Trentino, is the **largest Italian national park**. It was established in 1935 in an area that belongs partly to Lombardy and partly to Trentino and Alto Adige. In 1977 the park was enlarged and linked to the Swiss Engadin national park. It covers a total area of 134,620ha/520 sq mi, of which 61,823ha/240 sq mi belong to Lombardy. One of the attractions of the park is the 3899m/12,793ft peak Ortles in the Alto Adige region. The primary purpose of the national park is to protect the high-altitude Alpine environment of the

★ ★
Parco Nazionale dello Stelvio

> ! ***Baedeker* TIP**
>
> **Panoramic railway**
>
> From Tirano a famous railway line climbs to St Moritz in Switzerland, passing the 4000m/13,000ft Bernina range. Passengers enjoy superb panoramic views during the 2½-hour journey. Information from ATP offices or in the station at Tirano (tel. 03 42 70 13 53) or under www.glacier-express.de.

Ortles range, which is a habitat for stags, chamois, ibex, golden eagles, capercaillies and Alpine grouse. The vegetation partly derives from the ice age. There are also about 100 **glaciers** in the region.

The centre of the wooded Valfurva, a valley to the south-east of Bormio, is **S. Caterina Valfurva**, a place for summer and winter tourism. The largest glacier in Italy, Ghiacciaio dei Forni, can be seen from Albergo Ghiacciaio dei Forni (2176m/7139ft) at the end of the Forni valley, which borders Valfurva. From Bormio a road completed in 1825 with a gradient of up to 15% and 83 hairpin bends winds up to the famous Passo dello Stelvio (2757m/9046ft; its German name is Stilfser Joch), with fantastic panoramas along the way. This mountain road, built by the Austrians in the period when they ruled northern Italy in order to link Lombardy with the Inn valley and Vienna, is one of the greatest achievements of Alpine road building.

★
◄ Ghiacciaio dei Forni

★ ★
◄ Stelvio Pass

Livigno has a remote location at the extreme northern tip of Lombardy, 36km/22mi north-west of Bormio. It can be reached all year round from Münstertal in Switzerland through the Munt-la-Schera Tunnel. In summer it is also accessible from the Stelvio Pass and Tirano, from Val Poschiavo in Switzerland and across the Forcola di Livigno.

★
Livigno

Livigno is a little world of its own because of its remoteness and language. The people here speak Ladin, a language which has only about 500,000 native speakers. In recent years tourism has boomed in Livigno, partly because it is a **duty-free zone**. It attracts winter sports fans with 120km/75mi of pistes, of which about 40km/25mi are for cross-country skiing. As far back as the 16th century Livigno enjoyed privileges in the wine trade and freedom from customs duties. The duty-free zone was established in the 19th century under Napoleonic rule with the aim of preventing this remote place from becoming completely abandoned. The Eira Pass leads to Trepalle, at 2079m/6821ft the highest permanently occupied village in Italy.

✶ Varese

E/F 6

Provincial capital	**Altitude:** 382m/1253ft
Population: 82 900	

Varese, a provincial capital, nestles on the banks of the Olona in the outlying foothills of the Alps. Despite its dense population and a high degree of industrialization, the province still has wonderful scenery in a few places, and its northern part, where there are four small lakes with a superb mountain backdrop, is even praised as the »jewel of the Alpine foothills«.

Modern industrial region The industrialization of the region started with spinning mills on the banks of the Olona. In the last 120 years the whole province has experienced dramatic change, as the remarkable increase in its population shows. The inhabitants of Varese are amongst the highest earners in Italy. The name of the town is derived from the Roman name **Vallium exitus** (»exit from the valleys«), an accurate description of its location on the margins of the Alps. In the 13th century Varese became a **centre of government**. It is not a town with many historical sights, but has an attractive and lively town centre. Around **Corso Matteotti**, the main shopping street, there are a few lanes with the atmosphere of an old quarter.

What to See in Varese

S. Vittore The basilica of S. Vittore on the piazza of the same name was built between 1580 and 1615 to designs by **Pellegrino Tibaldi**. The conspicuously tall campanile dates from 1617, the Neoclassical façade from 1788. The interior of the basilica is magnificently decorated with 17th-century frescoes.

✶ Battistero di S. Giovanni Battista ► Directly behind the church is the plain late Romanesque baptistery of S. Giovanni Battista (c1230). The 14th-century figure in the gable represents John the Baptist; the remains of frescoes are from the same period.

Piazza Monte Grappa Go south-west from Piazza S. Vittore to reach Piazza Monte Grappa, which was remodelled between 1927 and 1935 by Marcello Piacentini, one of the leading architects of the Italian Fascist movement. Some of the original buildings on the piazza were sacrificed for this work.

✶ Palazzo Estense Palazzo Estense, west of Piazza S. Vittore on Via Sacco, is now the town hall. Francesco d'Este III, imperial regent in Lombardy, commissioned **Giuseppe Bianchi** to build it in 1766–73. It is distinguished by its late Baroque façade on the garden side and above all by its **wonderful gardens**, which were modelled on those of

Varese Map

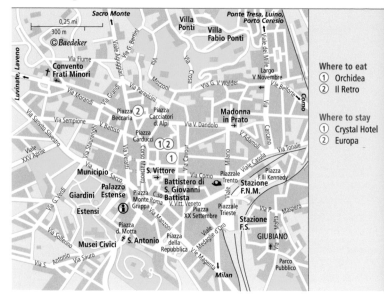

Where to eat
① Orchidea
② Il Retro

Where to stay
① Crystal Hotel
② Europa

Schönbrunn in Vienna. The path through the Giardini Estensi ascends slightly to the grotto, from where there is a fine view of the town and the nearby mountains.

The 18th-century **Villa Mirabello** in the neighbouring English-style gardens (entrance from Piazza della Motta) was greatly altered in 1843. It is now home to the municipal museum with its archaeological department and collection of paintings. Opening times: daily 10am–noon, 2pm–5pm. ⏱

Musei Civici

The northern suburb of Biumo Superiore takes its character from stately villas and old parks. A beautiful park, which is open to the public, is attached to **Villa Ponti** (1858). The 18th-century Villa Menafoglio Litta Panza houses the **museum of contemporary art**, which is mainly devoted to North American artists such as Dan Flavin and James Turrell. Exhibits from Africa and pre-Columbian America are also shown. Opening times: Feb–Dec Tue–Sun 10am–6pm. ⏱

Biumo Superiore

Around Varese

The outstanding sight in the region is without doubt Sacro Monte, a few miles north-west of Varese. It is the most important of ten holy mountains in northern Italy, places of pilgrimage during the Counter-Reformation on which churches and chapels were built as a sym-

✶✶
Sacro Monte

▶ VISITING VARESE

INFORMATION

I. A. T.
Via Carrobbio 2
I-21100 Varese
Tel. 03 32 28 36 04
Fax 03 32 28 36 04
www.turismo.provincia.va.it

WHERE TO EAT

▶ **Expensive**
① *Orchidea*
Via Donizetti 5
Tel. 03 32 28 51 19
www.orchidea-tre.it, closed Sun
For a discerning clientele; high-class ambience, many fish dishes and an extensive wine list. Reservations a must

▶ **Budget**
② *Il Retro*
Via Donizetti 5
Tel. 03 32 28 25 15
Closed Sun

If the Orchidea is too expensive, go next door to the simpler but attractive »back entrance« (retro) in the yard for a good pizza.

WHERE TO STAY

▶ **Mid-range**
① *Crystal Hotel (Best Western)*
Via Speroni 10
Tel. 03 32 23 11 45
Fax 03 32 23 71 81
www.crystal-varese.it, 44 rooms
Hotel in the centre of Varese in a sober-looking high-rise; tastefully appointed and pretty rooms.

② *Europa*
Piazza Beccaria 1
Tel. 03 32 28 01 70
Fax 03 32 23 43 25
www.hoteleuropavarese.it, 33 rooms
Very central location, though somewhat noisy, in a charming old building; parking spaces right by the hotel.

bolic defence against the threat of Lutheranism from the north. Bishop Ambrose (▶Famous People) is said to have built a chapel dedicated to the Virgin Mary on Sacro Monte as early as 389. Later a pilgrimage church and in 1452 a nunnery were established. In the 16th century, after the victory of the Holy League (Pope Pius V, Spain and Venice) over the Ottoman Turks, Carlo Borromeo, Archbishop of Milan, added 14 chapels and a small church to the processional way. As this superb path rises, the views of Varese and its surroundings, including the Lago di Varese, get better and better. The **chapels** were designed by Giuseppe Bernasconi and built from 1604. Each has a different plan: octagonal, square or circular. In the chapels, over life-size terracotta figures and murals represent the Mysteries of the Rosary: the Joyful Mysteries (Annunciation, Visitation, Nativity, Presentation in the Temple, Finding of the Child Jesus in the Temple), the Sorrowful Mysteries (Agony in the Garden, Scourging at the Pillar, Crowning with Thorns, Carrying the Cross, Crucifixion) and the Glorious Mysteries (Resurrection, Ascension of Christ, Descent of the Holy Spirit, Assumption of the Virgin). After the last chapel pil-

grims reach the Fontana del Mose with its figure of Moses (1831) by G. Monti.

In the **pilgrimage church of S. Maria del Monte**, which was built in 1473, and extended and altered several times, the final Mystery of the Rosary is depicted: the high altar is dedicated to the Coronation of the Virgin. The altar dates from 1660, the votive image from the 14th century. The church interior is richly decorated with paintings and stucco work, and late Gothic frescoes can be seen in the crypt. Former monastery buildings stand around the church.

From the last chapel, ascend a little to see the Casa-Museo Ludovico Pogliaghi, in which the Milanese **sculptor Ludovico Pogliaghi** lived from 1894 to 1906. It has been made into a small museum showing Greek, Egyptian and medieval sculpture, as well as the works of various artists of the 19th and 20th centuries. Opening times: Thu–Sun 10am–12.30pm, 3pm–5pm, Sun 10am–noon. ⏱

Casa-Museo Ludovico Pogliaghi

Some distance below the church the Museo Baroffio exhibits valuable medieval manuscripts and Lombard paintings of the 17th and 18th centuries. Opening times: Thu, Sat, Sun 9.30am–12.30pm, 3pm–6.30pm. ⏱

Museo Baroffio

Right next to the Sacro Monte, Campo dei Fiori (1226m/4023ft) looms over Varese to the north-west of the town. The area has been designated a parco regionale to protect its nature.

Campo dei Fiori

Lago di Varese nestles in gently rolling countryside to the west of Varese. It lacks the interest of the neighbouring north Italian lakes. When making a tour around the lake from Varese, stop on the north-eastern shore at **Voltorre** to see the pretty 12th-century church of S. Michele, where the atmospheric cloister has terracotta decoration.

Lago di Varese

Halfway between Varese and Porto Ceresio on Lago di Lugano, at **Bisuschio**, it is worth visiting the 16th-century Villa Cicogna-Mozzoni, which is regarded as one of the finest villas in the province of Varese and has a wonderful terraced garden with ponds, fountains and grottoes. Opening times: April–Oct Sun, holidays 9.30am–noon, 2.30pm–7pm; Aug daily 2.30pm–7pm. ⏱

★ Villa Cicogna-Mozzoni

★ Castiglione Olona and Surroundings

Castiglione Olona (10km/6mi south of Varese) is a remote mountain village that today reveals little of its former glory – apart from a fairly large number of small palazzi. However, its great cultural past makes it the main destination in the province of Varese for well-informed visitors. Castiglione Olona owes its golden age to Cardinal Branda Castiglione (1350–1443), who made it a centre for culture in the

Historic mountain village

15th century and brought in major artists from Tuscany for the purpose. In this way, from 1423 many Tuscan works were created here that bear witness to the period of transition from the late Gothic era to the Renaissance.

The most famous works here are **frescoes by the Florentine painter Masolino** (1383–*c*1440). The residence was destroyed by the Milanese Sforza as early as 1513 after the Castiglione family took the side of Louis XII of France when he occupied Milan.

What to see **Chiesa di Villa** on Piazza Garibaldi in the centre of Castiglione was built on a central plan between 1432 and 1443. Its similarity to the buildings of Brunelleschi in Florence, on which it was modelled, is obvious. The giant figures next to the entrance dominate the façade – St Christopher on the right, St Anthony the Great on the left. Inside, terracotta figures and 15th-century paintings have been preserved. **Palazzo Branda Castiglione** on the same square was the seat of the Castiglione. Cardinal Branda enlarged it in the 15th century. Today a small museum and an archive have been installed in the palazzo. Its noteworthy features are the cardinal's rooms and a house chapel, which are in part decorated with frescoes by Masolino. Follow the road past Chiesa di Villa to reach the **Collegiata della**

»Herod's Feast«: an important fresco by Masolino

Beata Vergine above the village. This church, too, was founded by Cardinal Branda Castiglione, who was depicted kneeling in front of the Madonna on the arch above the entrance in 1428 by a Veneto-Lombard artist. The tomb of the cardinal in the choir of the collegiate church is also in the Veneto-Lombard style. The frescoes in the choir, scenes from the life of the Virgin (c1435) and the martyrdoms of St Lawrence and St Stephen are by **Masolino** and his pupils. Opening times: April–Sept Tue–Sat 10am–1pm, 3pm–6pm; Oct–March Tue–Sat 9.30am–12.30, 2.30pm–5.30pm, Sun always 10am–1pm, 3pm–6pm.

The complex of buildings adjoining the Collegiata includes the baptistery, where the most famous work in Castiglione Olona, a **cycle of frescoes by Masolino** completed in 1435, can be seen. They depict episodes from the life of John the Baptist, including the well-known scene of Herod's banquet. Allow a little time to examine the frescoes. The fragile-looking, elegant figures were still painted in the late Gothic manner, but the onset of the Renaissance is already apparent in the perspective of the interior and the natural way of rendering landscape. Masolino's work demonstrates this change in style more clearly than that of almost any other painter. While the angels at the Baptism of Christ are still represented as delicate and pious, the coming of the Renaissance is apparent in the figures who are being baptized along with Christ, especially the figure with his back to the viewer.

★ ★
◀ Battistero

Castelseprio lies on a broad, high plateau above the river 4km/2.5mi south of Castiglione Olona. Just outside the village there is a strange sight: the remains of what was once a flourishing town with several churches. The Romans probably built **Castrum Sibrium** here in the 5th century as a bulwark against Germanic invaders. Under the Lombards Castelseprio was later the main town of a province that stretched from Milan to Lago Maggiore, and thus an important military and religious centre for the region. In the following centuries it gained further in importance, but was completely destroyed in 1287 in a raid by the Visconti, who saw Castelseprio as an undesirable rival. In the 19th century the site was used as a source of stone. In the Second World War partisans lived in this forgotten area. They drew attention to Castelseprio, and excavations began.

Castelseprio

Among the ruins and excavations, not only the defensive walls but also the remains of the church of S. Giovanni Evangelista, a 5th-century basilica, can be discerned. Next to it in the octagonal baptistery two baptismal basins were discovered. It is said that Arian Christians were baptized in one, and Athanasians in the other.

The main attraction is the little 7th-century church of S. Maria foris Portas, which lay outside the town walls and is still a little distance away from the other buildings. The exterior of the church, which has been rebuilt and restored, is not striking, but inside is a **cycle of frescoes** whose origins have not been fully explained. This incomplete

★
◀ S. Maria foris Portas

cycle is considered the most significant of its type between the 7th and 10th centuries, and represents in stylistic perfection the life of the Virgin from the Annunciation to the Flight into Egypt as well as the Nativity. It is unusual for its excellent execution, its late Roman or Byzantine style and its narrative not according to the canonical gospels but according to apocryphal gospels such as the Protoevangelium of St James. For example, a midwife is present at the scene of the Nativity, as related in this apocryphal gospel. The cycle is thought to have been the work of an itinerant Byzantine artist. Opening times: Tue–Sat 10am–6pm; Sun, Fri 9am–6pm.

✴ **Vigevano**

F 9

Province: Pavia
Population: 65,000

Altitude: 116m/380ft

Vigevano lies about 30km/20mi from Milan in the heart of Lomellina. This small town is the centre of the Italian shoe industry.

History
After the construction of a bridge across the Ticino in the Middle Ages bitter conflicts over Vigevano broke out between Milan and Pavia, as the town was now strategically important. Vigevano blossomed culturally in the time of the Visconti from the 14th century. In the 19th century it became the first place in Italy where shoes were industrially produced.

▶ VISITING VIGEVANO

INFORMATION

I. A. T.
Corso Emanuele 29
I-27029 Vigevano
Tel. 03 81 69 16 36

WHERE TO STAY

► **Mid-range**

Europa
Via Trivulzio 8
27029 Vigevano
Tel. 03 81 90 85 01
Fax 03 81 8 70 54
www.heuropa.it, 42 rooms
A hotel is located a good 100m/330ft from the Piazza Ducale and is frequented by trade fair visitors.

A jewel of Italian urban design: Piazza Ducale in Vigevano

What to See in Vigevano

It is worth visiting Vigevano just to see its wonderful Piazza Ducale, **the oldest Renaissance ensemble in Lombardy and one of the most beautiful in the whole country**. Ludovico il Moro commissioned the piazza in the late 15th century, probably from Donato Bramante or architects from the circle of his pupils. The large piazza is framed on three sides by uniform façades and arcades, which have polychrome fresco and sgraffito decoration. Under the arcades are inviting cafes and little shops. The **Duomo S. Ambrogio** on the east side of the piazza was built in 1532 to designs by Antonio da Lonate. The dilapidated Baroque façade with its concave curve was not added until the 17th century.

★ ★
Piazza Ducale

The castello in Vigevano essentially derives from a 14th-century Visconti fortification which occupies the south-eastern part of the site. The other buildings were constructed in the late 15th century for Ludovico il Moro, who established a hunting lodge here. The tower designed by Bramante, which visitors can climb, also dates from this period. Note also the magnificently decorated Loggia della Falconiera. From the Palazzo Ducale a long covered walkway leads to Rocca Vecchia, once the castle of Vigevano. Opening times: daily 9am–6pm, public holidays until 7pm.

★
Castello
Sforzesco

Museo della Calzatura The Museo della Calzatura (Via Cesarea) is dedicated to the history of the local shoe industry and the history of shoes in general. The exhibits include a great variety of footwear from Africa, Asia, America and Europe. Opening times: Tue–Fri 10am–12.30pm, 2pm–5pm; Sat 10am–6pm.

Around Vigevano

Abbiategrasso Abbiategrasso is situated a few miles north-east of Vigevano on the Naviglio Grande. For centuries it was an important trading post for provisioning Milan with agricultural products. On the canal bank a few villas built by the Milanese aristocracy have survived. Art-historical interest is provided by the **church of S. Maria Nuova** (Via Borsani). In 1497 Donato Bramante added a Renaissance porch to this Gothic columned structure. Opening times: daily 8am–noon, 3pm–6.30pm. Outside the town to the south-east, the **Cistercian monastery of Morimondo** has a 12th-century church with the straight east end typical of the Cistercian order. Little remains of the cloister, which was altered in the 15th and 16th centuries. Opening times: daily 9am–noon, 2pm–5pm.

Lomellina The flat and sparsely populated country west and south-west of Vigevano, the Lomellina, is »Italy's rice granary«. Once an enormous swamp, today it is Italy's second-largest area for rice growing. In spring the rice fields are flooded, and in early summer the country is carpeted in green. After the plants flower, the water is drained off again into the canals and the fields take on a straw-yellow colour. The rice is harvested in mid-September.

? DID YOU KNOW …?

- The 1949 film *Bitter Rice* by the neo-Realist director Giuseppe de Santin is a monument to rice cultivation in the Lomellina. It relates the hard life of the female rice workers – one of them played by Anna Magnani – who ruined their health in the flooded fields.

Mortara The sights in Mortara, a lively little centre of agriculture and industry 6km/4mi south-west of Vigevano, are the 14th-century **Duomo S. Lorenzo** and the **church of S. Croce**, which was founded in the 11th century. Out in the country 2km/1mi north-west of Mortara is the 15th-century **Santuario della Madonna del Campo**, with a 16th-century Madonna del Latte in the apse.

Lomello Lomello (15km/9mi south of Mortara) is a modest place today but has a significant past. The Roman settlement named Laumellum lay

INDEX

LIST OF MAPS AND ILLUSTRATIONS

PHOTO CREDITS

PUBLISHER'S INFORMATION

Illustrations etc: 170 illustrations, 26 maps and diagrams, one large map
Text: Dr. Eva Missler, Anja Schliebitz with contributions by Carmen Galenschovski and Reinhard Strüber
Editing: Baedeker editorial team (John Sykes, Robert Taylor)
Translation: John Sykes, Robert Taylor
Cartography: Christoph Gallus, Hohberg; Franz Huber, Munich; MAIRDUMONT/Falk Verlag, Ostfildern (map)
3D illustrations: jangled nerves, Stuttgart
Design: independent Medien-Design, Munich; Kathrin Schemel

Editor-in-chief: Rainer Eisenschmid, Baedeker Ostfildern

1st edition 2012
Based on Baedeker Allianz Reiseführer »Oberitalienische Seen«, 7. Auflage 2011

Copyright: Karl Baedeker Verlag, Ostfildern
Publication rights: MAIRDUMONT GmbH & Co; Ostfildern

Printed in China